DISPATCHES FROM DYSTOPIA

DISPATCHES FROM DYSTOPIA

Histories of Places Not Yet Forgotten

KATE BROWN

The University of Chicago Press   Chicago and London

Kate Brown is professor of history at the University of
Maryland, Baltimore County. She is the author of *Biography
of No Place: From Ethnic Borderland to Soviet Heartland* and
*Plutopia: Nuclear Families, Atomic Cities, and the Great Soviet
and American Plutonium Disasters.*

The University of Chicago Press, Chicago 60637
The University of Chicago Press, Ltd., London
© 2015 by Kate Brown
All rights reserved. Published 2015.
Printed in the United States of America

24 23 22 21 20 19 18 17 16 15   1 2 3 4 5

ISBN-13: 978-0-226-24279-8 (cloth)
ISBN-13: 978-0-226-24282-8 (e-book)
DOI: 10.7208/chicago/9780226242828.001.0001

Graphics by Andrew Umentum

Library of Congress Cataloging-in-Publication Data

Brown, Kate (Kathryn L.), author.
Dispatches from dystopia : histories of places not yet
forgotten / Kate Brown.
pages cm
Includes bibliographical references and index.
ISBN 978-0-226-24279-8 (cloth : alk. paper)
ISBN 978-0-226-24282-8 (e-book)
1. Hazardous geographic environments. 2. Historiography.
3. Disasters. 4. Travel. I. Title.
D16.B876 2015
907.2′02—dc23

2014044795

♾ This paper meets the requirements of ANSI/NISO
Z39.48-1992 (Permanence of Paper).

CONTENTS

1 Being There

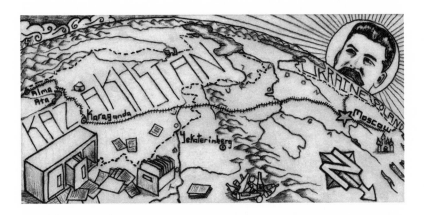

Writers rarely reveal the architecture behind their books. In this volume, I describe what happens when a researcher snaps shut her laptop, picks up a bag, and—nervously checking again for passport and tickets—boards a plane for a destination of which few have heard. Traveling to the story in the past two decades, I have drifted through parts of Eastern Europe, Central Asia, and the American West. Without intending to, I have become a professional disaster tourist. In writing history, I have ended up in a succession of modernist wastelands, each a bit more unsavory, a bit more desolate than the one before. My adventures have often gone calamitously wrong. I rarely find what I am seeking. I get lost, make mistakes, pursue foolish assumptions, and commit culturally insensitive blunders. In the course of these hapless misadventures I have relied on the kindness of strangers, as Tennessee Williams famously phrased it, to put me up, show me the road, and tell me their stories. I follow in a tradition of illustrious and daring adventurers, hardier and more courageous than I, more certain of what they encountered. They brought with them labels, which they applied to create maps, inventories, encyclopedias, censuses, and laws. But traveling is not always an act of appropriation. The premise of this book is that traveling can be a form of negotiation, an unraveling of certainties and convictions and a reassembling of the past, aided by strangers who generously open their doors to reveal histories that are in play, contingent, and subjective.

Each chapter of this book uses a particular place to explore the histories of communities and territories that have been silenced, broken, or contaminated. In telling these stories I narrate the history of places, their making and unmaking, and of the people who remain in the landscapes that are left behind. That may seem a simple statement, but places are often left out of nonfiction prose. Many writers presume that the site of action is a given, as if places were neutral containers of human interaction rather than dynamic agents in their own right. The core idea of what has been called the "spatial turn," by contrast, has been to explore how spatial arrangements shape the human, natural, and animal worlds, and do so in ways that are harder to see than the effects of published laws, market transactions, or social norms, because people often take spatial organization to be part of the natural (or given) world.[1] The motivation of this book, then, is to treat places as sources that are as rich, important, erratic, and unreliable as material that comes from archives filled with cataloged files.

Historians also tend to prioritize the textual and temporal over the spatial. They derive legitimacy from documented evidence that is closely linked to dates. But archivists and historians know that documents can be inaccurate, obscurantist, aspirational, and sometimes just plain false, written to deceive.[2] Historians are discovering that archives are not inert repositories, but contain their own narratives that are active in framing and determining the past.[3] In the following chapters, I explore how places as sources offer up in a similar way ambiguities and challenges for a researcher to decode.

The places I examine in this collection are those that have preoccupied me as a researcher in Russia, Ukraine, Kazakhstan, and the United States. Some are small and contained. In one essay, I explore the basement of a hotel in Seattle where Japanese Americans, on their way to internment camps in 1942, deposited their personal possessions and never returned. Others are limitless. I wander the Chernobyl Zone of Exclusion first on the World Wide Web and then in person, trying to figure out which version—the real or the virtual—is a forgery. In chapter 4, "Bodily Secrets," I revisit, in the small city of Kyshtym, in the Russian southern Urals, the nineteenth-century notion of "vapors" as it relates to invisible twentieth-century pollutants that mysteriously felled bodies and stunted family trees. In chapter 5, "Sacred Space in a Sullied Garden," I try to attend the annual Rosh Hashanah celebration of Hasidic Jews in Uman, Ukraine, but find I can penetrate the boundaries of sacred space only fleetingly, as an honorary child. I wrote chapter 6, "Gridded Lives," in 2000 because I was frustrated by what I saw as American triumphalism at having "won" the Cold War. Seeking to provoke Americans to think of their history on a different plane, alongside, rather than against, Russian history, I set out how, in the years following the end of the Cold War, the formerly sharp distinctions between a railroad city in Montana and a gulag city in Kazakhstan were substantially eroded. While the comparison may now read as overstated, I include the essay in this volume because it speaks to that period.[4] In the concluding chapter, I return to where I began life, in the Midwestern industrial rust belt, to investigate how my personal biography has inspired a long-term obsession with modernist wastelands.

As I go about the delicate business of stitching together narratives of territories that have been violently taken apart, I run into all kinds of problems. Places and the people in them tell many different, conflicting stories about the past. I puzzle over how to tell such multivocal or polyphonic stories yet still retain narrative form. Worse, what if there are no voices? What if everyone who remembers the history I pursue is gone or long dead? When I arrive someplace, the fact of my being there changes the place itself and the kinds of stories I can tell about it. How does a story mature when I acknowledge that my view is obstructed, my perspective land-bound and limited? Do those admissions undermine the authenticity and veracity of the stories I tell or enhance them? And in what voice do I write when I am part of the story? Questions like these eddy through the histories I navigate, often leaving me at sea. In the chapters that follow, I share the answers I have devised, answers that are not really solutions but jerry-rigged patches devised on the run for the problems of subjectivity raised by philosophers in the late twentieth century.

The Continental Divide

Geographers Robert Sack and J. E. Malpas write, "Place is primary because it is the experiential fact of our existence."[5] If they are right and place is vital for understanding human existence, why is it that when I show up somewhere, I often fail to grasp its meaning? Even a simple statement about location can point to this problem. Most of my research has taken place in Europe or Asia. That is a simple, factual declaration, until you start to question what exactly sets Europe apart geographically from Asia.

In the 1730s, the historian and geographer Vasilii Tatishchev drew a line, pregnant with significance, across the map and divided Europe from Asia along the spine of the Ural Mountains. Oceans divide all other continents, but Tatishchev's border partitioned the two continents across a great land mass. Marking the continental boundary at a low mountain range easily crossed in a horse and cart was a bold move. Tatishchev worked for Peter the Great, and much of Peter's memorialized greatness derived from his aspiration to push Russia out of an assumed Asiatic backwardness onto the map of Europe, which Peter, unlike tsars before him, recognized as superior. Before Tatishchev's line, European geographers had vaguely referenced the Don River, to the west of Moscow, as the endpoint of Europe, a boundary that placed Russia squarely in Asia. Peter wanted Russia to be part of Europe, and he also realized that all self-respecting eighteenth-century European monarchs had overseas colonies.[6] Pushing the continental divide east to the Urals not only cloaked Russia in the mantle of Europe but designated Siberia as Russia's hinterland, suddenly located in Asia as a dependency. With a stroke of his pen, then, Tatishchev gave Russia both European metropole and Asiatic colony.[7]

Today, this continental border can be straddled by two legs and just a bit of imagination. Long after Tatishchev reenvisioned Europe and Asia, twentieth-century physical geographers explained his border by imagining that three hundred million years ago the Siberian plate crashed into the eastern edge of the European platform. The impact pitched the landmass up, buckling over the Siberian segment, which dove under, forming a chain of low mountains from the Arctic pole to the deserts of Kazakhstan.[8] A number of markers in the Urals help visitors experience this border. I visited one with a group on a rainy, cold June day in 2007. Traveling an hour from Yekaterinburg, ascending a long, low incline that few people would recognize as a mountain, we finally pulled up at a roadside diner. It was a lonely place, cut out of a forest of pine and fir, which rose around us like a fortress wall, impenetrable, damp, and unwelcoming. From a kiosk, a man sold champagne to wedding parties and tourists. I looked around, searching for the reason we were there. I spotted in the small clearing a platform of red marble divided by a band of white stone—the continental divide. Several bridal parties milled about the platform waiting their turn for photographers to snap shots of the bride and groom kissing over two continents. From the size of the heap of bottles, it was clear that a lot of couples had similar snapshots in their wedding albums. I also went up to the pedestal to have my picture taken.

As I stepped onto the boundary marking the division between two great continents, nothing happened. No orchestral crescendo sounded from the dark wood, no grand vista announced my entry into Asia. Instead, someone in our party cracked a couple bottles of half-sweet Soviet champagne and poured it into plastic cups. Its bubbles were more evocative than the marble marker of the division so essential to contemporary categorizations of Russia as European and Kazakhstan as Asian. Raising our glasses, we hustled through a round of toasts, pitched the empties on the pile, and gladly retreated to the warm, dry bus, which sped us back to Yekaterinburg and Asia.

This is the dirty little secret: often places ostensibly rich with meaning have, at first glance, little power to narrate history and its significance. Place often disappoints, which is one reason it is overlooked, but a second, more pressing reason, for me, is that to describe the places I visit is to admit to the partialness and paltriness of the knowledge I distill from them. Places offer up only remnants, tattered, muddy, sunken, rusted, and despoiled. Once I am in place, things are out of place, disorganized and chaotic, like a box of files tossed in the air, all structure and order eradicated. Arriving at a site, I have little idea what else has been misplaced, stolen, destroyed, or buried. "Visibility," Bruno Latour writes, "is the consequence of lots of opaque and 'invisible' work."[9] No one has done that work before I arrive.

The usual place of historical inquiry is the archive or library. At first glance, archives appear more useful and complete than the places of past events. In an archive, documents are systematized into files, which are labeled and gathered into collections. Archivists do a great deal of the invisible work of making things visible and comprehensible by grouping and categorizing documents to frame knowledge, so that when a historian arrives there is a structure in place from which to make sense of the past. By filing and organizing, archivists squeeze vast territories into miniature, map-size icons that are more coherent and legible than the view you get standing in one spot, anxiously eyeing the horizon for clues. When a researcher appears on site, little organizational work has been done, which makes reading a place for the past a discouraging prospect. The scholar is largely alone in attempting to figure out what happened. Historians approach the archive with a critical eye as to the way some knowledge has been sorted and other knowledge silenced, but recognizing these problems does not mean they give up on them. Archives are still extremely useful. The same can be said of places. For all the problems in trying to see the past from the limited perspective of place, I don't think that is reason to give up.

For—think about it—history occurs in place, not, as historians commonly believe, in time. Or rather, time and place have been mixed together metaphorically so that everything, past and present, *takes place* in a particular *space* of time.[10] Philip Ethington notes how in Western culture people tend to imagine time as something spatial—time is a "line," a "frame," as people stand on a "threshold" of an era. "The past," he writes, "is behind us and the future is ahead."[11] The fusing of spatial and temporal metaphors derive from the fact that time is the tracking of human action across space, which itself is a moving target. For this reason, geographers argue that humans cannot create anything without first being in place, that place is essential to the construction of meaning and society, and, I would add, of history, sociology, literary criticism, and anthropology.[12] Plotting the past temporally only from sources in an archive is one of those movements that cloud the work of visibility. The absent place creates a noticeable gap in nonfiction narratives, one that readers comprehend when they complain of dry and lifeless texts. Readers grasp that something is missing.

Missing Unaccounted For

Officials at the U.S. Department of Energy (DOE) have an acronym, MUF, which means "missing unaccounted for." They use this term to describe plutonium that was processed at DOE sites but now cannot be found. Plutonium, an element that landed on the periodic table in the 1940s, is a manmade product. It is also humanity's most volatile and destructive creation. In trace amounts plutonium cannot be detected by the human senses, but amass enough in one spot and it can go critical, causing a chain reaction. Missing, unaccounted-for plutonium can be a big problem—and an appropriate metaphor for scholarly inquiry. There are a lot of MUFs in nonfiction narratives. Since the 1960s, historians have worked to uncover and present in their work voices long absent from national histories. New social histories emerged in American and European academies just after the riots of the sixties, when the rage of people who had long been missing and unaccounted for appeared on city streets as if out of nowhere and went critical, surprising those who had done the overlooking. Since that time, historians of labor, social, and environmental history, alongside historians of ethnic, racial, and sexual minorities, have penned whole new communities, movements, and identities into being. As a result, writers now can draw on a broader range of voices and topics than ever before. In looking for those voices, however, social scientists have discovered that written records do a poor job recovering the stories of people who were not literate, who lived on the margins, or whose histories were purposefully erased.

Frustrated by the paltry documentary record of people whose lives had fallen beneath metaphorical or actual bulldozers, I fell into the habit of going to the sites of past action. I followed the lead of historians of premodern history, who write about people who left no documentary history. They had figured out ways to read places, geology, climate, flora and fauna, as well as folklore and religious practice, for clues to the past.[13] One location I turn to repeatedly in this book is Kazakhstan, a territory violently dispossessed during the Soviet collectivization drive from 1928 to 1932, a period in which two million of a total four million Kazakhs died or fled. In their place in the subsequent decade, several million deportees, prisoners, and exiles were sent to Kazakhstan. Because of this history, I went to Kazakhstan too.

Where do I begin—with atmosphere?

At the bus stop, women selling dried fish call to me. They are wearing floral housecoats, the closest item in commercial markets to the *shapan* of wool and silk that used to be the mainstay of Kazakh dress. I walk through courtyards of the capital city, Almaty.[14] A man floats by singing three syllables, *mo-lo-ko*, in a doleful voice, but he has no milk to sell. Two girls sit on a bench and whisper as the moon stencils their shadows onto the darkened city walls.

Or maybe I should start with a telling snapshot. A Kazakh waitress in a small, downcast city on the northern steppe says she has never met an American before. She interrupts my dinner conversation: "Excuse me for asking, but do they really compare us to Africans?" A woman of Polish descent, deported in the 1930s for having been "Polish," greets me at the door of her sod house, swept and cool. She pulls out sentences in Polish as she would her Sunday china. After a few pleasantries, she slips back into her everyday Russian.

Mostly I want to tell you about Pani (Ms.) Janina who I knew for only six weeks in 1996 and haven't been able to get out of my mind since for one ignoble reason: I didn't like her. Pani Janina had the look of a nun, in gray pinafores and practical walking shoes, and the impatience of an admiral. She possessed a motor scooter, which she drove with feverish abandon through the dusty settlements inhabited by exiled Soviet citizens of Polish descent that ringed Almaty. She took me along on her furious mission to transform villagers deported from Ukraine in the 1930s into Poles in the 1990s. At the time, the postcommunist Polish government, struggling to pay back communist-era foreign loans, was loath to bestow Polish citizenship on this Russian-speaking community from Kazakhstan. Poland already had enough unemployed collective farmers. Nevertheless, this was Pani Janina's mission.

Speaking over the grinding gears of an aging municipal bus, Pani Janina summarized for me the history of Polish-Ukrainian-Russian encounters. Fluidly levitating between the sixteenth and twentieth centuries, she emphasized that the Ukrainians were a "primitive" nation, possessing no medieval history, no kings or literary tradition. "That is why they never stood up to fight for themselves." Pani Janina had a missionary's single-mindedness: the nation, which for her was a flowing synthesis of God, history, and language, was the defining prism by which to judge a person. A Pole was one kind of person. A Ukrainian was another. The hitch was that in Kazakhstan these discrete national boundaries made no sense.

We went to the Roman Catholic Church in a former deportee settlement on the outskirts of Almaty. The church had no steeple, no cupola, just a sign tacked up on a metal gate in front of an ordinary looking cottage. Pani Janina led me into a sanctuary of lace curtains and roughly sawed benches painted municipal green. In front stood a small altar in Baroque white and gold. Christ was a babe in the arms of Mary, looking European and kind. The priest was from Italy and spoke Russian haltingly. Pani Janina helped him, at first translating, then leaving his words behind to launch into her own sermon. Officially, Pani Janina served as a teacher of Polish appointed to the district schools by a joint Polish-Kazakh agreement, but in essence she was the spiritual and social leader of the exiled community of people of Polish descent in southern Kazakhstan. She worked among people who had not been aware of their status as Polish exiles until headlines broke the story in the early 1990s. In Poland, journalists and social activists made a lot of commotion about the "Poles of Kazakhstan." The exiles from Ukraine served as icons for decades of persecution of the Soviet state against Poland. Pani Janina buzzed around the former deportee settlements, rarely taking a day off, spending several nights a week away from home as an itinerant teacher and national awakener. Her work was paying off. "Before Pani Janina came, we didn't acknowledge our Polish roots," one woman deported as a child told me. "We were scattered about and had no idea about the other Poles around here. She went about on her motor scooter and connected us."

Even so, Pani Janina was displeased with her charges. They did not know the Catholic rites. They were slow to learn Polish and then spoke it with a heavy Russian accent. One day, in her apartment the size of a dorm room, Pani Janina got herself worked up describing the obstacles to her mission. She was angry about a lot of things: the Kazakh government, the Polish embassy, the Poles of Kazakhstan who were not Polish enough, the priest who did not care enough. No one cared as much as Pani Janina. She had an untiring zeal for her cause. I sat listening to her as she busily packed a bag for another trip to another deportee village. Suddenly her nose erupted in blood. As her hand shot up, a red stream trickled down her wrist and with it a hemorrhaging

Two sisters deported from Ukraine in Kazakhstan, 1997. Photo by author.

of emotions and tears. I persuaded her to sit, which was surprisingly difficult to do. I realized I had yet to see Pani Janina in any angle of repose. As she finally reclined on the couch, distraught, her head back, wrapped in a towel, eyes closed, she was for a moment dismantled and disarmed, which gave me a chance to put off disliking her and to grasp her frustrations. Racing around the dusty villages on her scooter, Pani Janina was grounded in one landscape, but as she went, she forced to the front the imagination of another, better place of aspiration. She imagined a verdant Poland, one that was unsettled and eclipsed in the twentieth century, and she wanted to suture it back together with the lives of the deportees of Kazakhstan.

The difficulty of this task drove her harried rushing, her impatience, judgments, anxieties, and anger. I was critical of Pani Janina because I felt she was using the former deportees as a backdrop for her own creation of an idyllic precommunist Poland. Yet, to be honest with myself, I was also using the former deportees to piece together a world that no longer existed. And like her, I would take the deportees' story and leave them behind in their semi-abandoned villages in the hollowed-out Kazakh agricultural economy of the mid-1990s. Pani Janina's anxieties played out against my own, which is why, I finally realized, I disliked her. She reminded me of the failures built into my own project. And my metaphorical scooter had an even greater chance of breaking down on the lonely road than hers.

Okay, so I admit I was there, in Kazakhstan, following the history of the deportees. I put myself in the story, akin to a stage actor turning to the audience and talking through the imaginary fourth wall of the set. Worse, I concede to having feelings about my subjects when I am supposed to be neutral and objective. Right here in the introduction of this book I have committed two major errors, violating a silent pact among historians that the narrative voice should be impartial, detached, and so in the third person.

What is wrong in acknowledging being there? I am confused by the notion that referring to oneself in scholarly writing is unprofessional or trivial or renders one's work tautological—"something we don't do." This question has long nagged me: Why, in disciplines that aspire to verifiable truth, do scholars sustain the fiction, when researching and writing, that they are not there?

Academics recoil from the first-person narrative, in part, because to confess to being there is to call into doubt one's objectivity and legitimacy. I find this strange because scholars readily admit to one another that there is no unmediated account, that each interpretation of reality is a highly specific and partial way of organizing the world. Most everyone in the business knows that writers are subjective, that the state of inhabiting a body grounds writers to a series of attachments, starting with the place where they stand.[15] Yet this is rarely stated in the output of academic work. Authors erasing themselves from their research and from their place—on the ground and in their prose—are often inhibited from telling what they know, a fuller version of the stories they are writing. Readers sense this underlying dissimulation and respond with resentment and frustration, feelings they label as "boredom."

Being detached translates grammatically into being disembodied ("one would think . . .") or multibodied ("we know that . . ."). Donna Haraway calls the scholarly practice of "seeing everything from nowhere" the "god trick." This narrative mode glosses over the fact that the writer, like everyone else, is rooted in a time and place, which greatly constrains what the researcher can see and how he or she sees it.[16] To put it another way, to live is to be somewhere and to be somewhere is to take a position. Narrative voice is telling in this endeavor.

I often wonder, as I read a third-person account, who is this narrator? How did he or she get there? Where, in fact, is this person?

Scientists have something called the "observer effect," which refers to the phenomenon of the observer, in the act of watching, altering the state of the object being studied. Anthropologists take the observer effect into account in participant observation.[17] Oral historians and anthropologists make a practice of describing the context of their interviews so that readers can judge the researchers' questions and the subjects' answers. Historians, journalists, political scientists, and literary critics generally have few such disciplinary practices to account for their presence in the acts of gathering materials, choosing some sources, rejecting others, and soliciting information from subjects, other scholars, and archivists. Nor is there a tradition of elaborating on the impact of the writer's career trajectory, biography, and personal skills (e.g., knowledge of languages or sciences, experience in nursing) on the kinds of questions and answers he or she devises. This too puzzles me. We are deeply embedded in creating and redefining notions of nation, community, personal identity, and biography, yet we lack the disciplinary rigor to reflect on that intimate and sensitive process.[18] We are not taught to meditate in writing on evidence we found but rejected; on doors opened or barred to us because of class, ethnicity, race, citizenship, sexuality, or gender; or on promising documents or subjects we encountered but did not have the language skills or technical knowledge to explore. Nor do we train ourselves to consider how being there—asking questions and shining a light on a subject—transforms both the subject and the terrain on which it exists.

One way to acknowledge these problems is to locate the researcher in place, whatever that place may be. "Embodying objectivity," as Donna Haraway phrased it, is a way to unmask the missing unaccounted for narrator in nonfiction prose. Haraway wrote about situated knowledge in 1988. In the subsequent decades, I started graduate school, read about the problems of subjectivity, read Haraway and others, and, inspired, set out to write a dissertation as an intermittent first-person travelogue. I thought that writing a history as a both a physical and intellectual journey would enable me to admit to the lost fragments I could not recover, to concede assumptions I held that fell away in the course of the work, and to come clean about the questionable qualities of my sources and conjectures. When I announced my intentions, I ran up against, not so much a wall as a prickling, startled hedge of resistance. The advice was meant to be helpful: "You won't get a job with that dissertation." "Other scholars will assign you, but not cite you." "The first person just isn't done after the introduction." With the help of a few senior scholars and a sympathetic editor, I carried on anyway, completing and publishing a monograph based on that dissertation. And my critics were partly right. I got a job in a good research university but one few have heard of (it has no football team), and it's true, professors assign that book (*A Biography of No Place*) more often than they cite it. Nor has that publication broadened the boundaries of acceptable historical prose. Since then, I have continued to collide with editors who wonder about the wisdom of writing myself in as a character in my history.

Embodied prose can change the way histories read. I find there are advantages to owning up to my position within the story. I am in place to see, hear, smell, and touch, and there to take a stand. I can admit to my limited, politicized, arranged-in-time perspective, and readers can see these biases not as faults but as opinion or option, as something to set alongside their own versions of reality. The first-person voice, I hope, makes my judgments more palatable in that it does not pass them off as claims to universal truth or utterances from on high. The first person has other uses too. Once in place, the narrative becomes writing-as-thinking, an exploration of places and people and the complexities of recovering them from the past.[19] In short, my embodied approach has three components—positioning the place as archive, locating the narrator in the place of intellectual quest with all its compromising, skewed qualities, and being there in the narrative.

While still in Central Asia, I showed up in a Kazakh settlement looking for a family that had migrated from Mongolia. The family lived in two yurts. One, with a gleaming plastic sheen, was factory-produced in Mongolia. Next to it stood a "Kazakh" yurt, handmade of boiled felt. The family had returned seven years before from six decades of exile in Mongolia after fleeing Kazakhstan during the collectivization drive in the 1930s. Akedey Touishi told his family history from a notebook full of dates, an ancestral accounting that went on for pages, tracing roots back to Genghis Khan. Touishi hardly needed notes, however. He spread his fingers and numbered off nine generations of his forefathers.

Family of Kazakh emigrants from Mongolia in front of their yurt, 1997.
Photo by author.

"Any son will know that," Touishi said. "We are always asked as children, who are you?" The answer lies in family genealogy matched to particular ancestral burial grounds on the Kazakh steppe to which the family ached to return throughout its years of exile. In Kazakh culture, places are stories, and stories are the geography of one's daily and ancestral life.[20]

"In Mongolia," Touishi laughed, "I always dreamed of returning to Soviet Kazakhstan. Everything Kazakh I thought was better. So I traded in my homemade leather suitcases for vinyl ones made in the USSR. Same with my boots and woolen coat, which I replaced with polyester Soviet equivalents. I didn't understand why those goods fell apart so fast."

Consuming Kazakhstan while in Mongolia became a problem for Touishi because, at the same time, Kazakhs in the USSR were becoming Soviet. That made the family's arrival in Kazakhstan in the 1990s a bitter disappointment. "We ask Kazakhs a question and they answer in Russian. They've forgotten their language and how to do anything." In Mongolia, the family had several hundred head of sheep, cows, and horses. That number had dwindled to a handful due to the difficulties

and expense of migrating. In Mongolia, Touishi's family were shep-
herds. In Kazakhstan they were largely unemployed welfare cases.
"There are no jobs for us here," he said, "No money. No land." Talking to Touishi, I learned that the dispossessed can become possessed—
haunted by the unbound fragments of their past, which greatly hinder
getting on with life in the present tense.[21]

Dispossession was a common feature of post-Soviet Kazakh life. The
republic had served as a dumping ground for several decades of deportees, prisoners, and exiles. Outside of Almaty, I interviewed an elderly
couple. Herbert Henke had been a member of the writer's union of
Ukraine in the 1930s. He wrote in German and was celebrated as a
Soviet-German author until he was deported to Kazakhstan in 1941 as
a potential German traitor.[22] His wife, Fana, had been a loyal communist. Her father had worked at the brutal job of collectivizing Ukraine
in the 1930s. I found the couple in a cramped, disheveled apartment in
an especially dingy housing block. Herbert was wearing a tie stained
with his afternoon soup. Fana had a quality about her reminiscent of
a bird about to take flight. She hopped about the apartment and spoke
rapidly, flitting from one topic to another.

Both husband and wife admired Stalin and all he had done for the
country. "Stalin was the sun. Without the sun [when Stalin died],
there was no life." Fana spoke loudly because she said Herbert was
going deaf. She shouted about Stalin, the war, her father the collectiv-
izer, but when she spoke about Kazakh president Nursultan Nazer-
baev and the "Kazakh takeover of Kazakhstan," her voice lowered to a
whisper. "The president passed a law that it is illegal to say anything
against him. All our neighbors are Kazakhs. Anyone could turn us in."

At the time, I thought Fana sounded crazy. Thinking back on it,
Fana, living in both past and present at once, performed for me in
real time the fears that enveloped her life as an ethnic German in the
Soviet Union, in Ukraine during the rise abroad of German fascism
and, later, in Kazakhstan as a disgraced deportee doing her best to hide
her ethnic origins and promote her more respectable (proletarian)
class origins.[23] People who have been uprooted—refugees, deportees,
the interned, but also the elderly, transitioning out of their homes or
out of life—often lack contexts that would tell them their place, both
metaphorically and physically, and so, I find, they turn to memory to

locate themselves. Unable to map their lives spatially, they chart it temporally, which leads many of the dispossessed to dwell in the past in unusually intense ways. Fana had that quality. I could believe or fact-check little of what she said, but the sentiments she expressed rang true. As geographers have pointed out, people live in multiple spatial and temporal realms simultaneously—in more than one place, in present, past, and future—and these realms come together in uncanny, sometimes haunting, but usually banal ways.[24] The everyday, historical register is a scale playing up and down our minds.

Fana Henke illustrates a common problem: witnesses often appear to be the by-product of their experiences. Fana can easily be seen, like the course of her life, as unhinged, and so unreliable as a source of testimony for a scholarly endeavor. Dispossession is spatial because, in our age of possessive individualism, people who lack property live as remnants, their dearth of possessions signaling that they are untrustworthy and unverifiable.[25] Deprived of property, the dispossessed have trouble making claims about their past lives.[26] One woman who grew up in a family of deportees in Kazakhstan told me she never believed her parents' stories of being dumped on the "naked steppe." "That just sounded insane," she remembered. Until the 1990s, there were no newspaper articles, books, exhibits, or accessible archives in Soviet society to support her parents' claims or verify their experience. The bizarre story of deportees left to fend for themselves on the Kazakh steppe simply didn't exist, and the people who whispered about it had no credibility. Since that time, I have been attentive to people who appear to be unreliable narrators, because it is the stifled voices, the words left unsaid, that haunt most societies. The known-but-unspoken stories are the unarticulated land mines we quietly fear, from which we shield our children and friends with well-intentioned words of caution: "You don't want to go there at night." "You should avoid that part of town." "You won't find much out from them."[27]

I once arranged for a group of graduate students to meet me in a Baltimore neighborhood that had suffered a half century of classic American urban decline. A local housing activist led us on a walking tour through the community. I thought we had a pleasant walk in the falling light of a hot Indian summer day. Lots of people cooling off in lawn chairs on the sidewalk hailed us, and a few came up to ask wry questions about our group of a dozen mostly white pedestrians. ("There's no ball game today. What are ya'all up to?") When we next met on campus, I was surprised to find that a handful of students were angry with me. They said I had put them in danger, that they had grown up in Baltimore—or rather, its suburbs—and knew ("everyone knows") you don't go to that neighborhood. One young man claimed to have counted six handguns. ("Six?" I asked, incredulous. "Yes, six," he affirmed with a grave expression.) Another student insisted that they would have learned more had we, instead of going there, just read histories about the neighborhood and stayed put safely in the seminar room on campus to talk about it.

Of course, my students were right. It is easier and safer to stay home, look at a map, read other explorers' accounts, and imagine that their organizing and mapping practices are definitive and conclusive. Knowing these traps and fearing these dangers, do I indeed stay home, or if I go, do I pretend I didn't? Do I write a history as if the answers were just something to be found, dusted off, and written up, rather than admit that my history entails a careful selection of some places, objects, and sources over others, which are then pondered over, pasted together, and intuited by no one other than me?

Obviously, I think not. I am interested in how spatial practices work to snare people into silence, invisibility, and diagnoses of menace and madness.[28] The reverse is also true. I want to know how, by means of spatial arrangements, humans assemble knowledge and possibility, credibility, visibility, and sanity. The following chapters offer snapshots of sources historians don't traditionally use, or admit to using, the kind picked up from a dusty floor, found lying at the bottom of a ditch, or heard over the noisy din of a rural coffee shop—orphan sources that come without identification numbers or certification. These remnants representing tossed-off people and places might serve as a portal into a new kind of discipline that redistricts the terrain of scholarly inquiry and narrative prose. My hope is these unconventional sources might release researchers from traps that arrest rather than emancipate knowledge and, in so doing, show how orphan sources might be prodded to speak, their emergent voices shaping narrative form out of formless ruins, dumps, and depopulated zones. These stories appear neither in a preordained fashion nor in random ways, but as the product of the author's particular mediation. In my most optimistic moments, I see this as a project of rebirth on two registers. I am looking both for a way to reanimate places and lives with stories that spring from them and for a means to reinvigorate history as an enterprise that has the capacity to excavate the depths and variety of human experience.

2 The Panama Hotel, Japanese America, and the Irrepressible Past

When I was living in Seattle in the 1990s, a friend told me of a place he was sure I'd want to visit. Just south of downtown, in the gray indecision of what Seattleites call the "International District," there was a transient hotel. Deep in the basement, behind a solid oak door with a rusty padlock, was a storage room, and in that room lay a massive cache of debris stashed in trunks, straw baskets, boxes, and crates. These were objects left by Japanese Americans deported from the West Coast in 1942. The pile of discarded possessions appeared, after fifty years of neglect and invisibility, to speak in an unorthodox way about the tentative nature of citizenship and welfare in twentieth-century American history.[1]

The facts of the case are well known. In April and May 1942, seven thousand Japanese Americans in Seattle were convicted without trial as "enemy aliens," given little more than a week to pack two suitcases, sell off their businesses, homes, and furniture, and report for what was optimistically called "evacuation" to a "relocation" camp on the withered, arid plain of central Idaho.[2] Many families left behind in the basement of the Panama Hotel whatever they couldn't carry or sell: trunks, furniture, clothes, dishes, family portraits, fishing poles, tool chests. A half century later the objects were dusty, moth-eaten, discarded, and forgotten. Their owners never returned to claim their possessions, nor could they reclaim their prewar state of innocence. History, especially repressed history, has an uncanny way of popping up in the most unexpected places.[3] For me, the storage basement promised to serve as a kind of archaeological dig. I sought out the fossilized objects in the basement in hopes they would describe a community and an everyday existence before both were shattered by deportation, imprisonment, and postwar assimilation.

The Panama Hotel is located on Main Street, not far from the Seattle port where, at the beginning of 1942, about fourteen thousand people lived, unofficially zoned off in a minority ghetto. Along with Japanese Americans lived Chinese, Filipinos, and African Americans, densely settled in a two-square-mile area called, by locals who wanted to be polite, "Japantown" or, in Japanese, *Nihonmachi*.[4] Since the war, the area has been retitled the International District, a vague name for an ambiguous sector that, amputated from the rest of Seattle by a web of highways and exit ramps, has been less an international zone than a no-man's land. In the mid-1990s, there seemed to be too few people on the streets, too little noise and bustle. Those I saw were mostly elderly, picking their way slowly among fruit stands, drifting along the sidewalks. Like the fish swimming aimlessly in the tanks of restaurant windows, few appeared to be in a rush to get anywhere. A tentative pause hung in the air, as if in hip and booming Seattle this part of town was suspended, awaiting either gentrification or demolition crews.

The Panama Hotel was built in 1910 as a boarding house for Japanese laborers. When I visited, it still served transient workers, but few were Japanese. Instead they came from Mexico and Guatemala or from the Midwestern rust belt. Some landed from Alaskan fishing ships or fruit-growing plantations on the dry side of the Cascade Mountains. Others arrived directly from unemployment lines, stopping at the Panama on their way up the West Coast looking for a change of luck. In 1995 at the Panama, a person could rent a room, clean and light with

Panama Hotel basement, Seattle, Washington. Photo by Gary Oliveira.

lace curtains on the windows, a wash basin in the corner, and a bathroom down the hall, for three hundred dollars a month.

Not much had changed inside since 1940, except that Jan Johnson,
the hotel's third owner, had added a coin-operated washer and dryer.
The hotel was a historic preservationist's dream, the product of a certain lack of prosperity that kept the hotel's managers from making
grand renovations, from gutting the dark, turn-of-the-century interior or sweeping out storage rooms full of potentially combustible
objects. At the same time, it had managed to stay in business, if only
modestly, so that all these years later, while surrounding buildings had
fallen to bulldozers to be replaced by sand-colored condos, the Panama
remained standing on its squat, architecturally unremarkable foundations.

To get to the trunks of the wartime deportees, Johnson led me on a
descent through sedimentary layers of the Panama's history—down
worn, gritty stairs, through a disused boiler room (the boiler man's
greasy coveralls still hanging on a peg), past World War I–era *sento*
(Japanese baths) where advertisements in Japanese and English ex-
claim the wonders of products long since forgotten. We walked by
huge, army-green drums filled with Cold War–era fallout-shelter
rations (forty pounds of salted crackers) and continued down a nar-

row and crumbling passage, deep into the spleen of the creaking hotel. The storage room was piled high with boxes, crates, straw baskets, and leather suitcases stamped with the names of foreign ports—Manila, Peking, Yokohama. Crumbling columns of sea trunks stood like old ruins between naked bulbs swinging on long cords from the ceiling. Clothes spilled onto the floor, pyramids of teakettles were lined up in rows, and a shroud of dust covered everything.

It was just a room of forgotten refuse, and I was transfixed. Saidiya Hartman argues that garbage is significant. "Waste," she writes, "is the interface of life and death. It incarnates all that has been rendered invisible, peripheral, or expendable to history writ large."[5] The basement of the resident hotel offered a snapshot of a portion of 1940s Seattle, where working people checked in and out on sinking and swelling tides of fortune. The location of the hotel—on the edge of the city, in a marginal zone—was itself reminiscent of the lives of Japanese Americans, existing in the interstices between American and Japanese cultures. As the war showed, their fate was linked integrally and impotently with the fortunes of both countries. These belongings left for decades in a gloomy spatial anarchy gave me a spooky sense of something about to happen, a feeling of the deportees' ever-present absence that penetrated the marble-gray columns of sunlit dust.

Most seductive was the fact that these objects were not "artifacts" that were purposefully preserved and cataloged. Because their preservation was accidental, I considered the forgotten possessions somehow had more truth to them. They had not been planted there for me to find decades later, to serve as the basis for "history." The happenstance quality gave me a sense that I was eavesdropping on something I wasn't meant to witness. It helped that access to the basement storeroom was limited. Few at the time knew what it held. Eventually media attention brought more inquiries than Johnson could handle, and she restricted visitors' entry. At the same time, she was reluctant to send materials to museums that requested them. I admit that I shamefully enjoyed my semi-exclusive access.

The storage room was a sort of reverse archive, the opposite of an official repository, a place to stash objects intended to be overlooked, a place to will them out of sight. Much like the unconscious, where the mind represses memories too painful to retain, the basement held possessions forgotten not accidentally but purposefully. White Seattleites in February 1942 voted overwhelming for the Japanese Americans' removal. Imagine their reaction if Japanese American deportees had left their possessions in plain sight: rain-soaked laundry dangling from clotheslines, produce rotting on fruit stands, goods in shop windows fading in the sun. The unrepressed possessions of suddenly absent fellow citizens would have told a story starkly divergent from newspaper accounts of "evacuation," safety, national security, and inevitable fealty to race.[6] The basement full of belongings underscores the myth of what was euphemistically called "evacuation," a term implying benevolence, a federal government seeking to remove Japanese Americans for their own safety.[7] Like the deportations—indeed, like the deportees—the stockpile was meant to be forgotten. To me, the Panama's storage room of locked-away possessions served as an icon for the quiet banishment of Japanese Americans from American society.

Seattle telephone directories show how neatly Japanese Americans were excised from the city population between 1942 and 1943. In the forties, the listings were arranged by street:

1942		1943	
Main St.		*Main St.*	
522	Mitswando Sagamiya Booksellers & confy mfrs	522	—
522a	Nikko-Low café	522a	Allison Birdie Mrs
527	Panama Pharmacy Izui M	527	—
	6th av S. intersects		*6th av S. intersects*
600	Mimbu Wm Y Lawyer	600	—
	Yoshihara Kenichi gen. insur.		
	Hara Iwao acct.		
601	Pacific Printing Co.	601	—
602	Yuasa H	602	—
603	vacant	603	—
604	Takahashi Yuri restaurant	604	—
604½	Oriental-American Bank Building	604½	Maine Hotel Lodgings
	Yuasa H Lodgings		Kobb Jos. G. mgr
605	Maki Kioyichi grocery	605	—
605½	Panama Hotel Lodgings	605½	Panama Hotel Lodgings
	Hori Takashi, owner		Monroe Alex D. G. mgr
606	Sato Kosaku 2d hand gds	606	—
607	Educational Society of Japanese Cannery Workers	607	—

Japanese Americans' disappearances were scarcely noticeable, an em dash in the phone book, a fleeting image on weekly newsreels. That 120,000 Japanese Americans, with only three exceptions, went quietly, showing up with the permitted two suitcases at the specified time and place, neatly dressed and orderly, to board Greyhound buses or waiting trains, made it seem like an auspicious beginning to a holiday rather than a forced deportation, the culmination of years of FBI surveillance, months of arrests and curfews, and an "anti-Jap" campaign growing daily in ferocity. The decorum with which Japanese Americans were deported and their belongings stowed away veils the unseemly violence of disrupted lives, severed families, and confiscated property.

The basement of the Panama Hotel contains things that could not be stuffed into two suitcases—fishing poles, dressers, family portraits, golf clubs, wingtip shoes. This mountain of family property speaks to how deprivation of such abstractions as citizenship and freedom is accompanied by forfeiture of concrete things—possessions, homes, jobs—which in turn strips people of other abstractions. Divested of books, they lose part of their knowledge. Confiscating letters and photographs speeds the dissolution of personal memories. Seizure of cars erodes mobility, independence, and adulthood. Depriving Japanese Americans of their possessions was a way of denying them the emblems that evinced their citizenship, reducing their status to that of the penniless alien immigrant, just off the boat, two straw suitcases in hand.

Sifting through trunks, opening drawers and diaries, I felt part time traveler and part voyeur. The street seemed far away. A silence stretched across the cavernous room. It was a blanket of timelessness that arrested any quick motions and muffled the ticking of my wristwatch. By making a fetish of the objects, I could read the basement like a travelogue, a memoir, or a random literary tract from another era. The things stowed there narrated daily life arrested in mid-act. In a tool chest I found the hand-carved neck of a violin, never finished. Diaries halted abruptly. Suits evoked the office jobs their owners had to give up when interned. The basement, this reverse archive, functioned like Proust's involuntary memory, where things once forgotten are randomly recalled: letters, garments, kitchen utensils—picked up

Kampkook, "America's Favorite Camp Stove," Panama Hotel.
Photo by Gary Oliveira.

in no particular order—offered clues to what he would call a not-yet-remembered-past.[8]

On one shelf was an unopened package of Dixie Dessert Dishes, twelve paper dishes stacked and wrapped in cellophane. The packaging is explicit: "For ice cream, puddings, fruits and frozen desserts." A product like this is purchased in anticipation of a party or an evening with friends around the kitchen table. The value of the unclaimed Dixie Dessert Dish lies in the undone: the get-together not held, the picnic canceled, the birthday celebration instead held around a plywood table at Camp Minidoka in central Idaho. Dixie Dessert Dishes were a tiny luxury, just a few pennies apiece, but their use was contingent upon greater amenities—the existence of puddings and frozen desserts, of refrigerators to keep them cold, of tables on which to serve them, and the stability all that implies.

In the middle of the storage room, on top of several crates, sat an old camp stove. The brand: American Kampkook. It had been used at least once, then carefully rewrapped in the original cardboard packaging and painstakingly bound with now-frayed twine. The butane still in its fuel tank had lingered for fifty years, while other less volatile substances had passed on. At a glance, the Kampkook was just another unremarkable product of American mass production, but to touch its dusty surface was to be washed in someone else's memories. Monica Sone recalls her family busily packing the car, driving out of town, and arriving at a majestic timber gateway that announced the entrance to an American national park. Her memoirs recount picnics by the lake, hot dogs roasting, children crying after playing so long and running so hard they can barely stand.[9] The only thing that could mar the day would be a popular wartime song on the radio: "We're Gonna Find a Fellow Who Is Yellow and Beat Him Red, White and Blue."[10]

The Kampkook stove tells the story of a failed American contract. Work hard, save, keep out of trouble, and you too can have the middle-class pleasures owed to every industrious American: a car, vacations in nature zones, camping equipment, and sturdy wool coats with aristocratic fur collars. The Japanese Americans whose possessions ended up in the basement of the Panama Hotel had worked hard, saved, and purchased goods that promised assimilation and normality, but then the war came (as it would), the "Japs" bombed Pearl Harbor, and after December 1941 being "Japanese" became a terrible liability.

In the memoirs of Japanese Americans, the family car is an item that was especially longed-for in the camps and, along with the kitchen, an object of the greatest nostalgia. Jeanne Wakatsuki Houston remembers old car trips, the smooth, seamless exterior and expansive interior of the car that was repossessed in 1942, and the junker with two flat tires purchased in 1945 in order to drive out of the camps with some dignity after three years imprisonment.[11] Perhaps the highway and the automobile are such intractable American icons because the act of driving allows one to simulate the elusive myth of the melting pot. On the highway, all cars fuse into one colorful stream, going at equal speed in the same direction, with great efficiency and ease. Perhaps the highway in the United States is revered, immortalized in book, song, and film, defended, cared for, and elaborated daily because it is one of the few sites in the American landscape where the myth of equality and social mobility can play out. Within the camps, however, even this automated promise of personal mobility was fictitious.

Buried in a chest of drawers was the last issue of the *North American Times*, dated Thursday, March 12, 1942, a few weeks before evacuation orders were posted on Seattle's telephone poles, addressed to "ALL

Chest of drawers, Panama Hotel. Photo by Gary Oliveira.

PERSONS OF / JAPANESE / ANCESTRY." By that time, the paper's editor had been incarcerated as a potentially dangerous enemy alien.[12] The lead article explains how the U.S. Treasury had ordered the paper, like all other Japanese-American papers on the West Coast, to cease publication. The newspaper's front page is in English and looks like any other paper at the newsstand, but inside Japanese characters surge up the page, swelling over photographs and around advertisements. English on the outside and Japanese on the inside—in the midst of the discrimination of prewar America, Japanese in Seattle maintained a schizophrenic existence.

Moving from object to object, I got a sense of the many borders Japanese Americans crossed every day. From the old to the new, the handmade to the mass-produced, from that which was interior, intimate, and often of Japanese origin to that which was public, social, and usually American-made. In the trunks were Western clothes, of the latest prewar style, with wide lapels, broad, zoot-suit shoulders. There were bits of Americana, trappings of apple-pie patriotism: American flags with gold-tipped wooden poles, a fringed, pink and green pillow from Mt. Rainier National Park, a comic book called *Air Adventures* about killing Nazis. These items symbolize citizenship, loyalty, and belonging. Only a few objects meant for private consumption hint at the

incriminating link with Japan that was the rationale for deportation—
a tiny teapot with a splash of leaves decorating its delicate porcelain; a
bucketful of handmade tempura fryers, their carved wooden handles
scorched black; a kimono, with tiny stitches holding velvet and silk
together. Perhaps it is here, in the intimacy of culinary cravings and
the privacy of family life, that culture resists the draw of assimilation
just a bit longer.

But there may be another reason for the absence of traditional Japanese possessions. Just as silences can be pregnant with meaning, what
was missing from the basement tells nearly as much about the deportations as what was there. Hearing of FBI searches in the frenzied,
banner-headline days following Pearl Harbor, Japanese Americans
burned many items that seemed too Japanese to pass a late-night in-
spection: silk national flags, kimonos with the notorious red dot on
a white field, hand-bound monographs, letters, maps, photographs.[13]
In what Henri Lefebvre calls a "society of bureaucratically controlled
consumption," the products of industrialized society are used to socialize and regulate. And to be effective, this regulation must have a flip
side, a latent violence that lends it force.[14] When Japanese Americans
carried out voluntary book burnings, destroying their own memorabilia and papers, it meant the diffuse control of consumer society was
no longer latent but boiling at the surface. At the same time, FBI agents
and police officers were making the rounds of Japantown, searching
houses, confiscating cameras, shortwave radios, and personal papers,
and detaining most of the community's male leaders.[15] The objects not
found in the Panama Hotel's basement describe a vortex of violence,
the point where coercion applied to maximum effect led to destruction. Obliteration, by its nature, hides the destructive moment, and
so it is that history often fails to record, in its chronicle of unchecked
progress, the quiet demolition of objects, values, and persons.

The metaphor of inside and outside continues in the parlance of
camp life. As a child in the Manzanar Camp in central California,
Jeanne Wakatsuki Houston sifted through a Sears Roebuck catalog
and longed for the objects of the outside: "dreaming of the dresses and
boots and coats that were out there, somewhere at the other end of the
highway beyond the gate."[16] For Wakatsuki Houston the world of consumer goods became the utopian world of acceptance and normality.
But once there, "at the other end of the highway," back in high school

in Los Angeles after internment, she found that even with the shortest skirt and the latest bobby-socked fashions, she could not get on the "inside"—into the girl scouts, the sororities, the cheerleading squad. The only way she found to unlock the Caucasian world was not via consumer goods and fashion but through white males, by playing into images of the mysterious and exotic "Oriental." When, during homecoming elections, she paraded onto the high school gym floor barefoot in a flower-print sarong with a hibiscus behind her ear, the boys in the school thundered applause and she won the crown. But it was a hollow victory, Wakatsuki Houston found, because being an exotic Oriental, even a popular one, was "just another form of invisibility."[17] Roland Barthes describes exoticism as "a figure for emergencies" when trying to assimilate the Other: "The Other becomes a pure object, a spectacle, a clown. Relegated to the confines of humanity, he no longer threatens the security of the home."[18] With this definition in mind, I recognize the affinity between prewar posters plastered around the city explaining "How to tell your friends from Japs" and the postwar election of a Japanese homecoming queen, who had, indeed, come home.[19]

There are a few traces in the basement of life in the internment camps. Hori Takashi, who owned the Panama Hotel from 1938 to 1985, returned from Camp Minidoka in the summer of 1945 to reclaim his hotel and his life in Seattle. He had acquired new possessions during his three years in the camp, more than would fit into his two original suitcases, so he packed them into U.S. Army rifle cases for the trip home. The wooden, casket-shaped boxes with Takashi's name and address stenciled on them contained papers, mostly records from meetings in the camp with U.S. government administrators.

Sifting through the documents I got a sense of the topography of camp life, and the internments took shape as a strange, regressive form of social engineering. The camps were designed on the principle of mass production, which the U.S. Navy builders, the Seabees, mastered during World War II.[20] Each block of barracks was identical to every other block, just as all ten camps, from California to Arkansas, were built according to one master plan. The camps operated on a system of enforced communality. Residents were packed into sparse sleeping quarters with households separated by army blankets strung between walls, porous to sound and smell. They ate in communal mess halls and relieved themselves in open toilets. The camps' planners did not consider issues of privacy and individuality, as if in categorizing all Japanese Americans as "enemy aliens," guilty by virtue of name and birth, they came to believe in their own representation of Japanese Americans as one big, extended family, one collective body.

Like many utopian projects, the internment camps embodied that which had been mythically projected, feared, and then disguised in the form of a positive solution for the future.[21] Japanese Americans, long accused of being "clannish" and refusing to assimilate, were placed in ghettos in desert landscapes where they had no choice but to socialize with other Japanese Americans in a clannish manner. Many, in fact, for the first time in their lives found themselves in a community of "Orientals." Wakatsuki Houston argues Japanese Americans went passively to the camps because they too believed the caricatures of themselves projected onto American popular culture. After the preceding years of less overt legal and physical discrimination and segregation, she writes, she and her family had assimilated the narrative of their inferiority and began to believe they deserved poor treatment. "You are going to be invisible anyway," Wakatsuki Houston writes, "so why not completely disappear?"[22]

When Albert Speer designed his grand scheme for Berlin as the capital of the "thousand year Reich," he calculated how it would look after two thousand years. Inspired by Roman ruins, he planned for Berlin to decay in a way that would speak to the grandeur of the Third Reich. Conversely, the Japanese American internment camps were built to disappear quickly and without a trace once their usefulness was exhausted. As a blemish in the American self-representation as a nation of individual civil liberties fighting in Europe and Asia for democracy, the camps, which imprisoned individuals because of a collective racial identity, were built using collapsible walls and un-fixed fences that army demolition crews could quickly disassemble. In architectural form, the internment camps were planned to be temporary, a fleeting moment in what contemporaries saw as an otherwise unblemished wartime record. Barbed wire—the same rambling barbed wire, which revolutionized the West, making cowboys obsolete by cheaply containing livestock—formed the structural backbone of the camps. Along with plywood barracks, it carved the camps out of otherwise unbroken, arid plains. The camps' formlessness and impermanence reflected the status of Japanese immigrants in American society, at once in and out; exiled to the desert and conscripted into the U.S. Army; banned from the coasts and propelled into the interior of the country. Japanese Americans possessed identities that, like the barbed wire borders, were hard to pin down and were suspected of being in a state of traitorous flux.

In 1945, then, the internment camps disappeared as quickly as they had come together three years before. Among Takashi's papers were the minutes from a meeting of Camp Minidoka's community council and block commissioners. The meeting was called to talk to a certain "Mr. Kimball from Washington," a representative of the War Relocation Authority (WRA). Kimball had the job of overseeing the closing of Camp Minidoka and the dispersal of the remaining Japanese Americans, who by that time consisted mostly of the elderly or the very young. At the meeting, the Issei, first-generation immigrants who by law had been banned from U.S. citizenship, were asking Kimball for help. They had been told they must leave Minidoka in a few months, but they were worried because they no longer had homes to which they might return. Kimball was saddled with explaining to the Issei the difference between the U.S. government's power (to uproot and deport) and its lack of obligation (to return and reestablish). In the contorted redundancy of bureaucratic speech, he provided the Issei a self-circling tautology for the opening and closing of the camps:

> The determination whether an emergency exists was first made by the government, and the government also determined whether it no longer existed. . . . When that emergency no longer existed, then it became necessary to consider liquidation, since the reason for continuance of the centers no longer existed.[23]

Kimball explained that his agency's responsibilities concluded at the end of the "emergency" (the war) and also at the camp gates. The WRA, he stated, was not responsible for finding Japanese Americans housing outside the camps, nor could it provide the requested reparations or loans to revive lost businesses and farms.[24]

When the WRA director, Dillon Myer, arrived later to speak to the interned Japanese Americans, he was even more adamant in asserting that the status of the internees had changed, meaning they were no longer wards of the WRA. "There are some people," Myer explained, "not only in Minidoka but in other centers, who get funds and incomes and are enjoying retired life in a relocation center."[25] For Myer, the Japanese Americans were no longer dangerous, potential spies and "enemy aliens," but, as persons refusing to leave the camps, had become loafers, welfare cases, and government freeloaders.[26]

Roland Barthes argues myths do not deny the existence of things; on the contrary, their function is to talk about objects in order to purify, make them innocent, and give them a natural justification and clarity so that interpretations become statements of fact.[27] These were in part the tasks of Myer and Kimball. Despite their good intentions, they could offer little in a concrete way to help the internees. But they could provide a new set of serviceable myths for the deportations. "Enemy alien" had left the vocabulary. The postwar interpretation viewed the immigrants and their offspring in terms of dependency and as a potential material drain on the nation's wealth. The rhetoric of "evacuation" as protection from irrational racists also disappeared. In fact, Myer expressed impatience with internees who said they were frightened to return to the West Coast, where the Anti-Japanese Leagues were still meeting. "There has been some anti-Japanese sentiment, but not nearly as much as a year ago or two years ago," Myer said. "This idea of their being evacuated for their own protection—that is a lot of bunk. That wasn't the reason. It has been said, but people now recognize the evacuation program. So we won't argue about that point. Let's wipe that one off."[28]

Myer and Kimball were not very good at mythmaking. Neither could offer more than elliptical sentences when explaining why Japanese Americans had been incarcerated in 1942. These men, who normally spoke in solid terms, wandered off into vague terminology when alluding to the motivations behind the deportations. Kimball talked about "that emergency" which did exist and then did not exist. Myer referred to Japanese Americans in the third person when speaking directly to them. He spoke about "their" protection and a general "recognition" by "people" of the evacuation. The officials did not speak directly to the Issei of their "enemy alien" status because, standing before the aging men, that charge appeared absurd. Kimball and Myer were confronted with the confusing discrepancy between the myth of the comic-book Japanese—arms up his sleeve, eyes slanted and savage, with a lascivious smile—and the benign, seemingly middle-class men before them who spoke in polite tones and seemed to possess very normal concerns about security, family, and welfare. To restate Barthes, mythmaking takes a good bit of distance, the distance necessary to blur details so that explanations can become clearer. Myer and Kimball were far too close.

Time also creates distance. Fifty years provide a safe remove from which to eulogize, simplify, and explain the deportations in terms clearer than those of Myer and Kimball. Why did the possessions in the basement of the Panama Hotel, having lain dormant for decades, suddenly become visible in the 1990s? Before that time, some people knew of them, but no one apparently thought the basement of junk was worthy of attention. Hori Takashi, who owned the Panama until 1985, saw nothing sacred about the old trunks in the basement. He told me he never meant to save them, just didn't want to pay to have them carted off to the dump. Takashi said the trunks belonged to people who, after the closing of the camps, went to other parts of the country to rebuild their lives, and explained in his matter-of-fact way how the Japanese community he grew up in failed to take shape again after the war. "People," he said, "went where they could to make a living."

Takashi preferred not to talk about his internment. When he did, his memory faltered and his sentences grew short. He could remember not only the name of his own grade school principal but that of the principal of his wife's school, yet he couldn't recall the day he was deported. "Ah, that was so long ago—who can remember?" As I pressed him, he stopped, lowered his head to think, and offered in a softer voice. "I figure we lost a lot of opportunities. But that's life."

Takashi rather liked to speak about the old days, before the war, when there were many resident hotels in the neighborhood, with steam pouring onto the streets from the underground baths, a Buddhist temple on the corner, and a Japanese theater down the street. Like Takashi, half of Seattle's Japanese American income earners owned independent businesses, which centered around the hotel on Jackson and Main Streets.[29] "After the internment," he repeated, "the Japanese community here was never the same again. Everybody scattered all over."

Memory is a state of mind. The storage room in the basement of the Panama Hotel, much like America's collective memory of the Japanese internments, existed for fifty years on the forgotten side of memory—stowed away within reach, but politely out of sight and out of mind. Takashi possessed his own memories, which he guarded closely, in his own cerebral storage vaults. For him the trunks were just that, old trunks. Takashi was not alone. For decades the internments were characterized by a legacy of silence, but silence that was evident. Janis Edwards calls the memory of the internments an "absent presence," one that was "simultaneously hidden and ubiquitous in popular culture."[30]

History takes a long time, public history even longer. In Seattle's International District, there was no public marker to commemorate the annihilation of *Nihonmachi*—nothing at the Buddhist temple, which served as a "Civil Control Station" at which several thousand deportees gathered before they departed by bus in May 1942; nothing too at other internment centers at 2100 Second Avenue, 1319 Rainier Avenue, or the Christian Youth Center at 2203 East Madison Street.[31] In the nineties, when I visited the Panama, there was just a mural, painted in 1977, with an image in the lower corner of a few people behind barbed wire. The untitled painting bore no caption. You had to know about the internments to decipher it.

At the turn of the twenty-first century, however, the Panama Hotel became a subject of interest, which grew in the subsequent decade. Journalists wrote about the hotel basement as a "discovery." A popular novel appeared about the hotel and its painful history.[32] In 2006 the Panama Hotel was declared a national landmark.[33] In 2010 residents dedicated a memorial; as with the Vietnam Veterans Memorial in Washington, D.C., the names of the internees are etched in stone, and visitors often make rubbings. By 2014 the hotel and the secrets of its basement had become a tourist destination, rated on Yelp, Yahoo, Trip Advisor, and Lonely Planet. Tourists now stay at the hotel instead of transients. They take their meals in a new tea house, where they can gaze down at the basement through a recently installed window in the floor. If they book in advance, guests can tour the bathhouse, which, according to the Panama's website, is the only remaining intact *sento* in the United States.[34] In ten years, the Panama Hotel has been transformed from a reverse archive into a landmark, a specific place of memory and site of popular culture.

In the 1930s, Walter Benjamin had the hope, if not the confidence, that by pointing out small, discarded objects, the "trash" of history, he could undermine the myth of progress that was wedded to capitalist expansion. Yet at some point even the wreckage progress leaves in its wake becomes profitable. Tour agencies, video game designers, and filmmakers sell the disaster of the Chernobyl Zone, the rubble of the American rust belt, and the poignant lessons of the Japanese American internments. Meanwhile, onetime American segregation and forced assimilation has flowed back to generate multiculturalism as a commercialized American product, sold to citizens and foreign tourists alike by spotlighting ethnic differences that make up the great nation: Italian pasta, African American blues, Indian powwows, Korean baths, Chinese dragons, and Jewish bagels for Sunday mornings. By the year 2000, the Panama Hotel had joined that pageant. Watching how small, formerly domestic objects are resurrected and paraded into public culture to be appropriated into a multicultural national self-conception intertwined with a myth of individual success, I wondered about the danger of conflating historical method and history itself.

I advocate in this book for multivocal historical narratives, but can a chorus of voices and found objects serve instead to mask segregation and racial disparities, while amplifying a resurgent American nationalism?[35] In the United States, neither the civil rights actions of the sixties nor the multicultural discourse begun in the seventies made a dent in residential and school segregation, which increased between black and white citizens in American cities and suburbs from 1950 to 2000. School segregation rose again from 2000 to 2010.[36] Residential segregation—which was pivotal in establishing the Panama Hotel as a repository for the possessions of deported Japanese Americans in 1942—remains a cornerstone of continuing racial disparities in health, poverty, employment, and education.[37] Now that most forms of national autonomy have been effectively suppressed in the United States, the narrative of an Ellis Island culture, even a critical one, is both safe and complementary, while it obscures a segregated reality.

But that is the most cynical interpretation of the unveiling of the Panama Hotel's accidentally preserved time capsule. There is also a personal side to memory. Jan Johnson, the self-proclaimed curator of this unofficial collection, bought the hotel from Hori Takashi in 1985. Johnson, who was born just as the war was ending, said she had fallen under the spell of the Panama's mysteries and didn't want it to see it plowed under by developers. When Takashi promised to clean out the crowded basement before handing over the title, she begged him to leave everything just as it was.

Under her watchful eye, fifty trunks were shipped off to a temporary exhibit, *America's Concentration Camps*, at the Japanese American National Museum in Los Angeles. When I met her, Johnson was anxious to get the trunks back to her labyrinthine basement, which, she said, is the place they belong, the place to see them.

"You know what I mean—you've been down there. Those things were put there by them. They are waiting."

I did know what she meant. There was an uncanny sense of time, or lack of it, in the basement. A sense of memories breathing out of the old clothes, a feeling I've never had looking at artifacts in a museum that are sanitized, archived, and placed behind glass with explanatory captions. Johnson describes the hotel as "her art." The concept of her art form is simple, if somewhat unconventional. Johnson intended not to touch a thing, not to move the slightest object if it could be helped. This has been a controversial position; local archivists and historians have criticized Johnson for refusing to hand over the whole mass of forgotten belongings to a museum, where the trunks could be cataloged in a climate-controlled room and safely preserved for public memory.

But who possesses memories? Over the decades, the internment of Japanese Americans has served public memory in a number of ways. During the war, the "evacuations" of Japanese Americans, while German Americans and Italian Americans remained at large, implicitly sent a message about the different, inherently racial war in the East.[38] Immediately after the war, American pundits viewed the camps as an isolated moment of wartime hysteria that pointed to the baseline American commitment to freedom and justice. The mantra starting in 1946 became "never again," sanctified by President Harry Truman's words of congratulation to the 442nd Regimental Combat Team, a segregated Japanese American unit: "You fought not only the enemy but you fought prejudice—and you won." Commentators also noted that the internments, in scattering former internees to new postwar homes, facilitated their rapid assimilation, which was taken as inherently good.[39] In subsequent years, historians have pointed out that though the internment experience was humiliating and painful, it led to a politically astute restitution movement that brought American

lawmakers to an awareness of racialized state policies. This awareness paved the way for the civil rights movement.[40]

Interpretations of the internments serve different purposes. Some
compensate descendants psychologically by giving meaning to the
losses of their parents and grandparents, who suffered quietly after
the war.[41] Politically, explanations have bolstered the sovereignty of
the state. Morally, they have charted out correct paths for the future.
But what if the objects in the basement of the Panama Hotel are not
required to serve any civic function at all? What if, as Johnson asserts,
they should remain as they are and speak for themselves? Although I
am paid to interpret artifacts and documents and give the past meaning, I like the fact that Johnson has resisted that impulse.

For Johnson the trunks are about discovery. Stacked on end, they
offer a bridge to the everyday existence of a community that was destroyed by executive order. Johnson did not resist the pull of time and
tragedy that makes a fetish out of the old things. She taught me how
it is possible to pick up objects, feel their contours, and put them back
down without encapsulating them in a new, carefully framed narrative. Johnson's resistance to the museum is a form of art that liberates
the lost and forgotten possessions from national, ethnic, and community narratives, freeing them to transmit messages (or not) idiosyn-
cratically to those who care to seek them out. As a place, the basement
under Johnson's curation remained a reverse archive. Subsequent historical narratives of the internments will shift on political and cultural tides, while the basement, if left undisturbed, as Johnson would
have it, remains to give testimony.

3 History (Im)possible in the Chernobyl Zone

The guards opened the trunk, glanced inside, closed it, checked our faxed letter of permission, and, with a wave, passed us on into the Chernobyl Zone of Exclusion. I had been thinking about the Zone for nearly a decade but had never before entered it.[1]

I carried with me a cinematic vision of Andrei Tarkovsky's wasteland, identified only as "the Zone" in the 1979 film *Stalker*. In Tarkovsky's fiction—and my imagination—the Zone spreads across a wreckage of rusted industrial plants, collapsing telephone lines, and buildings overtaken by dark forests. Abandoned, fenced-off, and guarded, the Zone emanates a mysterious and deadly force, one that threatens to kill or causes mutations in the offspring of those exposed. In Tarkovsky's version, the Stalker, for a small fee, secretly leads adventurers into the Zone to reveal its mysteries. They enter under cover of night and fog, dodging bullets amid the relics of industrial decay.

Author in front of the Chernobyl sarcophagus, 2004. Photo by Mary Mycio.

My two traveling companions and I heard no gunshots. We entered the Chernobyl Zone in the comforting sun of a balmy June day in 2004. Unlike Tarkovsky's tattooed and scarred Stalker, our guide, provided by the Chernobyl Zone information agency, was a bright-eyed Marilyn Monroe knockoff named Rimma Kiselitsa. After the genial guards opened the gates, the car steered us seamlessly through pine forests, past lazy streams and open marshes similar to those outside the Chernobyl Zone. While the Stalker and his charges slept wherever sleep overtook them, we checked into the Interinform hotel, a comfortable, if sterile, double-wide trailer, moved in since the nuclear explosion. The town of Chernobyl, where the hotel was located and where most of the people who legally work in the Zone live, appeared as just another tired, economically depressed Ukrainian town. A little shop on the corner did a brisk trade in sweets, sausages, and booze. In the evenings, we had our pick of two nightclubs. There the Zone workers gathered, many just past their prime, graying, bulging, and boogying in the dim light, twisting the way Elvis did, but in luxurious slow motion.

I had come to the Zone because I had seen a website called *Kiddofspeed* created by a certain elusive "Elena." Elena owned a motorcycle, a 147-horsepower viridescent Kawasaki Ninja. She had dark eyes and black hair. Her green leather biking jacket fit like a handmade Italian glove, and her voluptuous hips rode high on the racing bike. Elena's father had been a nuclear scientist at the Chernobyl Nuclear Power Plant, and he still worked there in the cleanup. Thanks to "Daddy," Elena had a special pass to enter the Zone whenever she wanted. And she did, taking long rides on the wide-open roads, where, as she put it, she had "the absolute freedom to ride [my motorcycle] wherever curiosity and the speed demon take me." No better place in the world to cycle, she claimed, the roads "are in the same condition they were 20 years ago—except for an occasional blade of grass that discovered a crack to spring through."[2] Within a few months of being posted in February 2004, Elena's site had drawn millions of visitors. From the chat rooms that cropped up, it became clear that many of the visitors were men from around the globe, swept up in the fantasy of a hot babe, on a hot bike, in a hot zone.

I had a different, less erotic fantasy. I had hopes of recovering history that had been forgotten in a place that time had left behind. As Elena rode, she stopped in abandoned villages and in the vacated modernist city of Pripyat, and she snapped photos. Her website was mostly about the photos: haunting shots narrating lives suspended the moment the roof of the reactor buckled and sent forth—invisibly, impossibly, inevitably—the toxin most feared in our nuclear age. The pictures showed disheveled apartments that looked as if people had left in a hurry and never glanced back: books scattered across the floor, family photos poured from a shoebox, clothes still hanging on the line, an issue of *Okhota i rybolovstvo* (*Hunt and Fish*) jammed in the mailbox. The magazine belonged, Elena speculated, to a man who had gone fishing and never come back. People could not take their irradiated possessions with them when they fled, she explained. Most were lucky to escape with their lives, if not their health.

I was taken in by Elena's website, seduced. Her voice was so confident, her subjectivity complete. She created an authorial narrative I longed to reproduce. She was there. She knew what she saw, and she could name it clearly, unfaltering, with confidence. In the way that blogs are often personal, Elena was up-front in her text, a witness giving testimony to the destruction of her native land. The intimate qualities of her voice, matched with on-site photos of herself, gave the blog poignancy and immediacy.

Right away, I started making plans to go to the Zone. For a historian of the Soviet Union, few sites could be more compelling than this, the world's largest time capsule, frozen at a critical moment in 1986—just before Mikhail Gorbachev experimented Soviet society into extinction. Thirteen years later, nothing was the same: the Zone was in an independent Ukraine, on the edge of a recently reconstituted Europe, struggling with a global capitalist economy that no longer produced the household appliances, canned goods, and Communist Party tracts that had contained and sustained the lives of the departed inhabitants of the ex-republic of the former empire. I wanted to find out, by sifting through the abandoned cottages and apartments, whether people knew their empire was about to crumble. I wanted to recapture stories that had been forgotten, along with household articles, in their haste to get away.

The problem was that my fantasy, like those of the millions of men hunkered over their computer screens, was just that—sheer imaginary. Elena's Web persona was a fake.[3] When Elena first posted the site, she had never been to the Zone. She scanned photos from coffee-table books on the accident, made up a narrative, and published it.

Little in Elena's story was true. There was no special pass. Her father had not worked at the power plant, even as a janitor. After her website gained notoriety, she evidently decided actually to go to the Zone. For the standard five-hour tour, she paid two hundred dollars. Her guide in the Zone had been the same Rimma Kiselitsa who served as our guide for a week as I toured the Zone with Mary Mycio, a writer working on a book about Chernobyl and a story for the *Los Angeles Times*.[4] Rimma told us that Elena had showed up with a canvas bag containing her helmet, which she pulled out so her husband could snap legitimizing photos to add to her *Kiddofspeed* website. There was no motorcycle. No one, Rimma said, can ride in the Zone in an open vehicle, let alone on a motorcycle. There are no wide-open roads. Guard posts punctuate the Zone every dozen or so miles. The roads, which are not in frequent use, have crumbled after two decades of neglect. Not just blades of grass, but whole saplings have come up through the cracks.

Driving in the Zone entails a mad scramble through sand and mud as the man-made landscape returns to the natural terrain of sandy pine forests and swamp.

Most important for me, there were no abandoned households. In the years since the explosion, nearly every home had been picked clean. Even the knobs on the kitchen cabinets were gone. Even the time capsule schoolchildren buried in the 1970s had been looted. (I know because I was hoping to dig it up and loot it myself.) Inhabitants had returned in the summer of 1986, after the radiation settled somewhat, to gather what they could of their belongings.[5] After that, soldiers dumped heavy appliances, furniture, machinery, and cars into great pits and buried them.[6] Pillagers followed in the hungry days during the transition to capitalism, selling any remaining radiated goods they could find in flea markets across Ukraine and Central Europe. In 2004, reportedly, people on the lam hid out in the Zone, surviving as poachers and thieves. They squatted in abandoned cottages, lit fires, and sometimes robbed travelers. Before I went to the Zone, Rostyslav Omeliashko, a Kiev archaeologist who made frequent expeditions there, told me he always traveled with an armed guard. He advised me to get one too.

After I learned of Elena's hoax, I revisited the *Kiddofspeed* website and now found it sensational and dishonest. I noticed much I had missed before. She included, for example, several aerial photos. How did I suppose she had taken those pictures? I traced several of her photos to the work of news photographer Ihor Kostin.[7] He started working the story the night of the explosion, when he joined a helicopter pilot and flew over the burning reactor. In the cabin, Kostin managed to click twenty frames before his camera failed. Most of those shots did not turn out. The plumes of radioactive gases that engulfed the helicopter (and Kostin's body within it) overexposed them. That Elena had appropriated Kostin's work after the risks he took seemed especially deceitful.

I also took note of the lurid nature of Elena's prose, written as if to attract disaster tourists and gamers, such as those who pay to play the online game S.T.A.L.K.E.R. In the game, players battle mutants, monsters, and shapeless blobs in a cyber version of the abandoned nuclear city of Pripyat. Elena emphasized the "silence" in the "unreal" "dead zone." "It is," she writes, "divinely eerie—like stepping into that Salvador Dali painting with the dripping clocks."[8] After being there myself, this prose rang false. People worked in the zone, guarding it, maintaining the still intact power plants, carrying out research, monitoring and cleanup operations. Several hundred elderly villagers had returned to the zone to live. Their family members came legally and illegally to visit. People dwelling on the perimeter of the Zone entered it to fish, hunt, and forage.[9] The zone isn't eerie and empty. It's just sad in a mundane way that a lot of struggling places are sad.

Why didn't I catch on to Elena's falsehoods before I arrived? I considered myself a somewhat savvy researcher. Why had I found her story so believable? Only slowly I grasped how I had been seduced. Elena's narrative was convincing because, when she first published her website, she had never been to the Chernobyl Zone. In her fiction, she had the pass, the motorcycle, and the open roads. She always traveled alone, she wrote, because she didn't want another cyclist raising dust in front of her. I envied that. Alone, Elena was free to go where she wanted, whenever she wanted, unguarded and unfettered, without the driver, guide, and fear that accompanied me. The fictional Elena was the autonomous, courageous, solitary author I could only fantasize being.

I might categorize Elena's narrative voice as that of the hero of a travel novel in which the narrator doesn't change ideologically, only the landscape around her does.[10] She stands firm, has no reservations or questions about what she sees, or rather, all that she sees confirms what she already knows. On her website, the narrator "Elena" conquers the truth with certainty, correcting all who have overlooked the Zone and her country's tragic history. The Russian philosopher Mikhail Bakhtin identified narrative form as a space writers create to sustain certain kinds of knowledge.[11] Bakhtin lived seventy years before Elena in Vilna, Odessa, and Vitebsk, multilingual cities like Elena's Kiev in what once was, like Kiev, the Russian empire's western borderlands. Bakhtin, walking mud-packed streets of sloping cottages and down-at-the-heel town houses, heard languages take shape, transform, and dissolve around him. In Vilna, a center of Polish arts and literature, Jewish writers were penning into being Yiddish literature. In Odessa, writers like Isaac Babel tangled Yiddish thieves' jargon with Russian prose. In Vitebsk, idealistic artists such as Marc Chagall and Kasimir Malevich opened an art school for poor students and asked townspeople to support the school by hiring the students to paint their houses. They did, and on the whitewashed walls strange, colorful angels and flying horses, inspired by Chagall, took shape alongside green circles, orange squares, and blue rectangles, painted by the disciples of Malevich.

In these borderland places, Bakhtin developed his idea of polyphonics. Polyphonic communication allowed for the mingling of language groups, cultures, and classes in a way, he imagined, that would guarantee a perpetual intellectual revolution and protect against the assertion of a "single language of truth."[12] Bakhtin would likely have called Elena's narrative mode "monologic," his label for texts that cut short dialog, attempting to fix truths, exclude other voices, and deny conflicting arguments.[13] Bakhtin came to know firsthand the violence of fixed truths and excluded voices. He was arrested in Petersburg in 1929 just before he published a book about the many, conflicting voices of Dostoyevsky's novels.[14] Sentenced and sent into exile, Bakhtin traveled from the creatively fertile, cacophonous Jewish-Ukrainian-Polish-Belorussian Vitebsk to what must have felt like the hushed quiet of Kazakhstan, where the great Kazakh famine was then well under way.[15]

Elena used her narrative mode to tell an inescapable truth about Ukraine and the Chernobyl tragedy, bringing "this issue the world wide attention it deserves." This claim comes from a second narrator on *Kiddofspeed*, identified as Elena's "only email contact," who manages her server. He or she places Elena's name inside quotation marks, acknowledging that "Elena," like every narrator, is a fictional character. Elena went to the trouble of committing a forgery, she wrote in a later version of *Kiddofspeed*, not for fame or profit, but "for the love of my country."[16] She could explore the Zone in absolute terms with absolute freedom because she had no troubling realities to cloud her version of patriotism, sacrifice, and victimization.

Although I was critical of Elena, it dawned on me that most nonfiction scholarship and journalism unfolds in a similar narrative mode. Elena presents herself as a coherent, stable subject, completely knowable to others and herself. This recognizable narrative form—that of the unchanging traveler, moving through a changing landscape—is part of what made *Kiddofspeed* convincing to her millions of readers, and to me. Taking a closer look at her website now, I started to think more about the narrative modes I use.[17] I have rarely mustered the classic nonfiction voice Elena employed. Most often I write in a confessional mode, in which I profess a certain guilt before the people I write about, whose lives amount to tragedy—tragedies I knowingly exploit in writing history. (The reader will find, and probably tire of, the confessional mode in this book.) Less often, I deploy the mode of the unreliable narrator. In this form, I undermine my credentials as a teller of nonfiction, delegitimizing my ability to produce truth-making claims as I come up against contradictions between my own limited vision and other people's diverging views. I use the unreliable narrator to point out the highly subjective qualities of historical research, which creates provisional truths about the past—truths that are certain to change. I am attempting to be truthful as I create these various narrative voices, but they are, in plain fact, as fictional as "Elena." I have made them up. Even when I write in straight, third-person prose, the narrator is my creation. Literary critiques study narrative voice in fiction, but the invented qualities of nonfiction narrators are usually left unquestioned. I would like to change that. In this particular story, largely in contrast to "Elena," the lone, intrepid explorer, "I" have invented for myself a new narrative voice—the coward.

On learning that Elena's website was fabricated, I resolved, having already traveled to central Ukraine, to make the best of the journey. Some remnants of the twilight years of the Soviet empire, I figured, must surely exist among the debris that was too worthless to plunder. So on my first morning in Chernobyl, I got up early, before breakfast in the canteen (promoted in an online tourist site for serving "unradiated" food), to take a look around. I was allowed to explore the town without a guide; at least, no one stopped me from doing so. Chernobyl was an old Polish-Jewish *shtetl* that before and during World War II had been "cleansed" of Poles and Jews. Before the accident in 1986, it was reportedly a quiet, pleasant, unremarkable Ukrainian town. In 2004 it still was, though even more quiet. I wandered over to the high bank of the Pripyat River, where the disorderly *shtetl* streets receded into a green wall of forest and vine before slipping to the lazy river far below. Looking more closely into the greenery, I glimpsed the outline of a window frame and realized a neighborhood of cottages existed beneath the verdant understory. I scrambled into the brush and came to the threshold of an abandoned house.

The threshold
of a Chernobyl
cottage, 2004.
Photo by author.

Inside I could see a dresser with some clothes pulled out. A dirty
plastic doll missing its limbs lay on the sill. Old shoes, which reminded
me of an exhibit from Auschwitz, and school notebooks spilled across
the floor. All junk too worthless to loot, but just the kind of "artifacts"
that might tell me about the past. I itched to enter and snoop. I didn't
have a facemask along to filter out radioactive dust, nor did I have
my Geiger counter with me. Though Chernobyl was considered one
of the safest areas in the Zone, it was hard to know for sure without
a dosimeter because radioactive isotopes tend to gather randomly in
hot spots. An area can be relatively clean, but within it one point can
measure very hot. After a rain or wind, the hot spots can shift. We
generally characterize the earth as terra firma—solid, stable, unmov-
ing. Environmental historians, however, are good at showing how the

visually static landscape is dramatically in motion.[18] Radioactive isotopes are especially mobile. They work as tracers on terrain as they do
in bodies, sketching out migration, movement, and impasses in three
dimensions. In contaminated landscapes such as northern Ukraine
and southern Belarus, the dynamism of these earthly bodies is especially dangerous to the unwary traveler.

Even without a dosimeter, I might have gone in, but eyeing the listing ceiling beams of the hundred-year-old clay, straw, and timber-
frame cottage, I worried that the whole structure might come down
once I crossed the threshold. And then, glancing around, I noticed the
rough scratching of the earth by wild boars. They paw around looking for insects and grubs, leaving behind large patches of raw earth.
This spot looked freshly scraped. I had been warned about the boars.
They had returned to the region since the retreat of human inhabitants. They would charge, I was told, if they felt threatened.

This wasn't the kind of research I was used to doing. Historians
work mostly in archives or museum collections. Once granted access,
we sit at a table and order objects brought to us by usually obliging
librarians. Historians work with documents and artifacts that have
been selected as significant and valuable. Each generation spends a
great deal of energy and money to collect, husband, label, and secure
cultural objects deemed important for posterity. Often those in posi-
tions of authority decide what is important, what is saved. If an item
is considered no longer valuable, or perhaps embarrassing, it may be
tossed. It's true: a lot is discarded. The vast majority of the past is lost to
historical research, to history. Most of what is jettisoned is the stories
of humble lives lived in marginal, unimportant backwaters such as
Chernobyl before it was radiated into infamy.

Usually the most arduous difficulties a historian encounters are
underheated archives, cranky archivists, and lousy food in the canteen. Speeding along on a motorbike across a radiated landscape in
order to narrate the history of forgotten lives, as "Elena" did, takes a
great deal of pluck—except, I had to remind myself, Elena didn't ride
her bike in the Zone. She, like the millions of visitors to her site, only
imagined wandering in the Zone. As I stood at the threshold of the cottage, they were all safely at home, in front of their computers, com-
fortably traveling through cyberspace. Only I was duped into this mis-

A wild Przhevalski horse in the town of Chernobyl. Photo by author.

adventure. Was I really supposed to gather up my scrawny frame and battle alone with the pitiless reality of time and transience—with the disintegration of a vast, irradiated landscape?

Predictably, I decided to pass on entering the cottage and instead retreated to the relative safety of the *shtetl* streets of Chernobyl. In the main square, I suddenly came face to face with a wild horse grazing on tender grass around a statue of Lenin. It was a Przhevalski horse, one of a herd imported from Mongolia after the accident to consume or trample the contaminated grass. The wild horse had a huge, pre-historic jaw. It stared at me and chewed furiously. That, too, made me nervous. I reeled away, back to the warm cafeteria and my radiation-free breakfast.

Later we drove to the city of Pripyat, near the power plant—what Elena had called a "ghost city." Pripyat lay in the path of the first clouds of radiation.[19] No one can live there anymore. Fittingly, it was the one place in the Chernobyl Zone, amid the old, quaint villages, where the swagger of the twentieth century could be firmly grasped. The city was constructed in the 1970s on empty land and incorporated in 1980 to accommodate the families of workers at the newly constructed

Panorama of downtown Pripyat, Ukraine. Photo by author.

nuclear power plant. These were professional-class engineers and technicians, so salaries were high and stores well stocked. Pripyat was built to order, according to plan, all in one style, as a modern garden city. Its forty-seven thousand inhabitants constituted what planners considered the optimal ratio of population to the supply of goods and services. A green "oxygen zone" surrounded the city in the form of miles of undisturbed pine forests, bogs, and lakes.[20] Since power came from abundant, cheap, and smog-free nuclear energy, the air and environment were pure and pristine, a haven for naturalists and outdoorsmen.

As planned, Pripyat was also a pedestrian's paradise. Builders had arranged it so that no walk for a major service would be more than fifty meters. Residential high-rises had schools, libraries, clinics, administrative offices, stores, and cafes at street level. Straight, tree-lined paths allowed people to complete their daily errands without the need for cars or buses. The town spread out from the main square, where the political and economic heartbeat of the community was situated: the local Communist Party headquarters, the Palace of Culture, a department store, a sports complex with an Olympic-size pool and soccer stadium, and a small amusement park with a new Ferris wheel that never revolved. (It was famously set to take its first spin as part of the May Day celebrations in 1986, a few days after the accident.) Pripyat, with one of the youngest populations in the USSR, was home to seventeen thousand children. On weekends, families walked from their apartments along the paths and, within minutes, arrived at unspoiled forests, meandering streams, and blue lakes. Pripyat was that kind of mushroom-berry-fish place that people in eastern Europe so love. And with it came the kind of culture promoted by Soviet officialdom. In Pripyat, people knew their neighbors and enjoyed sporting events, concerts, theater, and poetry readings, long after they had gone out of fashion in the rest of the Soviet Union.[21] As Elena reported from her imaginary childhood in Pripyat, it was a nice place to grow up, safe and clean—like, I imagined, childhood in an American suburb.

In many ways, Pripyat offered the late Soviet version of the prosperity and nuclear family–centered contentment epitomized by postwar American suburbs. The city was built at a time of unusual economic stability and political satisfaction among most Soviet citizens.[22] Life in comfortable, full-service Pripyat was good, though at the time of the Chernobyl disaster this was hard to believe for many Westerners, who were used to thinking of the USSR as a place of economic misery and simmering political dissent. In his memoir of the accident, Alexander Esaulov, a former vice-mayor, recounted how the television talk show host Phil Donahue showed up in Pripyat in 1987, about a year after the explosion. Donahue trooped around wearing old boots. Esaulov, serving as his guide, followed. Esaulov was surprised that Donahue was less interested in seeing the nuclear power plant or talking to people who worked there than in taking pictures of the most miserable villages he could find in the Polessian countryside. The more run-down the barn or hut, the better.

Esaulov was confused by Donahue's focus and tried to tell him that Pripyat was a modern city that had offered up a good life to its residents. Donahue had laughed at that and, on learning Esaulov was a vice-mayor of an evacuated city, exclaimed, "That must be an easy job!" Esaulov could not get the simpleminded Westerner to understand that managing an evacuated city is more difficult than managing one that is fully populated. Esaulov had all kinds of problems that no existing regulations or guidelines addressed. What do you do when you find a paralyzed grandmother left behind in an apartment, and the medical clinic is shut down? How do you pay workers with money that is too hot for banks to accept? Where can cleanup workers eat when all the cafeterias have been shuttered? Who will empty the trashcans and refrigerators stuffed with rotting food? And what of the documents—marriage, birth, and death certificates—stored in the city archive that are too contaminated to take along? Then there were the evacuated kids, sent to live a normal life in the Ukrainian city of Belyi Tsirkiv. Exhausted and frightened, they had disembarked from the evacuation bus to be met by men in gas masks and jumpsuits, equipped to handle the irradiated children of Chernobyl.[23]

Chernobyl was the most modern of catastrophes, a devastating slip of twentieth-century technology, but as an accident it had to be battled by extremely primitive means. West German, Japanese, and Soviet robots, deployed to clear radioactive graphite and dig tunnels under the boiling reactor, failed. The machines' electrical circuits quit working when exposed to Chernobyl's high levels of radiation. Soviet emergency teams had no recourse but to deploy "biological robots," men suited up in seventy pounds of lead armor held together with leather straps. These nuclear gladiators took turns running onto the roof of reactor number three to shovel one or two heaps of smoldering, searingly-radioactive graphite into the maw of the damaged reactor number four before falling heavily back downstairs. In twelve days in September 1987, five thousand soldiers lifted 170 tons of nuclear debris from the roof with shovels, wheelbarrows, gloved and bare hands.[24] Taking forty-second turns, the men shared among themselves exposures to the powerful gamma rays emanating from the smoking wreck. It was the very age-old, biological vulnerability of this most modern of disasters that was so unsettling.

Indeed, that was part of the problem. Pripyat was a modern city, one produced almost wholly by contemporary technologies and machinery, and in its plan and conception there was no room for human error or the human courage and sacrifice necessary to battle the disaster that was never supposed to happen. The reactors were originally designed for military use and so had no containment shelters to minimize an explosion. That fact was well known. Even so, city and plant leaders stalled out, paralyzed for several critical days after the accident, because they had no emergency plans or materials, such as protective suits to ward off gamma rays, iodine pills to protect human thyroids, chemical solvents to wash down equipment, buildings, and pavement, and disposable gloves and boots to shield workers. The very orderly modernity of Pripyat composed a confident, soothing spatial narrative that lulled to sleep healthy fears of nuclear catastrophe. Perhaps for this reason, few people noticed before the accident that the Chernobyl plant was poorly managed and leaking radioactive isotopes into the surrounding environment. When a lone KGB agent in the early 1980s and a journalist in 1986 warned of major safety violations and problems with the operating order of the plant, they were easily dismissed.[25]

Visiting abandoned Pripyat, the city's modernity made for a monochrome adventure. In Pripyat there was no vernacular or ecclesiastical architecture: no tiny cottage, garden shed, or hunter's shack, no synagogue, chapel, graveyard, or grotto dedicated to a forgotten God. Everything, absolutely everything, was built according to plan, a plan designed, approved, and stamped in Moscow. Until one entered private space, as far as the eye could see, there was nothing made by hand, nothing created outside of factory assembly lines. In the 1920s the philosopher Walter Benjamin wondered what life would be like once handmade products were wholly eclipsed by mass-produced goods.[26] Pripyat would have been a fine place to answer that question, except there was no one left to ask.

In Pripyat, doors were left standing open so that dust loaded with radioactive isotopes would not be trapped inside rooms and buildings. The open doors meant easy access for burglars and snooping historians. With our guide, Rimma, we stopped to look in abandoned apartments, hoping to find the intimate household objects Elena had promised on her website, though I knew I didn't have a prayer. While Mary Mycio waited below, Rimma and I wandered through one melancholy apartment after another. All empty.

Strangely, instead of leading me to sources that would illuminate the past—the lost dream of a planned socialist utopia—Rimma became my guide to the falsified dystopia of Elena's website. In one building, Rimma showed me the issue of *Okhota i rybolovstvo* that Elena's husband had brought with him and jammed into the mailbox to photograph. On a balcony, she pointed out a pair of pants that Elena and her husband had hung on a line and also photographed. We wound our

Clothes on a line,
arranged by "Elena,"
Pripyat, Ukraine.
Photo by author.

way up sixteen flights of a high-rise so that Rimma could show me the apartment where Elena and her husband had chosen to stage a photo shoot. They had collected some of the few forgotten snapshots, books, and Christmas ornaments from several apartments and arranged them in one apartment on an upright piano, the only remaining piece of furniture we found. Presumably the piano was too large to carry down the narrow steps, and the elevator that had brought it up had long since ceased to function. Since I was there, I dutifully snapped pictures of Elena's montage, knowing it was an artificial construct but beginning to wonder what wasn't.

Once a few doubters started to question the veracity of Elena's website, she became defensive and explained in chat rooms and later versions of her site that the truth is relative, that what was important was to capture the tragic and forgotten history of the Chernobyl Zone in her native Ukraine. In a way, that made sense to me. I had come for the same reason, taken in by the same fantasy, inclined toward a similar relativism. After all the debates on postmodernism, we have a harder

Piano with photos arranged by "Elena," Pripyat, Ukraine. Photo by author.

time than ever homing in on what is history and truth and where, if ever, the two meet. I had come to find what was not recorded in Communist Party newspapers or government documents, how people lived and what they said to each other or thought privately as they resided in the shadow of what was billed as a "completely safe" nuclear power plant in an "indivisible" Soviet Union. I wanted to focus on sources that had not been selected, edited, curated, and stored by official entities. I had sought to slip by the official historical gatekeepers the way Elena had glided into the Zone with her father's pass.

Yet it became starkly obvious that Elena's *ménage à trois* of truth, history, and representation became distorted precisely because the Zone was largely depopulated and uncared for. Truth disintegrates when the people disappear and the objects that sustain it (architecture, documents, photographs, household implements) fall apart. Elena could have her way with the "reality" of the Zone because no one among her online readers had been there to call her on it. No one but Rimma witnessed Elena's fabrications, and Rimma had not known of the *Kiddofspeed* website until her boss was reprimanded for allegedly allowing a lone motorcyclist into the Zone.

The past, like the Zone, is uninhabited. Once I stepped out of the archive and into the Zone, I was on my own, like Elena in the depths of her imagination, to make my way among the many conflicting truths of historical representation. There were no curators to verify the date and ownership of objects, no archivists to authenticate documents and keep collections together (or, at least, to give them the appearance of collections). There was no one to prevent me from randomly picking rain-washed documents up from the floor, blowing off the dust, and, after Rimma checked them for radiation, stashing them in my bag to take home.

The very freedom I sought in hunting down sources left me in limbo, with no way to check those sources. That is often the state of objects and papers before they have been selected, cleaned, and placed in a museum or archive to become "artifacts" and "documents."[27] The difference was that I found myself in the position of curator, archivist, and historian all at once. For anyone to believe me, they would just have to take my word for it.

When I entered the Zone, I had to check at the gate the tools of my profession, the rules by which historians agree to play to produce verifiable knowledge. And so the Zone becomes a metaphor for the kinds of debates that have reverberated in scholarship over the past few decades, about the links between power and the production of knowledge, and what occurs to "truth" when we no longer know how to authenticate it or when we falter in finding a voice to represent it. It is a disorderly, dangerous terrain, this metaphorical zone. That was the disturbing fact I took away. Certainly Elena had committed a fraud, but more generally I grasped how the past is staged in place as well as in archives. I realized, in other words, that in the belly of every truth I seek there lurks a hoax.

Still, although I am a timid traveler, I am not ready to turn my back on the Zone. Tarkovsky's Stalker was nervous too, continually urging his clients to be cautious. Like the Stalker, historians could learn to be more anxious in our metaphorical zone because we are working with powerful forces—knowledge, words, the encapsulation of lives lived. I hope that I do not treat that power lightly, as Elena did in her intrepid cyber wandering, nor am I willing to accept defeat and admit that we cannot tell the stories of people whose words and objects have not been considered important enough to record and catalog.

I have failed to mention what the seekers in the film *Stalker* were looking for in their Zone. It was rumored that in its depths was a room where people who managed to find it would be granted their innermost wish. After the Stalker guided his adventurers through terrifying hazards to finally reach the magical room, they faltered. They feared entering the room, as I was afraid to cross the threshold of the listing cottage. That struck me as telling. In my travels, I exchanged one stalker, the cyber-traveler Elena, for another, the dystopian debunker Rimma. But in writing about it, I too became a stalker, who — like every historian — can only lead her travelers to the threshold of truth.

4 Bodily Secrets

The provinces of Chelyabinsk and Sverdlovsk, deep in the Russian continent, used to be off-limits to foreigners. In the United States that would be like placing a ban on visits to Montana, Wyoming, and a good part of Idaho. The travel restriction was lifted in the early 1990s, but the city of Chelyabinsk is still no tourist destination. I met no other foreigners while I lived in Chelyabinsk, a Russian steel town of a million people and a million yards of rusting pipe and heavy machinery. In the courtyard of my apartment building, a neighbor inquired where I was from. She was asking, she said, because the last person who had lived in my furnished rental unit was from her hometown of Turgan and, it turned out, he knew her relatives. Perhaps we too might have a common connection? When I asked my neighbor if she had family in Chicago, a wave of dread crossed her face before she forced a laugh.

That look gave me a first glimpse of the vast and sweeping Russian nuclear security regime, of which Chelyabinsk is a small part. Security regimes are strange affairs. They sort knowledge and appear to prioritize and hide the most significant information. But that is a mirage. No security system does that. The most sequestered, top-secret information can be banal and inconsequential, while what is important to know can be right there, hidden by its very ordinariness. Even so, security regimes attract researchers who seek to break the code and learn the guarded secrets. Placing a territory in a classified zone is a sure way of drawing attention. Living in Chelyabinsk while researching a closed nuclear city, I got distracted by security regimes and the supposedly hidden secrets within them. It took me a long time to ask the most obvious question. Why draw attention with security restrictions to something you want to keep secret? I got caught believing in the veracity of the security state. It took an old woman and her scarred body to get me to see the real secrets. She taught me that the bigger story was right before me, in the bodies of the people I met, so close I could reach out and touch them.

I was in Chelyabinsk in order to find out more about Ozersk, a pretty little city in a northern birch and pine forest surrounded by wind-swept, gray-green lakes. The town is clean, orderly, leafy, with stately apartment buildings and shoreline summer cottages. At least, that's what Ozersk is said to look like. I wasn't able to enter Ozersk, or even get close to it. Formerly one of ten closed Soviet nuclear cities, Ozersk is now a closed Russian city, home to Russia's first plutonium plant, which reprocesses spent nuclear fuel for commercial reactors around the world. Both making plutonium and reprocessing fuel produce a great deal of radioactive waste. Ozersk is surrounded by a tall cyclone fence topped with barbed wire and patrolled by guards at gateposts, in boats on the lake, and on foot in the surrounding forests. During the Cold War, to enter the closed city, a person needed a thorough background check and a pass. A restricted buffer zone lined with missiles ringed Ozersk. The town was on no published map, and the address for the ninety thousand people who lived there was officially Chelyabinsk, some forty miles away. Ozersk was located in the center of a security network so vast, so cosseted with restrictions and defensive installations, that, as I learned more about it, I came to feel sorry for Gary Powers, sent confidently, blithely, like a lamb to slaughter, to fly a U-2 spy plane over this armed archipelago. Zenit rockets downed Powers's plane on May 1, 1960, just after he flew over Ozersk, then called by the few in the know (and Powers wasn't one), Chelyabinsk-40.

When I started visiting Chelyabinsk province sixteen years after the end of the Cold War, I was surprised to find that the habit of secrecy and intrigue was still going strong. When I showed up places, a mini-whirlwind surrounded me. People knew who I was before we had been introduced. Like a patient whom no one will tell has cancer, I felt there was important information I should know but wasn't privy to. I had strange encounters. An official at the archive invited me to her home, fed me borsch, told me about her marriage, her extramarital affairs, her children, and then announced that, at the archive, I was to pretend not to know her. Yet a few days later, while I was working in the archive's reading room, she invited me out for coffee, and as we strolled down the street she told me that her home, office, and cell phones were bugged, that if I needed to talk to her I should take her for a walk. I asked her why she was under surveillance. She said she had a top security clearance and access to a lot of state secrets. She lifted her chin, proud of her government's trust (and mistrust) in her.

Secrets! That is what historians yearn for, long-guarded secrets that make headlines. History holds out the promise that buried in archival storehouses are mysteries of the past that even people living through those events did not know. This quest gives historians authority and relevancy. Uncovering secrets was my mission too. As I worked through declassified files over the years, I learned a lot of details about life at this epicenter of the Cold War arms race, but I did not uncover any real secrets. What was there to learn? The most closely guarded knowledge—the location of the plant, formulas for bombs, and volumes of fissile material and radioactive waste—had long been fished out by spies, intelligence agents, journalists, and other historians. Though I was banned from entering Ozersk, I could zoom through it on Google Earth. I could find the formula for making a nuclear weapon in published sources and then order online enough radioactive materials to make a dirty bomb.[1] Why all the intrigue?

It took me several years to realize that the greatest mystery was not in the archives and never had been. I had thought I was going to expose the history of the national security state as it was being invented by those living at ground zero of the arms race. Strangely, seeking to peer through this elaborate security apparatus distracted me for a long time from seeing a major part of the story of the Maiak plutonium plant, which I missed because questions of access and secrecy loomed so large. Thinking back on it, the young archivist who handed me files, which I had not requested, about people living on the highly radioactive Techa River, should have clued me in. Surprised at the unexpected folders that landed on my desk, I looked up to notice that the young woman's eyes bulged and her fingers were swollen and blue. Had I yet any literacy in reading bodies as medical texts, I might have recognized these as symptoms possibly caused by an overactive thyroid and asked whether her unsolicited help had something to do with an illness associated with the plutonium plant. But I did not ask the archivist why she was surreptitiously aiding me. Instead, I continued on my way, doggedly pursuing my original research question, not wanting to get off track.

Seeking to talk to some former plant workers and neighbors of the plant, I got in touch with an Ozersk-based human rights lawyer, Nadezhda Kutepova. She connected me with over a dozen pensioners who had worked at the plant and were willing to tell me their stories, or parts of them. Unable to visit the closed city, I took up residence, in the summer of 2010, in nearby Kyshtym, a small city of heavy log houses on an isthmus between two northern lakes. I settled into a cottage to live. I also had a key to an office in a crumbling sanatorium for senior citizens. The spare, rectilinear room served as a neutral location for me to meet the veterans of the plutonium plant. I needed a "neutral" location because the owner of my borrowed cottage did not want me to meet guests there, as the neighbors might take note of my activities. That was the political climate. I was doing nothing illegal, but the idea of talking about the former nuclear arms complex made a lot of people nervous, including some of the people who came to see me.

One large, burly man, Sergei, walked in for our interview, folded his arms over his chest, and kept them there. He proclaimed that he didn't know why he had come or what the point of our meeting was. As a young conscripted soldier, Sergei had been sent to clean up radioactive debris and ash after a major explosion of an underground radioactive waste storage tank in September 1957, but he didn't want to talk about any of this with me. He told me he had signed security oaths designed to keep state secrets especially from American spies. There

I was speaking Russian with a thick American accent and holding our meeting in a "neutral" location. Who was to say I wasn't a spy?

Certainly not Sergei. After a few minutes, he got up and departed, in a huff. That left me alone with a handful of older women. Researching this sensitive topic, I often ended up speaking to women, not men. My story is biased that way. Like a morning spent at the bathhouse, sharing emotional intimacy with a stranger of the same gender came easily for many of the women with whom I spoke. Perhaps for that reason, after Sergei left we relaxed and got down to business. But to my chagrin, it turned out that our business was not state secrets but secret body parts—their genetic legacies, reproductive histories, and physical maladies. The women appeared to be far less concerned than Sergei about my nationality and the plant's security regime and more attentive to dog-eared papers they fingered in their laps. The papers were medical reports and legal petitions, and they wanted very much for me to look at them. But I was not interested in their papers. Instead I wanted them to tell me about their lives working at the plant and living in or near the closed city. I wanted to know what it felt like to be locked up in a zone, cut off from the larger world. I asked questions along those lines.

Anna Miliutina was eager to talk. Spry and energetic, Miliutina did not look her eighty years. She started at the plutonium plant when it was still in the construction phase, in 1947. For several decades, she worked as a shop clerk in the closed city, but in the late 1960s, she wanted to make more money and retire sooner so she took a job at the plant in production. Walking into a porcelain-lined tunnel to clock in for her first shift, the plant's security and safety regime impressed her:

> First we went to the hygiene control station, took off all our clothes and walked undressed into another room where we were given jumpsuits and cassettes to measure radiation. At the end of the day we gave back our cassettes and they returned our clothes. In the corridor was a soldier who let you into the workshop. We had numbers that indicated where you were allowed to go. There and nowhere else. We took a shower every day after work. When you left, the radiation monitor checked you and might hold you back. If I got too large a dose, I didn't know. They didn't tell you.

I had just started to work at the factory and there was an accident in 1968. It was a critical reaction. The first shift had cleaned it up. Maybe. Or maybe in the morning I did the cleaning. There were ten meters to clean, not a lot of space. So that was how I was related [to radioactive contamination].

"Were you afraid?" I asked.

No, no, no. What did we understand? How did we know we would get sick? Now I know. I cleaned it up. They threw a powder on the floor. If it was wet, they sopped it up. If it was acid, they washed. They had that kind of order.

Those events, of course, did not give us health. That accident [in 1968], which I cleaned up, meant I got a lot of radiation which I think is what gave me this chronic radiation disease, which doesn't show up on me [in the tests].[2]

Miliutina shuffled through her papers, worn, thumbed. She showed me a letter rejecting her requests for compensation and another denying her diagnosis of chronic radiation syndrome (CRS), a complex of symptoms assaulting multiple organs of the body. Soviet doctors first created the diagnosis of CRS in the mid-1950s when they noticed that young plant operators, who had started working at the plutonium plant in perfect health, were falling ill with a host of symptoms—chronic fatigue, loss of appetite, severe anemia, premature aging, aching joints, brittle teeth and bones, to name a few. They guessed that the prisoners and employees who first came down with these symptoms had been exposed for long periods to doses of radioactive isotopes that, while not enough to cause the immediate symptoms of severe radiation illness, mounted over several years to produce a general, debilitating malaise. A dozen of the first young women diagnosed with CRS grew too sick to work and died in their early thirties. Soviet doctors studying monthly blood tests learned to detect when workers were at risk of CRS, and they ordered the endangered workers transferred to cleaner working environments.[3]

Miliutina felt she should be included on the list of people with CRS, a diagnosis that would entitle her to compensation payments and state-paid medical treatment. As she pressed her papers on me, I attempted to direct her back to facts about her life, as I was intent on answering my research questions. Miliutina ignored my queries: "In the end, I was insulted," she said. "I did not get proper liquidator's status. I have gone everywhere and they will not give me this status." She showed me copies of the compensation law. She read from it aloud. I cut her off with my own questions: What year did she start work? What was her job title? I did not want her contemporary medical records but a record of her past, and I wanted her life story as unmediated and transparent as possible. Instead, Miliutina came out with sentences that I suspected she had uttered many times before. "We had twenty Chernobyls. It was a war. For others it wasn't a war, but for us it was."

Pulling out a new set of papers, she showed me how the radiobiology clinic had evaluated her with a dose of 24 to 27 nanocuries. That number meant nothing to me, and again I tried to return her attention to the 1960s. In that quiet office in Kyshtym we grappled, me steering Miliutina away from her papers and medical history and back to her biography, she returning to them. An interview is a negotiation. Both the interviewer and the subject have something they want to get out of it. I was dissatisfied with my end of the exchange. I'm sure Miliutina was too.

Another woman, Luibov Kuzminova started talking. She was, at age seventy-five, very beautiful, her face a soft peach centered on indigo eyes. In 1946 Kuzminova had worked as an agronomist in Metlino, a hamlet along a small lake with a handsome church and old stone mill. That was the year Soviet officers of the NKVD construction enterprise started building the Maiak plutonium plant, seven kilometers distant. In 1949, having run out of underground storage containers, the plant director ordered engineers to dump all the plant's waste, including a high-level radioactive slurry mixed with toxic chemicals, into the little Techa River. If ingested in undiluted form, the high-level radioactive waste was fatal in micro quantities. The Techa flowed past the plutonium plant and pooled into ponds, lakes, and swamps along its soggy course. Metlino was the first hydrological way station downstream from the plant. "We didn't know," Kuzminova recalled. "We drank and washed. We didn't know it was all dirty."

She narrated her biography as medical and reproductive record:

I was married in 1956. We had trouble conceiving. Then I managed to get pregnant but had first a miscarriage, then a stillborn. Finally I gave birth to three children in 1959, 1960 and 1963. The first child died at a year and a half of leukemia. The other two lived. They are sick a lot. My husband worked in the lab at the plant. He died in his fifties. I have female problems, and I have had a lot of operations.

In the 1950s plant radiation monitors realized that farmers living along the Techa River, into which engineers had dumped 3.2 million curies of high-level waste between 1949 and 1951, were dangerously exposed.[4] After several years of drinking and washing with contaminated water, villagers had symptoms similar to those of the first plant workers. In subsequent years, plant doctors carried out exams on seventy-nine hundred people in the downstream communities and clandestinely diagnosed over nine hundred cases of CRS.[5] Many of the twenty-eight thousand other people exposed but not tested might also have had the syndrome.

Like Miliutina, Kuzminova held tattered medical records, which she also pushed toward me, with the same effect on me as Miliutina's. Seeing my disinterest, Kuzminova put her papers aside, stood up, and before I could stop her, unbuttoned her shirt to show me the scars on her belly. Unlike the medical records, these markings finally drew my attention. On her abdomen, the thick chalk lines of the surgeon's knife scrawled a crosshatch—left and right, up and down. The marks looked as if they were graphically attempting to void her torso. I didn't know if the cause for those many surgeries were isotopes from the plant, but her pain, recorded in those bodily etchings, was simply, exhaustingly there. I could no longer doubt it, but confronted with this rendering of a body in pain, I wished it would go away.[6]

Miliutina wanted me to see her documents and Kuzminova her body in order to ratify a diagnosis—chronic radiation syndrome or some other medical verdict—so that they could feel justified, released from having to make an argument about their status as unwitting victims. I have no degree in law or medicine, nor did I have the authority to evaluate and certainly none to see that justice was done. Plant researchers and officials said the women were not sick from plutonium production, but the women said they were. Who was I to say which side was right? There we sat at cross-purposes. I wanted the women's life stories, and, unfairly, I wanted them without interfering self-interest. They wanted to hear that they were right in their decade-long quest for status as victims. They sought my help getting that recognition, and to do so they needed a diagnosis.

But the diagnosis of chronic radiation syndrome was a moving target. In the years that followed the Soviet government's release of information about the Techa River disaster, a furious debate flared up around the bodies of people who claimed they were sick from the plant's radioactive waste. Some doctors, backed by public interest groups, said villagers and former workers suffered illnesses associated with long-term, low doses of radiation. Other scientists, largely underwritten by nuclear weapons establishments, said the plaintiffs were in fact sick from poor diets, alcoholism, inbreeding, conventional illnesses, and stress. They argued that in suing for compensation, the plaintiffs were looking for handouts. I puzzled over the debate. Why so many opinions? After five decades of research, why was science unable to determine the reasons the plaintiffs were sick?

The controversy derived in part from the insensibility of radioactive isotopes. These ghostly historical agents shadowed the bodies of workers and villagers in ways nearly impossible to recover as historical record. Imperceptible isotopes require sensitive devices read by trained technicians to make them legible. Monitoring of regular workers at the Maiak plant became fairly consistent by the 1960s, but radiologists estimated the exposures of temporary workers (often soldiers and prisoners) and farming neighbors rarely and haphazardly. Clearly, hazardous radioactive isotopes remained in play even when there was no radiologist there to measure them, yet the record was sketchy at best.[7] Meanwhile, medical researchers largely dominated the debate. They had measuring devises to quantify the isotopes, and that gave them authority to make pronouncements on the health of bodies when they intersected with radioactive contamination. I had read a lot of these studies. I knew how many questions they begged, how equipment failed and data was incomplete.[8] I knew about the debates over "permissible doses" or "tolerance thresholds"—whether they meaningfully reflected acceptable exposures to hazardous chemicals and radioactive substances or existed merely to allow industries to continue producing toxic products and waste. In short, the disputes over the effects of ingested plutonium and other highly toxic isotopes were highly politicized, and uncertainty prevailed.[9] How then was I to account for these gaping silences in the record, the missing, unaccounted-for radioactive iodine, cesium, plutonium, and strontium slipping mysteriously through ecosystems, up food chains, and into human bloodstreams? In my research I had encountered ghosts, spirits of the forest, spectral nationalized identities, and other historical agents that I could not see, but this problem was of a different order. Though invisible, the isotopes were not ephemeral. They had a very real, material existence.

Here were the most elusive secrets of the Maiak plutonium plant, secrets that had nothing to do with formulas for bomb cores or blueprints for reactors, but instead involved mysteries that resided in the bodies of people exposed for decades to the plant's radioactive waste. How much they had ingested and what damage the bouquet of invisible isotopes had done to their health—that was the enigma, which after decades of research, no one in the United States or the Soviet Union had convincingly resolved. Bodies, it turns out, do not give up their secrets as easily as sequestered archives. The bodies of the women I talked to were archives after a fashion, storing strontium-90 and plutonium in bone marrow, iodine-131 in thyroids, cesium-137 in endocrine glands, hearts, spleens, soft tissue, and muscle. The problem is that unless the levels are very high, humans have very little capacity to read these corporal repositories.

In the early 1990s, when American doctors first visited the medical research institutes associated with the Maiak plant, they were impressed. Bruce Amundson, a senior cancer researcher, made a trip in 1992 to Ozersk, where he was amazed to find a vast body of research, thick files for each of thousands of people who lived along the Techa River. "In our open society," he told a reporter, "we made a conscious decision not to study our offsite [exposed] population. In a closed society, the Soviets were able to carry out extensive, secret studies over the same period. They are way ahead of us in understanding what may have happened to their people."[10] Unlike medical researchers near the American equivalent of Maiak, the plutonium plant at Hanford, Washington, Soviet doctors had kept a close eye on people exposed to their plant's radioactive waste. Since the early 1960s, Soviet researchers had collected blood and urine samples from residents of the Techa region.[11]

Patients had never been told of their exposures, but their Soviet medical handlers had been tracing them through their bodies for decades.

With this Soviet medical data and the new post–Cold War spirit of cooperation, American and Russian scientists eagerly began to collaborate. The U.S. Department of Energy pumped millions of dollars into Russian nuclear research installations, which were short of money in the failing post-Soviet economy. American and Russian scientists visited each other's nuclear sites. Most Americans, however, did not go to the Urals to learn from Soviet science, which they considered inferior. They came instead for the valuable Soviet "data sets," the medical files on three generations living on radiated territory, a collection of medical data unique in the world.[12] American doctors had no registry like it.

American researchers also had no medical equivalent of chronic radiation syndrome. To them it was a doubtful diagnosis, a vague complex of symptoms. Research in the United States, by contrast, had largely focused on a few cancers and thyroid disease as effects of exposure to radioactive isotopes.[13] Indeed, as American scientists came to lead joint research projects, CRS disappeared from the medical literature and gradually started to dissolve from the post-Soviet landscape too. By 2004 Russian researchers had reduced their original diagnoses of 937 cases of chronic radiation syndrome in the downstream Techa River population to 66 cases, and they ceased diagnosing new cases.[14] Miliutina and Kuzminova were angry because they felt that they and others had been squeezed out of this diagnosis and the benefits it entailed.

Long after meeting Miliutina and Kuzminova, I started to wonder about the discrepancy between Russian medical verdicts before and after their collaboration with American researchers supported by Department of Energy funds. Despite the Russian doctors' greater wealth of data and experience in treating people suffering from long-term low doses of radiation, the Americans' notions of "exposure," and "thresholds," and their more limited range of probable health effects (i.e., a handful of possible cancers) had prevailed.[15] Why?

In large part the decline in the diagnosis of chronic radiation syndrome before and after the arrival of the Americans is due to the very different uses of medicine in the Soviet and American nuclear research establishments. During the Cold War, American researchers worried a great deal about the "threat" of "public exposure."[16] They debated "permissible doses" and thresholds below which, they postulated, exposure would cause little or no bodily harm. Atomic Energy Commission policy turned on this understanding: the point of the threshold notion was to maintain that workers' exposures could be kept at safe levels and that nuclear installations, properly monitored, were not harmful. Workers whose exposure exceeded these thresholds during accidents were brought in to plant clinics and run through tests to try to determine how much radioactivity they had ingested or taken externally on the body. Doctors looked for signs of severe radiation illness and its related symptoms, which show up soon after exposure. They believed, however, that exposures below the threshold were relatively inconsequential, so they simply did not ask many questions about the long-term effect of low doses of radiation on the body.[17] American doctors, like Soviet doctors, took blood samples from nuclear workers and administered medical checkups, but they, unlike Soviet doctors, were not looking for a broad set of symptoms that might clue them in to medical problems associated with long-term exposure. Doctors working within the Atomic Energy Commission (the precursor to the Department of Energy) generally believed that if a body was exposed to no more than the "permissible dose" (which declined steadily from 1942 to the end of the century), that body was safe. Monitoring the environment, not bodies, they assumed, assured good health.

In the Soviet Union in the first decade of radiobiology, doctors at the prisoner-built, accident-prone Maiak plant faced a very different and immediate problem. They were not at all concerned about making an argument to a worried public about the safety of nuclear installations. In Soviet society, officialdom rarely had to answer to public scrutiny, and nuclear installations were so sequestered that officially they did not exist, having no presence on published maps or in public discussions. Instead, what vexed plant managers was how to keep valuable, trained employees working despite daily exposures to an alarming volume of fission products. Hungry prisoners and soldiers built the Maiak plant in a rush, and it suffered many more accidents than its American equivalent at Hanford. This meant that far more workers were exposed on a daily basis than at the American plant. Keeping workers healthy was especially difficult for Soviet doctors because the security officers who ran the plant did not allow them access to production records that could tell them how much of what kind of isotopes their worker-patients had been exposed.[18] Denied data on their patients' doses and from environmental monitoring—the very data at the center of American "health physics"—Soviet researchers focused on the specificity of the bodies they attended, looking for symptoms of radiation exposure on the body. The body, they hoped, could serve as a map encoding an individual's working environment and past exposures—if they could only decipher it.

Between 1950 and 1990, Soviet doctors at the Maiak plant took tens of thousands of blood samples and performed thousands of medical checkups.[19] Some workers underwent ten to fifteen blood tests a year. Some bodies, the doctors noticed, showed few signs of distress after chronic exposures; others, working in the same conditions, grew gravely ill. Soviet doctors became adept at detecting minute changes in blood cells and slippages in workers' cognitive and physical abilities, which they learned signaled the onset of chronic radiation syndrome. In the first decade, they diagnosed over two thousand cases of CRS, 23 percent of the plant staff.[20] In order to convince supervisors to remove these workers from hazardous shops, the doctors had to come up with a lot of evidence, all derived from workers' bodies.

Evaluating these two approaches, you might conclude that excessive Stalinist secrecy caused Soviet doctors to fall behind their Western peers, who enjoyed greater access to information in an open society. Lacking crucial information, Soviet doctors practiced blindly, while the Americans developed superior methods of evaluating radiation exposure and health. That was largely the conclusion American researchers came to in the 1990s. In the post–Cold War period, when everything Soviet was considered backward, the assumption that Soviet radiation medicine had little value made perfect sense. It is useful, however, to look at how American assumptions embedded in the practice of health physics had evolved out of an industrial-medical trajectory that plucked bodies from the environments in which they had grown ill.

In the eighteenth and nineteenth centuries, doctors and patients in the United States and Europe believed that disease was linked to the landscape. Disease was seen as an imbalance in the body related to changes in a complex of environmental and social factors. There were healthy places and sickly ones. Bodies were considered permeable and susceptible to environmental vapors, fogs, winds, and temperature. Nineteenth-century doctors kept records of barometric pressure, humidity, and other weather data in order to understand the health of their patients.[21] In the late nineteenth century, germ theory changed this understanding of disease. Instead of tracing illness to a mix of environmental and bodily factors, germ theory located single external agents as the source of illness. A germ could be anywhere and could penetrate the body regardless of ecological factors, which made disease placeless. Germ theory thus forged a trend in medical research that turned away from the study of how environmental factors determined health.[22] In the twentieth century, as doctors focused their research on singular causes of disease in bodies outside of place, other professionals—agronomists, hydraulic engineers, and soil scientists among them—stepped in to study the environment.[23] In this way, as a subject of attention, the body and the environment were divorced from one another.

In the 1940s, American researchers, concerned about worker health as plant operators on the Manhattan Project came in contact with industrial quantities of radioactive isotopes for the first time at the Hanford plutonium plant, used methods that grew out of the field of toxicology, which, in turn, had taken lessons from germ theory.[24] Industrial hygienists did not determine occupational illness based on workers' health complaints. Rather they fixed on measurements of toxins in the factory environment that could be linked to harmful physiological developments. Lead, for example, known to cause bodily harm, was found in samples of both factory air and workers' blood, making for a clear-cut case.[25] Following the same method, in 1944, American researchers first had to detect and measure the deposition of radioactive isotopes in bodies of test animals and then human subjects. This was a frustrating experience because they could not measure trace elements of radioactive isotopes but only larger "threshold" doses. For decades they worked on devising machinery sensitive enough to count isotopes buried in organs and bone marrow, with only limited success.

Atmospheric testing over Mt. Rainier to determine the dispersion of trace material in the atmosphere, 1970. Courtesy of the Department of Energy.

Another way to determine how large a dose a worker might be getting was to estimate exposure. At the Hanford plant, researchers put in place a monitoring program, attaching pencil-shaped radiation detectors to workers' bodies and placing monitoring devices in shops and labs. Taking lessons from industrial hygienists in the chemical industry, environmental researchers went outside, setting up filters, taking samples to study the spread and concentration of radioactive isotopes in soils, air, water, plants, and animals. Soil scientists looked at how a particular radioactive isotope, say cesium-137, soaked into soils, finding its way to the roots of plants and then into the plants' fruits.[26] Ichthyologists studied fish swimming in water laced with suspended radioactive isotopes.[27] Meteorologists examined the paths of isotopes in air currents. These "pathway" studies found that particular radioactive isotopes acted in unique ways depending on the specific environment—the mix of alkaline, sand, rock, and mineral in soils; the temperature and force of plumes in rivers; the vagaries of wind and

Dye tests conducted in the Columbia River near the Atomic Energy Commission's
Hanford plant (near Richland, Washington), ca. 1970. Courtesy of the Department
of Energy.

precipitation in air. Yet, because scientists of ecology had divided into
divergent disciplines and, likewise, from scientists studying human
bodies, this knowledge of the ways radioactive isotopes worked in particular environments scarcely made its way into medical studies of
radiation's effects on the body. This splintering of body and environment into discrete fields, historian Linda Nash notes, "made it difficult
to draw connections between environmental change and changes in
human health."[28]

American researchers were looking for cause and effect: singular radioactive isotopes assaulting singular bodily organs to produce
stand-alone diseases. It was important in the United States for doctors and lawyers to be able to prove in court that a certain agent (and
not others) caused bodily harm. Early nuclear workers complained
of health problems, which they suspected had something to do with
their jobs, but newly minted "health physicists," like industrial hygienists before them, generally assumed that workers were dissem-

bling and exaggerating their symptoms.[29] How a worker felt could not be diagnosed.[30] In the American tradition of toxicology, from which radiation biology or health physics emerged, only a link between a quantifiable exposure (i.e., a certain dose of radioactive iodine) and a known physiological effect (thyroid cancer or disease) constituted an occupational illness.

The archival record shows that American doctors were loath to link a worker's poor health or untimely death to the Hanford plant's leaking fission products and even more reluctant to relate effects on the bodies of neighbors to the plant's radioactive effluence.[31] While the Hanford plant was functioning, it had, officially, no recorded fatalities from radioactive isotopes.[32] Health physicists did not connect workers' exposure with occupational deaths until the 1990s.

The Soviet diagnosis of chronic radiation syndrome described a broad category of symptoms that were difficult to distinguish from symptoms of other major illnesses such as heart disease, hepatitis, rheumatism, and tuberculosis.[33] CRS never became a diagnosis in the American medical tradition largely because it would never hold up in court. There was no way in the American medical-juridical understanding of occupational illness, focused as it was on causal links between particular agents and particular diseases, to separate the complex of symptoms describing CRS from other illnesses with similar symptoms. Except for a few geneticists working in the late 1940s, I have found no evidence that American researchers thought in terms of radioactive isotopes assaulting multiple organs to weaken immune systems and cause a multiplex of debilitating symptoms.[34] Most researchers just didn't think that way. Their focus was on exposures, not on bodies and their symptoms, and they recorded long lists of estimated doses and depositions in isolated organs. To an amazing degree, in the studies that emerged from American nuclear installations, the bodies of patients—and certainly bodies in pain—are wholly invisible.

Historian Christopher Sellers situates a form of this "body blindness" in the early American environmental movement of the 1960s. The first activists, failing in court to draw a line between the coterie of vague human health effects associated with a chemical sensitivity to DDT turned instead to proving in court damages to animals and birds as "property" and natural resources. Winning these early court cases over contaminated environments, activists established the Environmental Defense Fund, but in so doing, Sellers argues, they turned their back on the humans threatened by environmental disasters to focus on land, animals, and property.[35] Cancer research shows a similar body blindness. Most cancer research has fixated on the cure rather than environmental causes of cancer, although such causes account for two-thirds of all cancers. Insurance companies will pay for genetic testing on women with breast cancer, but they refuse to use the body as an archive and analyze breast tissue for chemical carcinogens.[36] This is not just an American problem. Employers and insurers worldwide are reluctant to treat the body as a source of evidence of environmental contamination. Zhang Haichao, a migrant worker in China, was exposed to silica dust at the Zhendon Abrasion Proof Material Company in the Henan Province. Zhang contracted silicosis, but the official occupational disease hospital repeatedly refused to certify him as suffering from silicosis, diagnosing him instead with tuberculosis, which called for no compensation. To prove his case, Zhang had to go to extremes. He persuaded a doctor to perform a live lung biopsy to confirm his silicosis, although a simple X-ray had shown the disease clearly.[37] A failure to see bodies and to use them as archival maps of exposure helps explain the emphasis on cures, not the environmental causes, of a growing number of debilitating and deadly diseases.

In the late 1980s and early 1990s, the Department of Energy declassified tens of thousands of documents detailing the colossal volume of radioactive waste dumped into the interior western environment during the Cold War. When Americans living near the Hanford plant claimed that they and their offspring were ill with a variety of illnesses, which they blamed on the plant, DOE-funded researchers, tellingly, targeted the first large-scale health-effect studies not on bodies but on "dose estimates" from environmental monitoring. Using these estimates, calibrated from decades of ambient readings of radioactive isotopes in the environments, they guessed the doses residents received, then ran those numbers against the estimated exposures of Japanese survivors of the Hiroshima and Nagasaki bombings to come up with the probabilities of "downwinders" getting a couple specific cancers or thyroid disease.[38]

The Atomic Bomb Casualty Study serves to this day as the gold standard, for American medical and juridical panels, in determining how probable it is that an illness was caused by radiation exposure.[39] Of course, massive, one-off explosions in damp and coastal Japan differed greatly from the slow-drip exposure to a different cocktail of radioactive isotopes on the volcanic soils of the arid and continental Columbia Basin, and Japanese in the 1950s had very different diets and daily habits than residents of eastern Washington, but medical researchers rarely took those differences into account. Rather, they made models that regarded bodies and landscapes in Japan and the United States as interchangeable.[40] This is all the more remarkable considering how much hydrologists, ichthyologists, meteorologists, and soil scientists had discovered in four decades of research at the labs at Hanford about the locally contingent pathways of radioactive isotopes in the environment. Given this blind spot, it may not be surprising that regulatory and legal rulings concerning Hanford have produced bizarre conflicting diagnoses: while the federal government found the Hanford Nuclear Reservation to be severely contaminated and in need of a hundred-billion-dollar cleanup, federal courts determined that people living downwind and downstream of Hanford were largely unaffected.

These kinds of rulings reveal the moment when the bodies of exposed people disappeared, dissolved into the heavy physical and mental labor of trying to make insensible isotopes stand up and be counted. That had long puzzled me as I read through the published medical studies of people exposed near the Hanford and Maiak plants. The bodies—how they felt, their complaints, what they experienced as pain or illness—played no role in these records. There simply were no bodies, just counts of various isotopes, dose estimates, and probabilities of the emergence of various cancers in numerous organs extracted from a statistically configured composite body.

Invisibility takes a lot of work. The medical studies of the 1990s in the United States and then later in Russia, did just that, dematerializing the bodies exposed to the Soviet and American plutonium plants' radioactive waste. In pushing away my interview subjects' medical records, I too had exhibited this body blindness. Unable to judge, I did not know what to do with their vague complaints. When Luibov Kuzminova raised her shirt to show me her scars, tellingly I wanted nothing more than to make her body go away.

I puzzled over how to get past the obfuscating data and make those bodies appear again. One day I had an encounter that focused my thinking about bodies and health effects. While living in the cottage on the outskirts of Kyshtym, I got to know a neighbor, Ludmilla, who had a garden of potatoes she tended carefully. It was an unusually dry summer and every day, she and a friend, both in their sixties, carried buckets from the well to the garden to water their potato plants until they collapsed toward evening on a bench, fanning themselves. Sometimes I joined them in their watering, and Ludmilla gave me eggs and green onions in exchange. Ludmilla introduced me to her daughter, a slight woman with a pinched, worried face. I never caught her name. The daughter came to visit me unexpectedly one evening in my cottage. She said she wanted to meet an American. She had never met a foreigner before, and she thought she'd like to because she felt she didn't belong in Kyshtym. Over tea, she told me about her life: that she had a low-paying job; that she and her son lived in an apartment with no plumbing, just a courtyard outhouse; that she was tired of it all.

I asked her the age of her son. "Twenty-one," she said. "You know, the fellow who drives me here." I was astonished. I had taken her son, balding, blanched, and withered, to be her husband, an older husband. He looked like he'd been born at least a decade before his mother. She admitted his health was poor, due, she thought, to a copper-smelting factory within two hundred meters of their apartment building. I calculated other risks that might factor in. Kyshtym took a good hit over the decades from the radioactive effluent of the Maiak plant. As well, the young man was born in 1989, at the start of Russia's long economic crisis, a decade in which food, clothing, and health care were in scant supply.[41] A complex of factors likely sped the son past his mother in aging. His precise diagnosis will probably never be known, which does not change the fact that he is clearly very ill. There is as yet no medical study, historical inquiry, or epidemiological mapping that can place that boy back in his courtyard, where the smelting plant's gray fog trailed lead and arsenic, while he dug in earth watered by rain from clouds laced with fission products.[42] That sort of history is nowhere to be had, but the prematurely aged young man's body might give clues to such a history if there were a way to read it as a historical text.

This is a new frontier of scholarly inquiry, one that seeks to re-animate and recreate historically voided bodies, in a way that does not dismiss bodies in pain.[43] For the landscape most overlooked on the panorama of nuclear sacrifice zones is the landscape of the body. Human bodies—porous, renewing, and transforming—are as much a repository, a dump of manmade waste products, as are rivers, groundwater, soils, plants, and animals. Think of the tourists, people like myself who engaging in dark tourism, explore ghost towns, battlefields, and depopulated nuclear zones. The last stop of this tour should be reflective, a tour of human bodies, for they are the long-haul truckers of the vast transformations of human history on geology and biology.[44] Human history, in other words, is changing human bodies. Yet this bodily archive has scarcely been breached. In the search for secrets, the mysteries are right here with us.

5 Sacred Space in a Sullied Garden

There is no name for this season. I have in mind the lingering moment on the Eurasian steppe in the late twentieth century when the warm months yielded to the approaching frost, snow, and ice, when locals hoarded potatoes and casually spoke of famine. In this season, in late September 1998, I arrived in an old *shtetl*, named Uman, in central Ukraine. In the same week, an estimated ten thousand Hasidic Jews from across the world swept into Uman, as if carried by the powerful winds that rattled the tin roofs and sent dust curling round corners.[1] In their long black coats, the Hasids filled the narrow streets with song and a busy, rushing, closing-in sense of time. After the fall of the Soviet Union, thousands of Hasidic Jews of the Bratslaver sect started to arrive every year in this compact, remote Ukrainian city to celebrate Rosh Hashanah. They came from Israel, the United States, Canada, Africa, South America, and Australia. They traveled thousands of miles to spend the Jewish New Year at the grave of their spiritual leader, Nahman von Bratslav, who died in 1810.

I went to Uman, not for the religious holiday, but out of curiosity. I wanted to find out what it was about the grave that drew believers from distant homes to an otherwise unspectacular town with unreliable plumbing. At the time, I was writing about villagers—Jews and Christians—who, in the midst of famine in the 1920s, walked miles to pilgrimage sites to pray to the Virgin Mary, who they believed had appeared in a clearing on a hill in the central Ukrainian countryside. The pilgrims carried heavy crosses to plant at the site in an appeal to Mary for protection. In the space of a few months in 1923, hundreds of crosses came to dot the meadow, which locals renamed the Valley of Jehosephat.[2] The villagers' concept of sacred space was difficult for me to grasp. How would I write plausibly about a place that had the power to incubate faith and a belief in miracles?

I was at a loss for answers in part because I was a product of the modern era in which one spot hardly differs from any other. A housing development in Florida looks like a housing development in suburban Moscow—the same two-car garages, central air, and picture windows, despite vast differences in climate, culture, and topography. With technologies that can dry up swamps, turn deserts into green fields, vaporize hills, and send rivers underground, developers in search of profits have transformed places into commodities, repetitive, impersonal, and interchangeable. Yet, in the quiet towns of Central Europe in the 1990s, the free market was still a new and foreign innovation and the sacral qualities of religious sites, long suppressed by Soviet authorities, were vividly coming to life. In Uman, I talked to a thirteen-year-old boy from Toronto who had come to Nahman's grave for the fifth year in a row. He said his experience deepened every year, grew richer and more wondrous, and that he would try to visit the grave every year of his life. I marveled at the boy's conviction. He was one of many amid a rampant religious resurgence in eastern Europe at the time. In Częstochowa, Poland, a few summers before, I had stood shoulder to shoulder with a crowd of pilgrims in the bursting cathedral of the Jasna Góra Monastery. A trumpet sounded, chains rolled, and the believers gasped to see the icon of the Black Madonna revealed from behind doors of glimmering gold leaf. Like those around me, many of whom had walked for a month in August heat to reach the pilgrimage

Faithful praying at a Catholic Church, Zhitomir, Ukraine. Photo by author.

site, I had the impulse to fall hard, knees to cobblestone, at seeing the simple painting of a dark-skinned Mary on a cracked wooden board. I didn't, though. Alone in the crowd, I remained standing.

In the Kiev Lavre Monastery, I lit a candle and wandered into caves dug by eleventh-century Orthodox monks. The monks were still there, blackened, shriveled mummies reclining under glass on beds of stone. Believers bent over the corpses, kissed the glass, and whispered prayers to the men who had spent their lifetimes underground in service to an exacting God. When I wandered off the tourist route in the underground tunnels, a young priest stepped out of the dim light to block my path. "This place," he rumbled, "is only for Orthodox believers."

Ukrainian *shtetl* in the 1990s. Photo by author.

There I was, again on the outside. The sacral security regimes seemed as hermetic as the razor-wire fences and alarm systems of nuclear security zones. I was used to standing outside barriers, guessing at what occurred within, but if I ever procured a pass to a nuclear zone, I had a chance of grasping the secular rituals and traditions within. In front of these walls of devotion, I had few abilities to understand the fidelity, bordering on romantic love, that religious believers address to sacred sites. Peering in from a secular world, I puzzled over how I would describe these feelings and miraculous events. In Uman, I especially had trouble because I found little about the place to inspire passion.

Uman is a quiet murmur of a city in the midst of a rolling plain. It struck me as somehow misassembled. The architecture was neither tsarist nor Soviet, neither preserved nor bulldozed. Old, brick, never-finished buildings abutted aluminum kiosks selling cigarettes, candy, and cheap, local beer, smelling of vinegar and drawn from large steel barrels. The store windows, innocent of soap and water, bore faded advertisements for products no longer for sale, while on the sidewalk, women stood over card tables hawking plastic cookware and polyester lingerie that they had personally hauled, train-hopping, from the Chinese border. I was staying with a friend's mother, Dar'ya Semenovna, born in Uman seventy-five years before. She had left the region but once, to spend three years in Germany as a slave laborer during World War II. Dar'ya Semenovna said that Uman was much improved. "Before the war," she said, "the town was a dirty little thing."

It is easy to forget when in the strangely hushed towns in central Ukraine, towns such as Uman, Chernobyl, Bratslav, and Berdichev, that they were once centers of great and powerful Hasidic dynasties, hubs of scholarship and politics, to which thousands of pilgrims journeyed annually to see their leaders, the *tsadiks*. Uman and other Ukrainian *shtetls* are the birthplaces of Hasidism, an eighteenth-century movement that infused the central European landscape with a rich body of song, dance, and literature and a set of traditions that have refused to die. For Bratslavers the sacred qualities of Uman are not about the place itself but about a state of being—a condition of divine enlightenment and revelation.

The Hasidic *tsadiks* were the spiritual descendants of the founder of Hasidism, Israel ben Eliezer, better known as the Ba'al Shem (or Ba'al Shem-Tov), a Jewish scholar and hermit who lived in the first half of the eighteenth century in a *shtetl* not far from Uman. The Ba'al Shem traveled what is today central Ukraine, healed people, and preached an exultant message. According to Gershon David Hundert, the Ba'al Shem taught that there is no way to split the sacred from the profane, that the divine presence fills the world in all its aspects, and that no place—not even the lowliest hovel—exists without a spark of the divine. Of the Talmud and other sacred texts, the Ba'al Shem instructed that it was not the scriptural content but the words themselves that acquired divine grace when looked at or repeated in prayer or song. And so the Hasidim started a tradition of dancing and singing to reach God through ecstatic prayer. Hasidism is perhaps Ukraine's most lasting export. After the Ba'al Shem died, his fame grew still greater and his teaching spread from Ukraine to Poland, Galicia, Romania, and Hungary. His message caught on especially in humble towns and villages, where Jews welcomed the lesson that any ordinary person—one without great wealth, learning, or access to elaborate temples—could reach divine inspiration through everyday acts.[3]

Rabbi Nahman Bratslav was the great-grandson of the Ba'al Shem on his mother's side. Like the Ba'al Shem, Nahman sought solitude in the woods and on long canoe trips on tranquil Ukrainian rivers. Later in life, he claimed to have spoken to his great-grandfather in prayer during these retreats. To his followers, Nahman embodied the personal legacy of the Ba'al Shem. He defined Hasidic belief for his community and attracted a considerable following. In his mid-thirties, however, Rabbi Nahman contracted a fatal case of tuberculosis. He moved to Uman so he could die there and be buried in the mass grave of Jews who were massacred by Cossacks during the Khmelnitsky uprisings in the seventeenth century. Before he died, Nahman reportedly told his followers, "On Rosh Hashanah, I want you near me."

Nahman's disciples obeyed. They built a synagogue and formed a community in Uman, and for a century they kept up the tradition of spending Rosh Hashanah with the Rebbe at his grave. But after the Bolshevik Revolution in 1917, religion fell out of fashion and Communist revolutionaries closed the Bratslaver's synagogue in Uman. In 1937 Soviet town planners encircled the synagogue within the walls of a factory and turned it into a club for workers. In 1941 German troops and special killing squads brought a terrifying occupation and mass extermination to Soviet Ukraine. Members of the special killing squads herded Uman's Jews into open graves on the town's outskirts where they were shot and buried. Others drowned in the river, where Brastlaver pilgrims say the *tashlich* (a symbolic casting of sins upon the moving water, part of the New Year ritual). Nazis killed seventeen thousand of the city's twenty-two thousand Jews in mass shootings between 1941 and 1943. Before the war, Jews were a majority in Uman. After the war, very few Bratslavers remained to tend Nahman's grave and, as the city changed, the grave site languished on a slope sinking toward a muddy stream and a gravity-propelled trash dump.

For forty years after the war, Nahman's grave was quiet but not forgotten. I met, on a street leading to the busy grave site, a woman who introduced herself as Lena. She was a *znakharka*, a clairvoyant who healed with incantations and cured by laying hands on the sick. Lena said that Rabbi Nahman passed his hands over the womb of her great-great-grandmother, bestowing on her and her offspring the power to heal. In exchange for this gift, Lena tended Nahman's grave, as had her mother and grandmothers before her. At the grave, Lena talked to the Rabbi's spirit, and he answered, giving her advice. Once he appeared to her in a dream. She described him to me as a short man with piercing eyes and one graying ringlet slipping from under his hat. I found it appropriate that Lena spoke of Nahman in the present tense.

Central Ukraine is a landscape loaded with trauma. In the 1990s many people bore their memories of wartime and postwar suffering silently because Soviet officialdom had endorsed just a few narratives about the war: about heroism inspired by patriotism to the Soviet Union; about the sacrifice of, not a majority of Jews, but generic "victims of fascist aggression"; and about the suspected collaboration of a few.

My host, Dar'ya Semenovna, fell into the last category. In her small apartment, she pulled out postcards from a village in Bavaria where she had been incarcerated as a forced laborer during the war. In the first months of the two-and-a-half-year occupation, German officials encouraged young Ukrainians to sign up to work in Germany. Word soon got around that the jobs supplied no real wages and starvation rations. As volunteers dried up, German soldiers and their local auxiliaries held surprise roundups at the market on Saturdays to nab young, labor-ready bodies and push them, screaming and terrified, into waiting freight trains.[4] Dar'ya Semenovna was caught in such a raid, and the unheated stock car took her to southern Bavaria. At a public auction, she and the other *Ostarbeitern* (eastern laborers) were sold off to local German employers. Dar'ya got lucky. A factory owner purchased her to work in his factory, a slightly more merciful fate than those who landed in labor camps.[5]

The quiet village in Bavaria was the only place Dar'ya Semenovna had ever traveled outside Ukraine. She explained how the proprietor she worked for gave her pocket money and she saved up pennies to buy the postcards she showed me. After the war, Soviet security officials confiscated mail pouches filled with postcards from the men and women who had been stolen from their homes in Ukraine and sent to Germany. These plain, photoless postcards, which German officials printed in Ukrainian specifically for the *Ostarbeiter*, read like a folk lament. They include descriptions of aching loneliness and mournful inventories of the fathers, mothers, children, spouses, and siblings at home whom they missed every waking moment. "How is little Fedor without us?" one peasant mother wrote about her child. "Is he still alive? Here without all of you is just misery."[6]

Dar'ya Semenovna did not mail the postcards she purchased. She kept them because she cherished the images. She showed them to me—one of a rural Baroque church in the foreground of thatch cottages surrounded by cozy, lush gardens. There are no people in the photo, just a beckoning path ambling across and out of the frame.

Dar'ya Semenovna told me about "William," an American POW who worked in the same factory. He fell in love with her across the machinery and asked her to come to the United States with him after the war. "I turned him down," she remembered. "I was afraid. I only wanted home to mama, even if there was a famine there."

As she carefully stowed the cards in her bureau, Dar'ya Semenovna remarked that she had seen no place as beautiful as that Bavarian hamlet where she had been incarcerated during the war. I was stunned by the melancholy of her words. I imagined that in retrospect those years of imprisonment still held a promise of future freedom and happiness, a promise that did not pan out. After returning home to Uman in 1945, Dar'ya Semenovna's life never righted. Because she had been forced to work for the enemy, she was branded a collaborator and barred from finishing high school and going to university. While many of her contemporaries wore ribbons on their chests and stood honored in public ceremonies commemorating the Great Fatherland War, Dar'ya Semenovna spent her life as a cleaning lady, mopping floors and swabbing bathrooms in public buildings.

In the 1990s, after the collapse of the Soviet Union, former Soviet citizens were freed to reconceive of the past in richer ways, and World War II became a pivot around which people often told the story of their lives, even if they were too young to have experienced it firsthand. For Dar'ya Semenovna, looking back toward the end of her life, the war years became a form of tourism, if coerced, and represented a moment of adventure and passion in her long, disappointing life.

For Bratslavers, on the other hand, the war and the Holocaust made Uman sacred, a way to both commemorate and renounce the attempted genocide of European Jews. During the Soviet era, a few Bratslavers from Israel and the United States would slip into Uman each year for Rosh Hashanah to spend the holiday at Nahman's grave site. After the Berlin Wall came down, and with it Soviet restrictions on travel, more and more Bratslavers streamed into the town each fall. By 1998 a whole travel industry was in place, with chartered planes and buses to transport thousands of Hasids to Uman for the holiday.

The center of the action was the grave. The entrance to the sacred site started on a wide street of cracked cement lined with Brezhnevera apartment blocks. There, during the holiday, Uman residents and visiting Bratslavers milled around, hawking, selling, buying, and watching. The broad street narrowed to a path as it neared the covered grave. I wished to see it, and started walking that way, into a throng of believers pacing and praying at the foot of the grave. As I approached, some men turned on me, hissing and making motions as if shooing away a cat. I stopped, confused, seeing the faces of the men redden, lips curling. A minute passed and finally a man came up and whispered in English with a Brooklyn accent, "They are really serious about the ban on women. If you go farther, you could get hurt."

I looked around and noticed for the first time that all the eyes watching me were male. I felt a fool. Devout Hasidim are forbidden to look upon women during the holiday. During the major holidays the grave becomes the preserve of men arriving from abroad. For those acquainted with Jewish religious tradition, it appears absurd that I let slip that one, important fact before I made the trip from Kiev. But I did. I learned later that among the ten thousand visiting male Bratslavers in Uman that year, there was only one Orthodox woman—who, like me, was barred from the grave and the synagogue.

I had come to watch. But I was not allowed anywhere within eyesight. I returned to Dar'ya Semenovna's apartment disappointed. Over potatoes and cherry wine I told her my problem. "Why don't you dress as a boy?" she suggested. I shook my head, replying I thought it would be disrespectful to the Hasids. "A shame," Dar'ya Semenovna replied, "you have come so far."

I had only traveled two hours on a bus from Kiev, where I was living at the time, but I saw her point. I had come a long way in trying to understand this kind of pilgrimage, and sitting in Dar'ya's apartment, I was no closer to grasping the experience.

"Go there at night," she tried again, "and watch from behind a bush." That struck me as a better idea. It was still sneaky, but if I wasn't seen, then I broke no sacred law. Right? My logic was doubtful, but it was good enough for me at the time.

Late on the eve of Rosh Hashanah, I made my way back to the grave. I was aided by the fact that Ukrainian cities, short of cash and thus electricity, skimped on street lighting. In the dark, I slipped up to the courtyard just above the path approaching the holy site, and climbed a tree. The tree's canopy offered good cover. From my perch on the branch, feeling powerfully invisible, I watched.

In the balmy night, the small clay and wattle cottage built around the grave glowed fluorescent. Songs and shouts came from the pavilion covering the holy site. The wind blew vigorously as a young man with the first tufts of hair on his chin tapped by in delicate high-heeled shoes, his long white stockings smudged and disheveled. A broad-brimmed *streumel* engulfed his crown in a halo of mink. An elderly man aided by another boy slowly followed, moving with arachnid precision—spine bent at a right angle, right leg carefully unfolding, cane in pursuit, neck extended—downhill toward the grave. As the prayer service ended, more men poured along the narrow, littered street; men in long robes and ringlets alit in the silty gusts. Boys followed the men, twitching behind their fathers. Men silvered at the sideburns and in elegant suits passed, succeeded by younger, poorer Hasids shuffling by in hand-me-down suits and broken loafers.

Although few of the Bratslavers spoke Russian or Ukrainian, the men moving back and forth seemed very much at home in Uman. The street between the grave of Nahman von Bratslav and the new synagogue looked more like a street in Jerusalem than one in the former Soviet Union. Unlike the wide parade routes favored by Soviet planners, this street narrowed to a crowded and twisting footpath pitted with peddlers selling yarmulkes, portraits of the *tsadik*, prayer books, and shawls. The men and boys, hands on each other's shoulders, caught up in song, filled the space with sound and motion. It was haunting to witness, as if the prewar photographs of Ukrainian *shtetls* had come to life. As if the Hasids innately knew their sacred place in this distant land.

As I watched the procession, I fell into a transcendent state of heightened sensory apprehension. The evening breeze pulled toward me the scent of autumn leaves mixed with frying onions. Voices rose and fell in and out of earshot, occasionally overtaken by the bleating traffic on the artery above. The pale lights of cozy, compartmentalized, family life in the surrounding apartment blocks circled the gravesite, sheltering the men and boys lost to their ancient prayers. I came to a moment when the strangeness of the place gave way to familiar and intimate sensations of childhood, my legs dangling from a tree, spying from above on the life I could not join. At that moment, that's all there was: this place, the balmy wind, the song-filled vibrations of the air, and me.

Listening and sensing, from my branch, the universe expanding outward, becoming grander and more magnificent, I suddenly felt a sharp pull on my leg. Grabbing the trunk to keep from falling, I looked down to see two policemen in Ukrainian uniform. They were looking up at me, and they were angry. They ordered me to climb out of the tree. I packed my notebook and slipped to the ground, trying not to look sheepish. Once I was brought back down to earth, they started in the way cops do, telling me about the regulations on trespassing and the ban on women at the site. I protested weakly, saying I was just there to watch, as if watching were not a violation of the Hasids' sacred law. They lectured some more on law and order in general, and then changed tactic, "We're doing this for your own protection," one of the police officers said. "Last year a few Hasids beat up three women who got too close." The second officer looked at me sharply. "Who are you anyway, some kind of journalist?" I admitted I was a sort of journalist. They asked about my accent. I conceded I was American.

At once we were on friendly terms. "Oh, well. You are American? Why didn't you say so? I am Yuri and this is Sasha. We are from Cherkassy." It had happened many times before, this quick familiarity. Once they learned I was a foreigner, the two men no longer worried about my presence at the grave and their job of preserving the peace but instead told me about their lives as cops: the long hours, how they didn't always get paid, and when they did, how meager their wages were to support a family. These stories were familiar. On meeting a foreigner in post-Soviet Europe, many people wanted to narrate their existence, as if to tell me was to broadcast their troubles for all the world to hear. I listened absently and nodded, wishing to be back in the tree returned to my broken reverie.

I kept looking past the policemen, trying to take a measure of the Bratslavers' activities. Yuri noticed. "It is a shame you can't go in there." He said, pointing over his shoulder to the new synagogue, built to hold ten thousand visitors. "It is really interesting. They sing and dance, shout and cry." Yuri observed the look of regret that walked across my face and smiled sympathetically. Then he had an idea. "Wait right here," he said, "I'll be back," and he dashed off to a mobile home set up as a police station, while Sasha and I stood on the spot in silence. In a few minutes, Yuri returned with a policeman's peaked cap and a rubber cape. "Put this on."

"You want me to dress as a police officer?"

I eyed the two men, each over six feet and weighing in around two hundred pounds. Given my size, Dar'ya Semenovna's idea of dressing as a boy made much more sense.

"Seriously?" I considered turning them down, but then I thought of how often I had failed to get the story, arriving home empty-handed. My moral doubts as to passing myself off as someone else ebbed. Or, maybe, it was just easier to let it happen.

"It will be fine." Yuri tenderly arranged the cape around my shoulders and placed the officer's hat on my head. "You will walk between us, and no one will ask questions."

There I stood, the heavy macintosh cascading past my hands and falling to my feet, the officer's cap swallowing my skull and one eye. I was fooling no one. I made for a very short cop with a bad tailor.

Sasha appraised me doubtfully. "Just make sure you stay between us and don't say a word."

We headed off. The two men kept their shoulders pressed to mine. I had to walk carefully so as not to trip on the cape, while I tilted my chin to prevent the cap from slipping over my forehead. Huddled together, we set off awkwardly down the ramp toward the grave. Seeing a dense crowd of men, the more cautious Sasha lost nerve and veered off toward a large, tensile structure, the synagogue, which up close looked curious, a cross between a big box store and a religious revival field tent. As we walked, the Hasids made way for us. I tried to look at no one, in the childish hope that by not seeing, I myself would not be seen.

I had an idea what I would witness in the synagogue—swaying men, singing, and speaking in tongues. In my mind's eye, these snapshots occurred slowly in a musty sepia with the sound muffled. I did not expect the bawdy nightclub atmosphere that materialized before me. Young men with electric guitars and keyboards pumped out a loud, fast-paced klezmer, while men and boys, dressed in the fashion of eighteenth-century Polish nobility, arms locked, moved chaotically in a mosh pit of jumping, spinning, gyrating bodies. The crowd parted for teenagers who cartwheeled and spun on their shoulders break-dance style. The sound was almighty, the energy contagious. I understood why Yuri had wanted me to see this. I itched to join in with the dancing believers. I got the feeling Yuri did too. Cops and historians stand around and observe, though sometimes they crave to take part, knowing, however, that to give in to that feeling can get a person in trouble professionally.

As it was, I was already in professional trouble. I should not have gone into the synagogue, where I was not invited, even though I considered my goal worthwhile. I wanted to witness in order to write a more sympathetic account of the history of religious Jews and Christians in Right Bank Ukraine. Too often, I thought at the time, Jewish history in modern eastern Europe was written as if in a separate ghetto of historical literature.[7] In these accounts, historians depict Jews as under siege from their aggressive, anti-Semitic neighbors. I wanted to see Jews in Ukraine in context, in a way that reflected what they shared with their neighbors and showed their cultural impact and spiritual leadership in the former Pale of Settlement. In order to write more sensitive prose, however, I committed an insensitive act. Crossing into the tensile synagogue, I entered a gray zone from which I have never really emerged. There is no clear line that demarcates where historians overstep the boundaries of privacy. Historians read intimate letters and diaries, which the authors never meant to be public, and somehow the fact that the reading is posthumous (sometimes by centuries) softens the violation. I didn't have even that consolation. My intrusion was direct and immediate and forced to the surface the recognition of the voyeuristic qualities of historical research.

But standing in the synagogue, I had none of these thoughts. I was just nervous about getting caught. So, apparently, was Sasha. After about ten minutes, he cut our tour short, and we returned to the mobile police quarters where I handed in my borrowed uniform.

There it was. I had witnessed what I had come to see, or at least something of it. What did my adventure tell me about Ukrainian *shtetls* before the Holocaust and about villagers who believed in a Virgin Mary freely roaming the countryside?

Not much. The high-pitched squawking of the sound system, the swiveling teens, and the bargaining over tourist memorabilia were particular to the late twentieth century. I had been wrong in my expectations. There was no nostalgia, longing, or mournfulness in the synagogue's sacred discotheque. Nothing sepia anywhere. The dancing men clapped their hands on each other's shoulders, smiled broadly, and joyfully expressed their spiritual union in that moment on that spot. Hasids believe that their leaders who have died are just as present in daily life as those who are alive. In Uman, centuries after Nahman's death and forty years after the Holocaust, the dance at Nahman's grave was a declaration of life, which, as Nahman had taught, transcends the limits of this world. In short, religious belief is the immediate product of its time and place. I cannot say that the Bratslavers dancing before me had an affinity with the Bratslavers in Uman in the 1920s, nor that the Ukrainian Christians I met who were fascinated with the Rabbi's mythical powers had much to do with Ukrainian peasants in that period who sought out *tsadiks* for advice and help with fertility and health problems.

Yet this chronological incompatibility doesn't mean that my mission was a failure. I took from my stolen glimpse into the synagogue one small insight. In the synagogue, I was struck by the Bratslavers' straightforward elation in the celebration of Nahman's (continuing) existence. Their joy seemed discordant with scholarly explanations of irrational religious faith. Ethnographers in the 1920s and historians later explained away villagers' belief in miraculous occurrences with interpretations that drew from the medical and psychological literature of the time. For example, after years of war and civil war, some scholars postulated that villagers in times of stress and famine placed their faith in miracles as an articulation of fear and distress.[8] Other scholars suggested that uneducated people were easily fooled by charismatic charlatans, who sold them notions and miracles, or that poorly educated and frightened believers used a faith in miracles as a way to make sense of a confusing, dynamic world.[9] Some saw religious believers as caught up in mass hysteria, as sick people in need of a cure.[10] What I had witnessed, however, did not appear to be emotions born of fear or illness, confusion or ignorance. None of these descriptions of feelings tracked with the simple joy I witnessed in the Bratslavers' synagogue. Neither my expectations nor the analysis of other historians made sense once I had a street-level view of the Bratslavers' religious practices. Put simply, I didn't know what I was going to experience and feel until I got there.

A hundred years before I watched the Bratslavers from the tree branch in Uman, a Kiev psychiatrist also made contact with a group of religious believers in a state of ecstatic prayer. He too was sure he knew what he would find when he went to watch, and, like me, he was taken by surprise. The story goes like this. In 1892 peasants in parts of Kiev province were flocking in great numbers to a new religious sect called the Maliovantsy. Its adherents behaved strangely, radically altering their way of life after conversion. Peasant believers sold off their possessions, quit work, and remained in a state of idle expectation, awaiting the end of the world, which they believed was imminent. Worried, tsarist officials asked a psychiatrist, Ivan Sikorskii, to study the sect. Sikorskii began by detaining Kondrat Maliovannyi, the man whose name the others ascribed to the new sect. Sikorskii had Maliovannyi committed to the psychiatric ward of a Kiev hospital. Several other men picked up while preaching were also incarcerated.[11]

Sikorskii reported that almost all members of the sect experienced deteriorating health, characterized by a poor diet, spasms, hysterical attacks, olfactory hallucinations, and a refusal to work. Strangely, these symptoms were accompanied by an abnormally happy disposition. The last two indications—idleness and happiness—were especially alarming in a peasant population typically characterized in tsarist Russia by never-ending toil and a "dark" or sadly resigned disposition.[12] Sikorskii quickly came to a diagnosis; the men and their "followers" were suffering from a "mass psychosis." In describing his patients' cases, Sikorskii portrayed men who were intellectually and physically on the move. All were peasants. Some had been baptized Orthodox, others Catholic. All had left their inherited religions on spiritual quests. The men recounted to Sikorskii dreams and visions that led them to an ever more radical divergence from established religious communities. Eventually each of the men began to travel and preach independently. As they did, they drew few boundaries in the region's multivalent religious terrain. They preached to Christian communities regardless of orientation: Catholics, Orthodox, Uniates, Old Believers, and Protestants. They crossed the threshold of Christianity and appeared in Jewish synagogues and heders. A few of the patients, unschooled and illiterate, claimed to have divinely acquired the ability to read the bible and other texts. Sikorskii tested them and was mystified to find that, indeed, several of the men who had no formal education could read quite well.

The patients recounted to Sikorskii encounters with the Holy Spirit, which came in many forms: visions, dreams, bodily sensations, and otherworldly scents. The men stated that they were the physical manifestation of Christ on earth. This was not an exclusive state of being, they said. Christ could inhabit many men at once. The Virgin Mary could possess women, and many women had also started to preach and lead communities. Once possessed with the Holy Spirit, a person became infallible. He or she no longer needed to confess or go to church for holy rites. All his or her actions and utterances were a manifestation of God's wisdom. This divine confidence Sikorskii found most irritating. His prisoners answered his queries with a self-assurance Sikorskii reserved singularly for his class.[13] Self-confidence in ignorant peasants he labeled "arrogant" and "impertinent."

Sikorskii was clearly bothered by this "epidemic." In his lengthy study, he returned repeatedly to the fact that members of the sect refused to work, that they adopted the dress, civility, and manners of educated bourgeoisie, and that they were so inanely joyful. In their madness, they renounced all that defined them as peasants: their rough clothing, brusque manners, social inferiority, gloomy disposition, and, especially, their incessant labor. Sikorskii tried to behead the movement, committing the preachers, mostly male, whom he perceived as leaders to the asylum, but to no avail. Without their preachers, the sectarians continued to meet, pray, and remain blissfully idle. New leaders, male and female, recently infused with the voice of God, emerged to take their place. Confounded by the persistence of the movement, Sikorskii took the unusual step of going to a meeting to observe the contagion in action. What he witnessed there bothered him even more.

As Sikorskii described it, the meeting of the faithful began quietly enough. In the packed room, someone began to sing. Other voices joined in. The sound of murmured prayers mingled with song. A short time passed and then someone started to twitch. Several quivering hands flew into the air. Legs, as if independent of the body, shifted into motion, swaying and twisting in involuntary spasms. A shout crashed into song. A man gave himself over to tears, breaking down, awash in brine, his powerful body trembling beneath him. As if the tears were a signal, the room filled with the sound of sighs, hiccups, belching, and more sobbing, and the crowd collapsed into a frenzy, jumping, clapping, beating faces, pulling hair, pounding chests, and stomping feet. Sikorskii wrote that the faces expressed the full range of emotions: joy, exhilaration, disappointment, fear, surprise, bitterness, horror, physical pain. But mostly, he observed, the tears and shouts were of jubilation. In their euphoria, a few women stripped down to their girdles and, embracing men near them, planted long, passionate kisses on their lips. Yet in the mass "hysteria," no one, Sikorskii marveled, lost control. This was not mayhem. Mothers holding babies in their arms and children by the hand did not lose their grip. Sikorskii, growing intensely curious, got as close as he could, wading into the crowd of inflamed believers, trying to see if they would touch him. He puzzled over the fact that, although most people had their eyes closed and seemed to be in another world, not one person bumped or jostled him.[14]

A diagnosis can take a bit of distance. Going to the religious gathering, the physician had become an ethnographer, and though he took just a few steps into the crowd, his experience was enough to soften his judgment. Up close, Sikorskii became less sure of his assertion of pathology. After his visit, he basically let the matter drop, forgetting his diagnosis of "mass psychosis," and released the captured peasants from the Kiev asylum. I had noticed this kind of dissolving skepticism before in the work of a Soviet ethnographer in the 1920s who watched peasants hitch girls to a plow to circle the village cross in order to call down rain in a drought. The ethnographer had stood back, arms folded at the villagers' foolishness, only to have to admit to seeing, after the third pass around the cross, large drops fall from the sky.[15]

Traveling to the sites of impossible miracles, the physician, the ethnographer, and me, the historian, changed position. We no longer watched from on high or a distance, and that gave us access to insights we did not have before. Judgment and verdict transformed into understanding and a suspension of disbelief.[16]

I returned to Dar'ya Semenovna's after my misadventure with Yuri and Sasha. Her apartment building's water heater was on the blink, and as I was in the bathroom cleaning up for bed, Dar'ya Semenovna brought in a boiling kettle and poured it in the basin. I stood waiting for her to step out of the small bathroom, but she lingered, looking at me broadly and holding out a warm sponge. She said she would help me bathe. I gave her a puzzled look.

"Well, you need to, no?" she said and gestured with the soapy sponge to the place between my legs. Once again that day, I stood mystified. This woman, who I had only just met, wanted to bathe me as if I were a child. She had spent the previous evening telling me about her life, sharing confidences of decades past. I understood her gesture as a desire to reciprocate, or continue with intimacy, now of a bodily nature. So, as I had allowed Yuri to dress me as a police officer, this too I let happen with a shrug. I slipped off my clothes, and her furrowed hands gently worked from my legs up my torso. Her work drew us into a communion. From her touch I felt that I grasped her loneliness, courage, humility, and a compassion that surpassed most any I had known before.

Dar'ya Semenovna's care for my body reminded me of my status in post-Soviet society as an honorary child. As a foreigner it was assumed I had a child's naiveté and ignorance. Sure that I knew nothing of what had gone on in their country before I arrived, a lot of people, like Dar'ya Semenovna, Sasha, and Yuri wanted to tell me about their lives, to give me an education. If I accepted this role passively, relinquishing my status as an autonomous adult and the critical rationality of a researcher, they often let me in, if fleetingly, for a closer look. By becoming childlike—susceptible, disabled, and dependent—I became a temporary member of their community, which in the Soviet Union was defined by an understanding of biological vulnerability, mutual interdependence, and obligation. And it was that generosity in receiving a stranger that guided me, and I would argue the concerned Dr. Sikorskii, to a higher plateau of knowing.

Of course, I am not a child, just as the Hasids had not returned "home" to Uman. They and I were strangers in this land, and were seen as such. Ukrainians milling around the holiday happening complained to me of the religious tourists who rented rooms from them, how slovenly and messy they were, how they littered the streets and damaged their rented apartments. The message behind these complaints was that the Hasids stayed in Uman but no longer had a stake in it; they lingered there but did not live there, were not at home. The Hasids, in turn, were sure the Ukrainians were charging them too much and cheating them. For me, the essence of that narrative was that although the Hasids had lost the language of their grandfathers and lived far from the daily life of Ukraine, they had not forgotten their dispossession and estrangement.

Yet despite this distance, there was something to being in the place. As a secular person I can't call it magic, but I have no other descriptor for the transformative experience of being there. Plato taught that humans are distinct from the animal world because they possess a soul detached from their bodies. Kant explained that humans are unique because they have the power of reason that can overcome bodily drives. Religion is founded on these supposed distinctions of humans from the animal kingdom, and the critique of religion comes from a similar philosophical trajectory, but the experience of ecstatic religion reminded me that the mind (and the soul, if there is one) are essentially linked to a body, which is vulnerably, pleasurably, dependently connected to a place. The body, in fact, is the first place of earthly existence.[17]

What I mean to say is that there are two aspects to being in place. One is simply the location. The other is a corporal state of being that reminds a person of his or her biological position within the animal kingdom and the natural world. For both myself and the Hasids this was an experience of transcendence—theirs born of faith and prayer, mine emanating from a return to a childlike perceptual awareness. For all the vocabulary set to print in scholarly literature, we are poor in words for this sort of experience. The Hasids could have prayed elsewhere. I could have read about pilgrimages and the loss of the multilingual, multicreed communities of central Ukraine from a library in Kiev or the United States. But it would not have been the same. I, and presumably the Bratslavers, would not have had the same complex of feeling, the same revelations, transmitted somehow by the act of being there, in dirty little Uman at the end of a terrible century.

6 Gridded Lives: Why Kazakhstan and Montana Are Nearly the Same Place

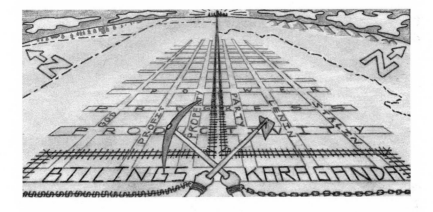

From the map of Karaganda, it appears that its city plan was based on the model of the old Roman military camp—set up along a grid, the old Stalin Prospect running north to south, the former Lenin Prospect bisecting it east to west. The grid makes sense for a prison city. It creates wide-open spaces and straight lines, an architecture designed not to be seen but to facilitate seeing, to support surveillance of the city's inhabitants so as to regulate and contain their conduct. Karaganda, located on the arid steppe of northern Kazakhstan, was founded in the early 1930s alongside KarLag, one of the largest labor camps in the Soviet Union. Karaganda was a prison city in that it was built largely by convicts and fed on crops grown in the labor camp's farms, while prisoners and deportees worked in the mines and factories of its blossoming industries.[1] In 1930, Karaganda was not even a point on the map. By 1939, the city had 100,000 inhabitants, half of them wards (prisoners or deportees) of the Ministry of Interior's Gulag division (NKVD-Gulag).[2]

I had expected Karaganda to have that smoke-belching, wrecked look of the industrial cities of Soviet Russia to the north. But I was surprised. After Joseph Stalin died in 1953, the prisoners were gradually given amnesty, the barracks dismantled, the barbed wire lifted, and, curiously, what remains is a neatly ordered city of broad avenues and shady sidewalks, monumental squares and symmetrically plotted parks, ample and verdant. There is plenty of parking, convenient shopping, and no cramped corners. No sign of the gulag's secrecy or human suffering is written into the urban landscape. Instead, Karaganda is an open-armed embrace that says it has nothing to hide. There are no old shops to dig out of back alleys, no tenements or crowded nineteenth-century courtyards of the kind Dostoyevsky haunted. In fact, Karaganda is so well-ordered, there is no great need to explore it on foot. It can be read easily from the upholstered comfort of a car at cruising speed.

The car slides by long columns of housing blocks, which replaced the prisoners' barracks in the 1950s. The residential tracts, built with assembly-line efficiency, are the Soviet equivalent of the American suburban development. The same three blueprints echo in row after row, the same efficient economy of occupancy and technology behind the lace curtains, the same segregation of space based on the daily repetition of meals, commuting, and recreation around which American homes are also designed. Built rapidly, rapidly looking obsolete, the buildings radiate that temporal quality of much of American architecture, as if designed not for generations of a family but for cycles of a professional career, a familiar architecture responding to the unmatched social mobility of the twentieth century.[3]

One evening, I stood on the balcony of my Karaganda hotel room, looking at neon signs glistening along the rain-soaked streets. The October wind breathed the first frost of winter and sent skyward small wrappers of candy imported from North America. In the distance, the comforting lights of thousands of living rooms lit up the expanse, revealing the soothing grid as it marched up and down, partitioning the electrified urban spaces from the black void of the steppe beyond. Here, far from home, in the midst of a former gulag on the Kazakh steppe, I had the uncanny feeling that I had seen this city before. Karaganda, with its gridded composure, easy repetition of residential units, carefully swept walks and after-school dance classes, seemed oddly familiar, as if I had landed not in Central Asia but in the American middle west, in Wichita, Topeka, Bismarck, or Billings.

Billings, Montana. Like most railroad cities, Billings can be navigated without a map. Broad arteries cut north and south, avenues east and west. The streets are platted out and conveniently numbered, beginning at one and continuing, hypothetically, to infinity, in keeping with the grand aspirations of the founding fathers. The Yellowstone River flows unnoted on the outskirts of town, beyond the grain elevators, railroad switching yards, and oil refineries. Looking at Billings from the height of the cliffs above it, the mind drifts off to high-school geometry, trying to take in the ever-divisible asphalt grid of smaller and smaller blocks that break down to rectangular spaces etched with yellow paint on the parking lots. Fly over Billings, and this chessboard divisibility of space expands to cover the whole land: squared-off fields contained within square-mile sections fit into angular counties in the washboard abdomen of the country, where the states break up into rectangles and trapezoids.

Standing on the bluff overlooking Billings, I was better able to decipher what it was that made it feel like Karaganda: the divisibility and hierarchy of space, the abrupt, fortresslike partition of urban from agricultural territory, the lonely feeling of a city adrift like a ship on a sea of land that is inhospitable and unpredictable. Yet, historically, these similarities didn't make sense. Karaganda is a city erected in the midst of a vast labor camp, a city where in the 1990s children planting trees in the schoolyard would come across human bones. Billings, by contrast, was founded by railroad entrepreneurs, farmers, miners, and businessmen on the American frontier. One city is the product of an authoritarian state that employed and ruled everyone who toiled there; the other, a conglomerate of competing business interests and individual farmers. Two countries, worlds apart, two different histories, yet cities in the American West share the same modern, expansive, modular feel as Karaganda because Karaganda, like every western American railroad city, is built along a grid.

The fact of the grid may seem like no fact at all. For the grid is no novelty; it has been used as an architectural model for centuries, and

KarLag guard
tower. Photo
by author.

it does not necessarily follow that all gridded cities are born of the
same motivations. Kazakhstan and the Great Plains fall in the same
topographical zone of vast, arid, high plateaus. One could argue that
the flat, endless landscapes lend themselves easily to geometric dis-
section.[4] Yet it seems logical that two such contrasting societies—the
communist Soviet Union and democratic United States—would natu-
rally develop cities in distinct patterns expressing the vast differences
between the two countries in ideas, politics, and economic structure.
For if one believes that form relates to content—that cities contain
their histories, as Italo Calvino writes, "like the lines of a hand, written
in the corners of the streets and the gratings of the windows"—then

can it be purely coincidental that Karaganda, a prison city, and Billings, a railroad town, look alike?[5]

To attempt any kind of analogy between Karaganda and Billings is to ignore the polarities between the two places. For at least in terms of imagery, one can conceive of few regions more dissimilar. The American West represents the last, inexhaustible frontier of American individualism, the place where people went to be free. Northern Kazakhstan, conversely, conjures an image similar to that of Siberia; it is a place of unfreedom, exile, and imprisonment, a place where masses of undifferentiated people were sent against their will to serve a monolithic state. Placed in the larger context of the United States and the Soviet Union, the contrasts between the two cities intensify: the free market versus the planned economy, the democracy of the people versus the dictatorship of the proletariat, the pioneer versus the exile, the self-made man and free labor versus the machinated relationship of prison guard and convict. To liken Billings to Karaganda is to blur the domains, as we have defined them, of freedom and bondage, liberty and oppression. People were deported to Karaganda against their will. They were either sentenced to hard labor in camps or exiled to special settlements, and they starved, froze, and worked until they dropped from exhaustion. Of course, it is true that on the Great Plains people also starved, froze, and worked until they dropped from exhaustion, but in the American Plains they did it of their own free will; they bought their own train tickets. Is that difference of free will essential?

Just by posing the question, I threaten to relativize the oppression of the Soviet penal system and the suffering of millions of people sent into exile or to the gulag. Certainly, there is a difference between Billings and Karaganda, a difference calculable in both magnitude and outcome. As Soviet archives have been opened, documentary evidence has confirmed survivor accounts that narrate how Soviet security forces—the OGPU, NKVD, and MVD[6]—uprooted millions of peaceful citizens and subjected them to physical and psychological abuse, starvation, and conditions ripe for disease, from which hundreds of thousands of people died.[7] The years of arrest and deportation tore apart families, destroyed communities, and changed permanently both social relations and the landscape.

Yet setting aside for a moment the well-documented differences between the penal Kazakh steppe and free-market American frontier, I wonder if there is significance to the spatial similarities of the grid in Montana and Kazakhstan.

Maybe. Comparisons can be fruitful. They can also be misleading or overtly political.[8] Anything can be compared to anything. It is a trick of historians to juxtapose historic eras or regimes to point out similarities or differences and thus win an argument. Since the onset of the Cold War, for example, Stalin's Soviet Union has often been likened to Hitler's Nazi regime. The extremes of left and right are seen to fuse at one common point of total communist/fascist social control, illustrating the apex of state terror.[9] Contrasts, too, can be used for polemical effect. In the same Cold War years, historians, journalists, and politicians in the United States have focused on Soviet transgressions such as the purge trials, collectivization, and the suppression of dissidents as a way to spell out what democratic America is not or should never become.[10] Conversely, Soviet historians and journalists for decades fixated on American ghettos, racial strife, social unrest, and rising crime rates as a sign that Soviet socialism was on the right track.[11]

Now, with the threat of the Cold War faded, there is more room to question whether knowledge itself has not been gridded into neat polarities, communist and democratic. Histories tend to prioritize texts, written matter, and ideological categorizations. And certainly, in the heated debates of the Cold War, words, rhetoric, and ideologies were highly evaluated, perhaps overvalued, at the cost of ignoring and diminishing the history of the production of spaces and the lives that have been forged by and for those spaces. This is no new idea. Several decades ago, Henri Lefebvre asserted that there is no communism, just two myths: "that of anti-communism, on the one hand, and the myth that communism had been carried out somewhere on the other." Lefebvre doubted the existence of communism because it had led to no architectural innovation, no creation of specifically socialist spaces.[12] In other words, in the history of space, communism and capitalism have produced no qualities that distinguish one from the other.

What would happen, then, if I discarded all that is commonly known about the polarities of communism and capitalism and, just for the sake of argument, explored the spatial affinities? With this approach, it may turn out that historians and politicians in both countries have focused to the point of obfuscation on the differences between Soviet

communism and American capitalism and ignored the parallels produced by the industrial-capital expansions of the twentieth century.[13]
After all, a mirror image, as the Soviet Union has been purported to
be to the United States, is just the same form reflected backward. We
may even recognize in the two countries similar paths of development and destruction that differ more in scale than form. If that is so,
then the decades of fixing on political systems and ideology appear in
retrospect as a prolonged exercise in self-definition. Neither country
could have existed without the other, because each country used its
communist/capitalist nemesis as a self-justifying point of departure;
each country projected a mirror image of the other in order to define
and produce itself so as to rule. Without the specter of the counter-
revolutionary capitalist or the subversive communist, each country
would have had a much harder time defining the abnormal and the
dangerous; thus, it would have been more difficult to appropriate the
power to condemn and exclude, to coax and coerce into conformity.[14]
In short, if we strain away the mountains of verbiage encircling the
Cold War, it might appear that the Soviet Union and the United States
share a great deal in common.

Or perhaps we are still too close to the twentieth century to see
how greater forces have, over the last hundred years, put disparate
lives in sync in strange ways. To do so requires a different set of questions than those the Cold War theoreticians posed. Rather than asking where is freedom and where is bondage, who has choices and who
does not, who wields power and who is powerless, I might question,
more simply, *how* is power produced?[15] And once that question flutters
down to eye level, the gaze is drawn to spaces that once seemed innocent of manipulation—urban architecture, transportation routes,
lines of communication, patterns of production—all of which represent a particular political and economic logic that has inhabited our
societies, both Soviet and American, for the bulk of the century—
inhabited them with an encompassing opacity.[16]

My question, then, is—is it possible to write the history of gridded spaces? If so, do the gridded spaces of Kazakhstan and Montana
constitute the endpoint of larger processes that the United States
and Soviet Union shared? Lefebvre sees the grid as an abstraction, "a
superstructure foreign to the original space," that serves as a foothold
to establish the basis of rule.[17] James C. Scott understands the grid as a

way to simplify the opaque and complex quality of indigenous social practices so as to enhance centralized power at the cost of local rule.[18] In short, the grid can serve as an apparatus for conquest, as a way to dominate space. Narrated together, the histories of Karaganda in Kazakhstan and Billings and Butte in Montana illustrate how the grid evolved just as the territories were being swept into the larger industrial and agricultural economies of their respective expanding states in eras of superlative industrial and bureaucratic expansion. During North America's second industrial revolution, which preceded World War I, the railroad, America's first national bureaucracy, put Billings, Butte, and other cities in Montana on the map. In northern Kazakhstan, the Communist Party, and specifically the NKVD, charted out Karaganda and many Soviet cities during the industrialization drive of the 1930s, which foreshadowed World War II, at a time when the Soviet state first became an industrialized and bureaucratized power. In both places, political forces produced gridded space, often violently, to serve economic and political goals.

But that is getting ahead of the story. To start from the beginning — there were no cities in northern Kazakhstan or the Great Plains before the steam engine and railroad. The populations of preindustrial cities in Central Asia and the American plains were largely supported by surrounding agricultural communities, and grew only so large as the limits of the land, the reach of walled fortifications, and scarce supplies of food, water, and cultivable soil allowed. Without technology, the short grasslands of the steppe and range, the dry, continental climates, could support no more than small communities of sedentary peoples tilling the soil, and were best suited for nomads living off the migratory grazing of range animals adapted to the extreme cold, heat, and aridity of the climate.

All of this changed in the industrial age. Cities no longer needed to follow the lay of the land or to rely on locally produced foodstuffs to feed their populations. Montana and Kazakhstan could support urban populations by means of technologies such as railroad networks, steam engines, irrigation systems, and the telegraph and telephone, all of which required a concentration of capital investment so large that in both regions it fell to a small group of managers to direct from afar the means of production and labor that kept everything going.

The managers in both places oversaw these vast networks with the help of time schedules, statistics, and production plans, and with the regimentation and subjection of labor.[19] In both Montana and Karaganda, the rush for land, water, minerals, and cash crops displaced indigenous peoples who had formerly inhabited the territories, while the European populations that replaced them were sorted according to contrived understandings of race, class, and loyalty.

These patterns of production created corresponding patterns of subjection, which determined that people settled the American high plains and Central Asian steppe in similar ways by carving land into economic units for efficient exploitation. New towns, located for the benefit of commerce and the quick extraction of resources at railheads, responded not to ecological limits but to the surveyor's rational grid.[20] The grid made space modular and repetitious. The urban grid was a concentration of the expanding rural grid, which linked the hinterland economically and spatially with cities. As a consequence, there were no topographical limits to urban space, and the cities grew and multiplied, supplanting the nomadic cultures that came before. In fact, the cities born during this century gave new meaning to nomadism by ambling across the flat plains wherever transportation routes wandered, with nothing to stop them but sheer loneliness.

In both countries, as a result, conquest meant consumption; the newcomers ingested—in coal, copper, wheat, sugar beets, ore—the territories they desired. In short, the histories of cities in Montana and Kazakhstan complement one another. Taken in tandem, they tell not two stories but one—the history of gridded space.

The sun reaches low for the horizon, the exhaust rises up from the valley, and gazing down on Billings the mind wanders to childhood stories about the frontier—tales of "hardy pioneers," "bringing civilization," "displacing savagery." These brave and arrogant aphorisms lay on the hardened sand before me like the rusted carcasses of the tin cans that followed European settlers wherever they traveled. American historians have discarded most of the myths of winning the West, and indeed it is hard to see that legend in the small corporate city of Billings.[21] In fact, Billings seems to have no history at all written into its carefully measured right angles. Or rather, its history might be sought in the wake of the bulldozer and the moving van—in the vacated lots and disowned possessions of the long row of thrift stores—which makes sense, because Billings was not founded on precedent or history. Its story, instead, like that of many western cities, is located in a vaporously elusive understanding of the future. As an early settler of Kansas instructed his readers: "The American of today must find his enjoyment in anticipating the future. He must look beyond the unsightly beginnings of civilization and prefigure the state of things a century hence."[22] The trick in the Great Plains involved overlooking the present to gaze at the future, but a future that never arrived, whether it be in steers, coal, or grain.

This myopia for the present tense helped give Billings its start. In 1881 the land on which Billings stands today was considered worthless. It was a barren, waterless alkali flat with here and there an oasis of sagebrush. The settlers and traders who first came to the region settled upstream at Clark's Fork Bottom, where the confluence of two rivers made a good trading post and where the land was fertile and water more plentiful. The residents of Clark's Fork assumed that when the railroad came through it would logically create a terminal in their little settlement, where there were a few traders and farmers already waiting for trains to bring in goods and ship their produce to market. But railroad executives in St. Paul and New York had a different set of priorities. The federal government had deeded the Northern Pacific line alternating townships of forty square miles on either side of the tracks to help offset the cost of building a transcontinental railroad. Frederick Billings, the president of the Northern Pacific, and his engineers studied the U.S. survey maps and determined that, at a certain point, the odd-numbered townships lay next to each other across the line of the railroad, instead of connecting at the corners as they did elsewhere.[23] Sensibly, Mr. Billings decided to locate the new city at that point where the railroad owned twice as much land as usual.

Then Frederick Billings did something even more sensible. He and a few associates formed a real estate development company and bought from the railroad 29,394 acres in the city-to-be for less than four dollars an acre. It made no difference to Mr. Billings that the site for the new city planned for twenty thousand residents would be established on barren flats, somewhat removed from the swampy edges of the river, without drinking water, two miles north of the closest human habitation. Within the four walls of real estate speculation, the siting of Billings made sense; the fact that the site was barely habitable mattered little to Mr. Billings. After all, Frederick Billings never dreamed of living in Billings.

After the Minnesota and Montana Land and Improvement Company chose the site for Billings, the company designed the city plan, with the railroad at its center, allocated building lots, and proposed future industrial development before any actual building took place, before the "city" was anything but a thicket of squatters' tents.[24] Nonetheless, the founding of the new city was trumpeted for hundreds of miles, and the profits to be made were fabulous. Once it was announced that Billings was going to be the next "Magic City," Frederick Billings's land development company began selling off the alkali flats at $250 for a quarter-acre lot. Whole blocks were sold in New York and Chicago, and within a few months the price had risen to $1,200.[25] By the summer of 1882, most of the city property was purchased, yet two-thirds of the owners were absentee; people who bought lots never planned to live in the hot, dry, treeless flats but to resell them later at a profit.[26]

The cosmology that ordained the grid in Billings pivoted around economics and administration. Billings's real estate company subdivided land into parcels, uniform and commercially interchangeable, because it made for efficient marketing and sales, especially from remote offices in St. Paul and Chicago. In this way, engineers, land agents, and railroad executives established, planned, and promoted towns identical to Billings throughout the West—Laramie, Reno, Bismarck, Cheyenne. The pioneering homesteader, the cowboy, and the lonesome miner are essential figures in American mythology and self-identity, but historians of the American West have argued that the vanguard of settlement in the West were these corporate-owned towns, run by businessmen who operated on the profits from real estate speculation fueled by federal land grants and the promise of future growth and industrial development.[27]

Karaganda, like Billings, was an unmarked void on the map before its founding as a city in 1930. It consisted of a ramble of shacks, a few abandoned buildings from a tsarist-era coal mine, and a small and occasional market where Kazakhs would come to trade sheep pelts and mutton steaks for salt, flour, and other necessities. In the late 1920s, Soviet geologists rediscovered the Karaganda coal basin, after which the Moscow-based Department of Mines set up the Karaganda

Coal Trust and determined that the site would be home to a major new industrial city. Without visiting the region, architects in Moscow drew up plans for a city of forty thousand workers who would dig out a projected twelve new mines. Within the year, several thousand miners, most of them Kazakhs, began working underground in Karaganda. But the Coal Trust found that it could not keep its stores stocked with enough food to feed the miners, and despite a city plan calling for seven square meters of sanitary housing per person, housing conditions stumbled into proletarian disgrace, with most of the miners living in yurts or tents scattered near the mine shafts. In search of food, the Kazakh miners drifted to and from their native *auls* (villages), which made for a sporadic and ill-disciplined labor force, and coal production sagged below prerevolutionary figures.[28]

In February 1931, however, the railroad arrived in Karaganda and with it a whole new form of discipline. The railroad brought supplies, geologists, and experienced miners from the Donbass in Ukraine, and it also brought NKVD officers, who quickly realized the limitless possibilities of establishing a labor camp next to the Karaganda mines. Sounding as optimistic as a Billings railroad associate, an NKVD officer wrote that the combination of virgin land, mineral resources, and a rail connection meant that "Kazakhstan offers remarkable potential for the creation of a powerful agricultural base. Only a labor reserve is needed due to the sparsely populated territory."[29] A labor camp, NKVD officials proposed, would funnel a plentiful supply of workers to Karaganda to till the virgin soil and produce food for the miners. In 1931 the Gulag division of the NKVD set up KarLag on 281,000 acres of land around the growing settlement of Karaganda and began to import labor.[30]

The labor camp helped solved Karaganda's shortage of workers and food. City leaders made use of prison labor to grow crops on the outskirts of the city and to work on construction sites in the city to build housing for the miners. To supervise the prisoner-laborers, NKVD guards walled districts into "zones" separated with barbed wire, each about the size of a city block. The guards required avenues straight and broad enough to march prisoners in columns to work sites and enough visibility to shoot in case anyone made a run for it. It is tempting to postulate that Karaganda's grid grew out of the demands of prison architecture, except for the fact that most modern Soviet cities are likewise platted in a grid. Soviet planners in the 1930s designed and created many other industrial cities—ones not intended for prisoners—that are nearly interchangeable with Karaganda.[31]

In the early 1930s, Soviet planners dreamed of building an entirely new kind of "socialist city" that would express the principles of socialism in every line of every building. A socialist city, they postulated, would demonstrate the antithesis of the confusion and grime of a capitalist city. Soviet architects dreamed of "modernization without urbanism" and preferred to build cities from the ground up, on virgin soil.[32] They sought to design rational landscapes in which people would live safely and equitably, with plenty of light, space, and visibility. Architects from as far away as Germany submitted blueprints for cities that did not look like cities at all, but more like parks, spaceships, or modern art. Once built, however, the new socialist cities all looked alike, heedless of climate and topography; they were plotted symmetrically along a grid, Lenin Prospect running east-west, Stalin Prospect north-south. What motivated the grid in the Soviet context?

Even though private property was outlawed in Soviet socialism, concepts of ownership and management determined the shape of Karaganda, much as they did Billings. Individuals in the Soviet Union could not own land, but after the Soviet government nationalized all property, it allocated territory in vast swaths to state enterprises. The NKVD became a major recipient of land in northern Kazakhstan and one of the major exploiters of natural resources. By 1936 the NKVD controlled 795,600 acres of what had previously been Kazakh pastureland. By 1941 it was responsible for 12 percent of all Soviet lumber, 54 percent of all nickel, 75 percent of all molybdenum, and 37 percent of all tungsten production. The total value of gulag industrial production between 1941 and 1944 reached 3.6 billion rubles.[33] Land that to Kazakh nomads had been a flowing body of winter and summer pastures marked with ancestral burial grounds became to the Europeans who conquered it a series of parcels, surveyed in square meters and assigned value in rubles.[34]

To effect the transformation from ancestral land to commodified space, European settlers first envisioned indigenous land as empty, waiting to be populated. Billings and Karaganda were conceived in the minds of people who first saw the territories as representations on a map. The land for both cities was granted by federal governments to growing bureaucracies charged with settling the territories for the production of raw materials. In both cases, cities were platted by planners in remote locations who, drawing a series of lines on paper, finalized century-long processes of transferring territory from indigenous to European hands. The first blueprints for Billings posited a city for twenty thousand residents; Karaganda, fifty years later, was to have forty thousand. Once the transactions were complete, the cities came into being, contemporaries in Billings noted, like "magic": "the thoroughfares of Billings present a scene of business activity such as is not witnessed in any other town of Montana. The change seems almost as wonderful as some of those related in the old time tales of Eastern magic."[35] In Karaganda, historians also marveled at how the city sprang to life: "Great changes have taken place under Soviet rule on the Kazakh steppe. Where there used to be a few felt yurts and adobe huts, now a beautiful city has arisen . . . We see wide, tree-lined streets, avenues, parks and squares."[36]

One can read into this narrative on progress the classic subtext of the Soviet command economy at work: the city, planned from afar—but far from planned in actuality, significantly funded by the central coffers of the ominously expanding Soviet bureaucracy whose task it was to industrialize at all cost—but primarily built by cheap or unpaid manual labor. The years of hard work and spent lives that went into making Karaganda are summed up in a brief origin story describing one seemingly effortless leap from empty steppe to modern city.

Both Soviet and American proselytizers emphasize origins. What had been empty was filled in, the barren made green, the primitive sophisticated. Europeans arrived, found places empty of history, and gave them a beginning, and thus meaning. And they did it, the writers stress, quickly. In these new places, in the dawning age of fossil-fuel technology, civilization did not need centuries to ripen, as it had in Europe. There was no time for that. The promoters of Soviet and American insta-cities were drunk on speed, efficiency, the "magic" of machines.[37] They threw up hospitals, schools, courthouses, and libraries so that each new city would look like "a city," built not in decades, years, or even months, but weeks. Labor crews in Karaganda competed with builders in Leningrad in a construction race and won.[38] In the American West, the English scholar James Bryce wrote critically of the pace of expansion: "Why sacrifice the present to the future? Why seek to complete in a few decades what the other nations of the world took thousands of years over in the older continents? Why do things rudely and ill which need to be done well, seeing that the welfare of your descendants may turn upon them? . . . the unrestfulness, the passion for speculation, the feverish eagerness for quick and showy results, may so soak into the texture of the popular mind as to color it for centuries to come."[39]

Leaders in both countries set out to colonize vast new territories immediately, conquering by consuming land, crops, and minerals in assembly-line fashion. The problem was, although Soviet and American planners could imagine these insta-cities, they could not orchestrate enough bricks, laborers, and lumber to build them. In this sense, the American booster press and Soviet propaganda read like science fiction. The words describe a possible, even plausible, future, but one that did not yet exist.

T. C. Armitage discovered this fictional quality of the new urban spaces the hard way. He was an insurance man who worked in the Northern Pacific engineering office in St. Paul. He worked for the railroad and should have known better than to believe the booster press campaigns coming from Billings. Armitage put cash down on a few lots, sight unseen, choosing a prime location by the Yellowstone River. Soon after, he boarded the Northern Pacific to Billings. When he arrived, he was dismayed to find no depot, no real city, no town, not even an outpost, just a "dreary expanse, white with alkali flats." When Armitage inspected his lots, he found a good deal of his real estate was flooded, and he needed a boat to locate the corners of his property.[40]

Fifty years later, a Soviet journalist, Semyon Nariniani, had a similar experience. He was sent on assignment to central Siberia, a few hundred miles north of Karaganda, to report on the newly built steel town of Magnitogorsk. As historian Stephen Kotkin tells the story, Nariniani rode the train for eight days, making five changes and waiting through many delays. One day, the train slowed in the midst of the empty steppe. Nariniani thought it was another breakdown, but the conductor called out, "Magnitogorsk!" Nariniani disembarked, looked around at the empty landscape, turned to the stationmaster and asked, "Is it far to the city?" "Two years," the man answered.[41]

In memoir after memoir, what seems to have bothered European

settlers of the plains and steppe the most was the emptiness: "the still-
ness with nothing behind it."[42] Soviet deportees refer automatically to
the land they first encountered as "the naked steppe," devoid of water,
trees, streams, houses, people—geography itself—empty of everything but space.[43] What most failed to mention was that the land was
not empty but *emptied*.[44] They came to territory that had recently been
cleared of the nomadic pastoralists and hunters who once populated
it, people who lived off the arid grasslands by moving through them,
following herds that grazed on a carpet of grasses and plants. Since
humans cannot digest grass, exploiting animals that do is a rational
way to use the dry range and steppe not suited for agriculture or in-
tensive husbandry.[45] As the first settlers appeared in Kazakhstan and
Montana and took up homesteads in fertile land along rivers, Kazakhs
and Indians adjusted their economies accordingly, trading fur and
meat with the newcomers for tools and commodities. It wasn't harmony and it wasn't an idyll of pastoral unity with nature, but it was
life—a social system and economy that adapted adequately to the conditions of the plains and steppe.

But that is not the way Kazakhs and Indians were seen by the Europeans who came to colonize them. Nomadic pastoralists were understood as part of the landscape. They came to symbolize the savage and
precarious past, which still loomed over the present on the frontier
with terrifying force. When, for instance, high winds blew and unsettled the tent cities of Billings or Karaganda, or winter blizzards
stranded people and livestock in blinding white confusion, it became
clear how flimsy was the edifice white settlers occupied, an edifice
linked only by a thin lifeline of steel rails to the distant sources of food
and energy that kept their economies going. To Europeans, the unsettled nomad came to embody this cruel and undiscriminating nature. And so European colonizers constructed an ideological and prin-
cipled crusade, casting themselves in the role of civilized man against
primitive nature.

Most histories of Karaganda begin with the simple story of the Kazakh
shepherd Appak Baizhanov, who one summer day in 1833 chased a fox
into a hole.[46] Appak dismounted, dropped to his knees, and started
digging out the foxhole. As he dug, he came across a piece of rock,

black as a raven and of a puzzling texture. He brought it back to the elders at camp, who could make nothing of the black stone and tossed it into the fire. The rock blazed up unnaturally and they grew frightened. The elders ruled that the stone must be a bad force and should not be touched again. "Of course, the nomads did not recognize coal," one Soviet historian instructs, "because the young shepherd and his elders were illiterate."[47]

The moral of the story is that Kazakhs lived in cruel ignorance, and it took the arrival of Russians, armed with science, to help them realize the potential of the riches that existed beneath their "barren land." In Soviet texts, Russians are "the big brothers" come to help Kazakhs, who are "one of the most backward nations in the prerevolutionary empire."[48] This is another way of saying the Kazakhs made poor subjects because they rode fast horses, fought well, and managed with their nomadic elusiveness to evade the tax collectors.[49] And so Soviet officials had no choice but to continue the work begun by tsarist officials, who had been trying for decades to colonize the Kazakhs by settling them and using the land suitable for tilling to grow cash crops for export. Since the Russian empire first took control of Kazakh territory in the 1820s, Kazakhs had been gradually pushed off good pastureland into the desert interior of Kazakhstan. The final blow, the equivalent of George Armstrong Custer's buffalo-slaughtering hunting trips, came in the early and mid-1930s, when Soviet reformers decided to collectivize Kazakh nomads and thus rationalize the production of meat and dairy products on sedentary collective farms.

Not far from Billings, a small marble marker stands in the brown grass, embossed with a simple Christian cross above the name George A. Custer, Major General. The story of Custer and his defeat by Crazy Horse at the battle of Little Big Horn is well known. So, too, are his infamous trips through the plains shooting bison and leaving behind the stench of rotting flesh. These ventures cloud his memorialization as a martyr on the battlefield. Custer was one of a number of Americans who felt that the extermination of the buffalo would inspire Indians to settle down.[50] He understood, as did Soviet collectivizers later, that to take away the roving sustenance of the indigenous grasslanders was a sure way to root them. In turn, rooting nomads and transforming the landscape would make it hard to remember "a time," as David Rollison puts it, "when the land was anything other than a commodity to be converted to cash."[51]

But even after the bison were turned into bleached bone, their memory brushed onto canvas, and the remaining Indians settled on the reservation to a form of semi-dependency, the neighboring Crow, who had served as allies of the U.S. Army fighting the Sioux and Cheyenne, came to represent a threat and nuisance to the leaders of Billings. Before all the original lots and homesteads were inhabited by white settlers, city leaders in Billings started itching for more *Lebensraum* and petitioned Congress to move the Crow from their territory south of Billings and open the land for settlement.[52] Frederick Billings and other entrepreneurs of the area wanted the Crow territory in order to build rail lines across it to the coal fields in Red Lodge, and, just as important, they sought to sanitize the valley of "troublesome Indians" who were held responsible for missing cattle. An editorialist wrote in the *Billings Post* in 1884, "It will be a great boon to this section, when these miserable, idle dogs are moved away, and this valuable section of land thrown open to the use of people who will utilize it."[53]

Perhaps neither Americans nor Soviets anticipated the extent to which forced settlement would exterminate not only the nomadic way of life but nomadic lives as well. Collectivization brought disaster to Kazakh pastoralists. Between 1929 and 1932, the livestock count dropped from 6.5 million head to 965,000. Of the total population of Kazakhs, estimated at 4.4 million in the late 1920s, by the mid-1930s 2 million were missing, having either died from famine or fled across the borders to China, Mongolia, or Afghanistan.[54] In Karaganda, by January 1933, only 15 percent of the indigenous Kazakhs remained.[55] In the Great Plains, the bison, which once roamed in immense black clouds totaling around twenty-five million, had by the 1880s been all but exterminated. Among American Indians, of the estimated precolonial population of 5 to 7 million, only 150,000 remained in 1900, 7 percent of the original population.[56]

American and Soviet reformers created the savage and the primitive by defining it against the civilized and the advanced, and in so doing they appropriated the power to exclude Indians and Kazakhs from their land and livelihood—a power deployed with destructive results. The project, however, did not cease with mass fatalities.

Surviving Indians and Kazakhs became subjects of social programs aimed at supervising and correcting their primitive ways. In Montana, the Bureau of Indian of Affairs sought to make Christians out of Indian pagans and farmers out of Indian hunters. Bureau agents banned sacred dances and seized religious objects in a demonstration of authority that often turned violent. Instead of the old traditions, Indians were to learn the new orthodoxies of American hard work by becoming private landowners and farmers in ideal Jeffersonian independence. In 1904 Montana governor S. C. Reynolds created the Crow Indian Industrial Fair, modeled on the Midwestern county fair, where Crow contestants won prizes for the best farm teams, biggest cabbages, and best-kept tipis. Meanwhile, at missionary boarding schools, Crow children learned to can fruits, milk cows, speak English, and recite the dictums of American Protestant values. The policy was successful, in part. By 1896 half the Crow lived in houses and grew their own food. But that statistic reveals only a fleeting moment of triumph. By the 1920s poverty, malnutrition, tuberculosis, and trachoma were so chronic on the Crow reservation that local agents calculated to a "mathematical certainty" that the Crow Indian would soon cease to exist.[57]

Like Indians, Kazakhs did not own land and tended to view ownership in communal terms. Even so, Soviet ethnographers found Kazakh tribal life to be poisoned by class relations and the feudal exploitation of the poor by the rich. And so Soviet reformers focused on disentangling Kazakh nomads from their livestock in order to affix the nomads to Soviet institutions, where they would learn true communal values, proletarian discipline, the Russian language, personal hygiene, and wage labor. Soviet reformers separated recalcitrant parents from their children, the best of whom were sent to orphanages to be retooled for life in a society based on science and technology. Anyone whom the NKVD suspected of holding back socialist development became a target for suppression. NKVD agents banned Kazakh mullahs from teaching Muslim texts, and disenfranchised and later arrested Kazakh leaders, the *aksakal* and *bai*.[58] They shut down mosques and opened in their stead "red yurts," where women and children learned to write, clean, and farm. Soviet communists photographed the happy Kazakhs swinging their pitchforks on the way to the fields, and they too held fairs where the grower of the biggest melon and thresher of the most wheat mounted a bunting-festooned dais to receive a red ribbon with Lenin's profile looking forward to the future.[59]

Once European settlers had marginalized indigenous populations, the emptied spaces needed to be refashioned, and because the land was vacant (or vacated), there was nothing to stop its wholesale appropriation as productive, agricultural, and industrial territory. After the arrival of the railroad in Billings and Karaganda, European colonizers no longer occupied new land in a piecemeal fashion—a bend in the river here, a river valley there—but implanted a wholly new figurative and physical architecture on the landscapes. Railroad executives, U.S. Geological Survey officials, and Soviet officials spread out a purposeful map blanketing the landscape, dividing and subdividing territory according to function and use—mining, farming, ranching. And once space was divided according to function, so too were the lives that inhabited that space. Indians were to become farmers on land designated for that purpose. Kazakhs were to become collective farm members on land designated for that purpose. And new people were to be imported to fill the recently emptied spaces and implement the destiny described by the maps.

It is logical to think that cities emerge after the accumulation of a critical mass of people, but in Montana and Kazakhstan, this pattern was reversed. Cities came first, then people. Most of the settlers to the Yellowstone Valley arrived a full two decades after the founding of the Magic City. Saddled with a great deal of land bought on speculation, the founders of Billings worked in tandem with the railroad to entice homesteaders to the valley. Booster propaganda lied outright only at times; it usually misled by innuendo and cheerful exaggeration. The *Billings Gazette*:

> Below you lies miles and miles of cultivated farm land, the beautiful Yellowstone Valley, entrancing vistas of woodland and river greets the eye. Delightful attractions of well-laden orchards, with green and brown and yellow fields all dotted with dainty looking farm buildings and pretty red-roofed school houses, form a picture not readily forgotten. And at your feet, the loveliest gem in the beautiful setting, behold the charming city of Billings.[60]

The photo that accompanied this journalistic account shows a waterfall and thick forest, suggesting a shady, refreshing mountain idyll. Imagine the surprise of homesteaders when they arrived in Billings. Mrs. T. W. Wilkinson Polly, a Missouri native, remembered her first night: "It was a tearful set of women and children that evening. There was not a tree, hardly a blade of grass, only sagebrush and dusty streets and untidy surroundings, making it seem as if we had come to the last place on Earth."[61]

Mrs. Wilkinson Polly's tears flowed out of the realization that she and her family had been duped; they had spent their savings and gambled their singular futures on a swindle. The sun-baked flats and tent city could not be recognized as the Eden of the railroad ads and booster press accounts. Yet Mrs. Wilkinson Polly is written into history as a pioneering homesteader because she and her kin made their future themselves. Once they willingly entered the ideological frame of private property and Jeffersonian independence promoted by the railroad and real estate developers, they became the principal force of their own misery.

A few decades after the railroads went into the business of producing homesteaders for Montana, the NKVD took up the task of supplying deportees for the agricultural settlement of Kazakhstan.[62] In addition to KarLag, the NKVD deported tens of thousands of people to northern Kazakhstan to till the virgin but often agriculturally marginal land around growing new industrial centers like Karaganda.[63] To colonize and utilize the land most effectively, the Labor Colony department of the NKVD-Gulag gridded the land into 240,000 or 480,000-acre parcels for prospective collective farms, assigning an average of three hundred deported families to each farm.[64]

Maria Andzejevskaya was born in a Ukrainian village in the 1920s. One summer day in 1936, NKVD security agents knocked on the door and told Maria's parents they had a week to pack their things and report for resettlement in Kazakhstan. No one in the village knew where Kazakhstan was, but they were told it was to the south, where there was plenty of land for everyone to farm.[65] To many, resettlement, even if by force, sounded like good news; overcrowding and land hunger had plagued the sandy, swampy regions of central Ukraine for decades.[66] Maria and her family joined about half her village in packing up and loading their tools, furniture, and livestock on a train to Kazakhstan.

They were part of a mass deportation of over seventy thousand Soviet citizens of Polish and German descent, who in 1936 were deemed suspect of collusion with bourgeois Poland and Nazi Germany.[67] Maria's family rode the train for nearly a month, and when they finally disembarked from the cramped cattle cars in mid-September, the landscape had changed drastically. Maria described terrain that was empty except for a tall pole with a sign on it, labeled "settlement number two": "They told us we were going to Kazakhstan, and they would give us land and homes and we would live well. 'There's no winter, it's the south [they said],' 'everything will be perfect,' and then they dropped us off and there was nothing. The five of us children, mamma and papa, everyone cried, and then it was something horrible, night was coming, what would we do?"[68] Maria's family did what Mrs. Wilkinson Polly did. They built houses out of sod, and in their mud homes they put up with the dampness, snakes, and bugs. They made it through the first winter on their dwindling food stocks, and when those were gone they traded their clothing and dishes to Kazakhs for meat and flour. They learned how to gather up manure and brushwood to burn for heat in the long, subzero winters. They figured out the signs of a blizzard and how maybe to survive one if caught outside. In short, they learned to endure.

What is the difference between the homesteader and the deportee? At first glance, the two do not belong in the same category. Homesteaders went to Montana voluntarily to break the soil; deportees were rudely coerced from their homes and driven to the virgin Kazakh steppe. Yet, looked at more closely, the categories of free will and coercion begin to fuse. Mrs. Wilkinson Polly's family chose to move based on the hopeful view of Montana advertised by civic boosters and railroad advertisers; an NKVD officer conjured up a similarly rosy picture of Kazakhstan for Maria Andzejevskaya's family. Maria's family was offered no choice but to leave, but there is evidence that many of her neighbors were willing to go, and some even asked to be put on the deportation list so they could also try their fortunes in Central Asia, where there was plenty of untilled land—virgin soil, the same motivation for which Mrs. Wilkinson Polly made the long trek to Montana.[69]

Not to overdraw the comparison, once in Kazakhstan, Maria's family was legally restricted from leaving their village and had to report to a local commandant every month.[70] Mrs. Wilkinson Polly's family could leave if they had someplace else to go and money to get there. In fact, they could be forced to leave if the crops failed and the bank foreclosed on their loans. Many will argue this difference in free will is essential, that to be held in place by decree is entirely different than to be held, or propelled, by debt. And they are quite right, yet these differences themselves point to a set of similarities that cast doubt on assumptions of incommensurability between the Soviet Union and United States. For in both categories, people became the willing and unwilling tools of larger projects to control huge territories by turning grassland into cash crops. In both territories, families were hoodwinked by visions of a better future. Once they arrived, both homesteaders and deportees expressed a sense of powerlessness, a hazy feeling that their lives were being controlled by outside forces.

Montanans regularly railed against the power of the corporations and the railroads, forces that seemed to seep everywhere, controlling them by setting prices, hiring, firing, overcharging, and underpaying them. In 1912 J. C. Murphy published a book-length diatribe against the corporations in Montana. An excerpt:

> Less than a decade of time had been required to bring the material wealth of the state under combine control . . . to acquire most of the tremendous water power and electric power resources of the state to one ownership . . . to bring the banking interests of the state practically under the domination of a single chain of banks owned by the same interest, to reduce the profits of wage earners and to make their condition in industrial centers little better than bond slaves, to transform the functions of a public press . . . into a perfectly organized machine for the suppression of knowledge . . . all this by lawless corporate combination . . . exercised by absentee bosses.[71]

The corporations remained incorporate, the bosses absentee. Murphy could not visualize the source of his subjection; it came from everywhere and embraced everything at once. In Karaganda, I asked a group of elderly people, former deportees, who was responsible for their imprisonment. The voices rang out immediately: "The System." "The Party." "Stalin." "Moscow." And what about the guards, the people who are your neighbors now? Again, a chorus of replies: "It is not their fault. They had no choice. They were good people. They only did what they were ordered to do."[72]

Former deportees in Karaganda saw their lives caught in a "system" so immense it swallowed everyone, even the guards. Settlers in Montana at the turn of the century expressed a similar uneasiness about the corporations that seemed to overtake them at every turn. The "Company" and the "Party," two faceless, diffuse entities, encircled, or so it seemed, the lives of the people who lived in Kazakhstan and Montana so fully that they never caught sight of the incorporeal, ephemeral forces ruling them.

The first years the settlers and deportees plowed up the mineral-rich, virgin grasslands, crops grew impressively. During years of relatively high rainfall and mild temperatures, crops also thrived. Settlers in Kazakhstan remember fondly the years between 1937 and 1939, much as the boom years between 1909 and 1917 are still talked of in Montana.[73] But inevitably, drought followed rain. And with drought came dust. Soil, overtilled and uncovered, went airborne in the dry years. Settlers in Kazakhstan and Montana remark on dust so thick "you couldn't see the horses' ears." They mention the dust storms nearly as much as they do the locusts that fed mostly on the weakened crops but also ate through clothes and leather. Those were hungry years. And to make matters worse, when the price of wheat fell after World War I, dry land farmers in Montana were shadowed by bankers. Bernice McGee's father, a Norwegian immigrant, homesteaded a farm in the foothills above Billings. Every autumn, she said, her father would sell his crops and head for the bank to pay off the loan he had taken for seed and supplies the spring before. But after he paid the bank, there was no money left for the family to make it through the winter, so he would take out another loan, and the cycle of interests, payments, and anxiety would begin again.[74] For the deportees in Kazakhstan, tax rates rose each year, especially as World War II drew closer. Fifty years later, Maria still knows the tax rates by heart: "Thirty-six liters of milk. Eight kilos of refined butter a year. Two hundred kilograms of meat for every family a year. That was a whole cow!"[75]

The biggest obstacles to farming and living on the steppe and plains involved water, or the lack of it. Karaganda and Billings fall into the same precipitation zone, where rainfall ranges from a drought-level eight inches to a cultivable seventeen inches a year. It was decided that farming could only be secured through irrigation, but irrigation seemed a fantasy when even drinking water was in short supply. In Karaganda, people had to cart water for miles by horse or camel. In Billings, residents paid fifty cents a barrel for water hauled from the Yellowstone River. Water was all that was needed to make the land fertile, but large-scale irrigation demanded a concentration of capital and labor well beyond the means of an individual farmer or even the collective energies of the surrounding urban communities. In Billings, the managers of the land company attracted settlers with the promise of "the Big Ditch" for two decades, but they never succeeded in building it. Only in 1900, when the federal government backed irrigation projects, was there enough capital to build a series of canals and reservoirs.[76] In Karaganda, where the central government dedicated hundreds of thousands of rubles to a twenty-four-kilometer canal, and KarLag had at its disposal a growing labor force swelling into the thousands, digging it still took four years and then supplied only the city and a few hundred acres of farmland.[77] Irrigation presents a metaphor for the large-scale settlement of the continental steppe. It takes the kind of money and concentration of labor and machinery that only government budgets, outside capital, and expertise could provide, which left the farmers of the arid steppe and plains in a state of dependency, waiting on the largesse of the state.[78]

In other words, small family farms, the kind Thomas Jefferson envisioned, did not prosper in the Great Plains. To have a predictably profitable crop year after year, farmers needed to irrigate, ideally employing heavy machinery and fortifying the soils with fertilizers. The long arch of agricultural development in Montana points to the replacement of small homesteads with large agribusiness farms, an American version of the collective farm, where fields are huge, machinery is a must, and a mobile labor force is needed to produce high-yield cash crops to pay for it all. At KarLag, the NKVD specialized in setting up large-scale farm-factories and even ran a model farm that pioneered dry-land farming techniques, much as Frederick Billings's son Parmly turned the family ranch into a model "scientific" operation.[79]

The experience of working on these large, corporate farms did not

Author with gulag survivor and Labor Army worker Ella Schmidt, at the KarLag site. Photo by David Bamford.

differ greatly between Kazakhstan and Montana. Margarete Buber, a German socialist living in the Soviet Union during the 1930s, was arrested and sent to KarLag in 1938, convicted of treasonous activity. Her story—that of a Soviet prisoner—has been told many times. She suffered cold and hunger, slept on hard planks in dirty huts infested with bugs. She worked in the beet fields in KarLag, harvested and threshed grain, hauled water to the fields, shoveled manure, dug ditches on a railroad crew, sorted vegetables, and weeded a truck garden. She recounts the two years she spent in KarLag as a time of perpetual motion. As one job finished, she would be marched with a gang of fellow prisoners to another location in the vast camp and assigned a new job. The gulag system she described as a "slave trust": "Wherever labor is needed, the GPU [State Political Police] sends its prisoners. They fell timber in Central Siberia and Karelia, work in heavy industries in the Urals, cultivate the steppes of Kazakhstan, mine gold in Kolyma, build towns in the Far East of Siberia."[80]

In 1942 the NKVD created a second, even larger "slave trust," a migratory stratum of workers called the "Labor Army." On August 28, 1941, a date nearly every adult in Karaganda knows, the Supreme Soviet sent out an executive order to deport people of German heritage east, to Kazakhstan and Siberia. The government feared these Soviet citizens would serve as a fifth column for the invading German army.[81] As a consequence, more than a million citizens of German descent were uprooted and transferred thousands of miles during the first months of war. The NKVD conscripted the transplanted Soviet-German deportees, among others, into a Labor Army to serve in the Asiatic rear of the country manufacturing, mining, and farming to support the Red Army at the front.

In Billings, of course, there was no NKVD to organize labor. But there were large beet farms and far more beets than any single farming family could sow, weed, harvest, and ship to the Billings sugar refinery. Meanwhile, in New York at the turn of the century, relatives of the same families of Russian-Germans were arriving on Ellis Island in their homespun clothes, speaking an archaic German dialect. Few knew English, but some saw the Milwaukee Railroad posters of the farmer, biceps bulging, plowing up a field of gold coins over a map of the railroad running straight through Billings. Others were enticed by a railroad recruiter in Russia with a cheap ticket to the Great Plains. The Russian-Germans came most often with no cash or assets, and few could afford to buy land and establish their own farms. Instead, colonies of Russian-Germans became part of the sugar-beet labor force throughout the Great Plains, working the fields in Nebraska, Kansas, Idaho, and Montana.[82] In Russia, they had farmed independently; in North America, they entered the world of agricultural wage labor.

It was a precarious world to inhabit. Work came sporadically and was remunerated halfheartedly. The winters were long, unproductive, and unpaid. In the summers, parents and their children spent the daylight hours in the fields crawling along the rows of beets, blocking, thinning, and weeding. The backbreaking, punishing hours in the fields paid off for some families, who managed to save enough to buy their own farms. But other families remained on the migrant labor circuit for decades, and their ranks grew in the drought periods when farms were lost to banks. The family of "David K.," for instance, emigrated from south Russia in 1903. Three decades later, in 1936, a social worker for the state relief administration found the family "living in a dilapidated, two-room shack," unheated and so cold she had to keep her coat on during the interview. In the 1920s David K. and his wife had bought a small farm on credit. "But one year there was no rain, so there was no crop; next year there was too much rain and black rust ruined the crop; next year frost destroyed much of the crop, and each year thereafter some reverse caused loss."[83] Once, cholera killed the hogs, and later a train ran over the horses. In short, the farm had not prospered. David K. had sold it, bought a used car, and set out with his family, rolling through the fields of North Dakota, Idaho, and California as migrant laborers, where they farmed "onions, potatoes and especially beets." David K.'s wife bore eleven children, and the interviewer found her "in poor health, physically run-down and very shabbily dressed," her youngest child nursing at the breast. Three boys were undernourished and "so poorly clad as to be conspicuous." The little girl, Rose, was "unkempt and suffered from a cold and skin ailment." No one in the family had finished grade school. Most had not made it past the third grade.[84]

Germans from Russia weed beet fields just beyond Billings; Germans from Russia weed beet fields near Karaganda. The processes by which the two groups became migrant laborers were quite different, and again the difference hinges on the element of coercion and free will. However, the outcome—membership in a migrant labor force—was quite similar, as was the quality of life. Russian-Germans in Karaganda and Montana were related not only by family ties but also as subjects of a new kind of expanding agricultural discipline based on cheap and mobile labor.[85] The conditions that encompassed their lives—meager living quarters, long work hours, low pay, few chances for advancement, and continual mobility—bonded them long after time and events broke up their German colonies in Russia. Thanks to migration, legal and illegal, there has never been a sustained shortage of unskilled laborers in the United States. The glut of immigrants and all the disparate, untamed forces of the market produced the same kind of mobile, inexpensive labor force that the NKVD generated with its centrally planned charts, mobilization orders, requisitioned trains, and armed soldiers. The invisible hand of the market and the whimsical breezes of U.S. immigration policy sutured together a migrant labor force on the level of that conscripted by the NKVD, with hardly a flourish of weapons.

There are, of course, other differences between deportees to Kazakhstan and homesteaders of Montana. A major difference is memory. Montana pioneers are lionized as men and women who, with courage and the sweat of their brow and a heap of other slogans, remade the West, fought off Indians, broke the virgin soil, and in so doing symbolized the freedom and independence of the American way. The deportees, on the other hand, are memorialized as victims of a heartless, impersonal regime. They stand as an icon of suffering in histories of the Soviet Union.[86] Driven across the steppe and deposited on a windswept plain, they are often shown in photographs as hungry children with ribs like knives and pinched women burdened with crying infants. The pioneer, by contrast, is a man, axe in hand, jaw jutting, all determination. No one needed to help a pioneer; he did for himself.

Ex-convicts and deportees in Kazakhstan are attached to the memory of themselves as victims of a cruel regime. This is the metanarrative of their lives, and they feel no remorse for the loss of the nomad, nor do they romanticize life on the agricultural and industrial frontier. The difference in the West lies in the impulse to remember. If you travel through Montana, the stylized ghosts of the past haunt billboards and roadside stands: the dead Indian, the dead pioneer, the long-gone cowboy, the withered family farm, the displaced miner. Teenagers in American cities, most of whom will never exchange their sweat for wages, walk about in the heavy denim of the farmers' Carhartts; suburbanites negotiate manicured avenues in the rugged jeeps of ranchers. James Bryce's premonition has come true: America's restless, feverish passion for quick results has kicked up a nostalgia for a past plowed under to make room for an ever-receding future. This grief for what has been paved over is integral to modern life; it is a sign that in the United States, more than in the former Soviet Union, the destruction that accompanies a successfully expanding modernity has been far more complete.

On a cold, rainy Sunday, the first winter winds drive the rain like lead pellets against the windows of the German Cultural Center of Karaganda. A group of senior citizens who were once conscripts in the Labor Army sit around a long table. They all have stories to tell about their role in the creation of industrial space in Kazakhstan, and they tell them all at once, in a chorus of voices describing the long years of work, insults, want, and need, as well as the small acts of kindness and camaraderie that helped them survive. From the corner, a small woman began to speak, Maria Weimar:

> They brought us here [to Karaganda] to Mine Number 89. As soon as
> we arrived they placed us in the zone. There was a high fence, on top,
> three rows of barbed wire. On every corner there were guard towers,
> and there was a checkpoint. We were escorted to work, at the mine
> where all of us lined up for roll call. At seven in the morning we were
> led out and at eight we were already supposed to be at work in the
> mine. We worked twelve-hour shifts . . . We worked from eight in the
> morning until eight at night . . . The conveyor went by and we picked
> out slag. You had to grab the rocks quickly all day. Twelve hours with-
> out a break.[87]

In Pittsburgh, Polish immigrants worked in steel mills, twelve hours
a day, seven days a week. If they wanted a day off, they worked a
twenty-four-hour shift. In the Urals, Soviet-Polish conscripts mined
ore in twelve-hour shifts, the same period Maria Weimar spent daily
underground, every day but one, from 1943 until 1947. In Virginia, during World War I, boys in the coal breakers, their shoulders hunched
in the chill and for fear of the foreman, bent over the conveyor belts
and picked through slag. Decades later, the children-turned-old-men
describe the breakers as "hell" and complain most, as does Maria
Weimar, of blistered, cut hands, ripped hour after hour on the jagged
rocks. The boys worked out of need and fear, much like Maria did in
Mine Number 89 in Karaganda. The same machines, the same hierarchies and rush for production, the same endless days and fatal accidents, clogged air, ragged lungs, fragmented bodies, and flat, beaten
stares. It comes as no surprise that in the realm of labor history the
names, dates, and places begin to blur into one long, muscle-aching
sigh.

A sigh that indicates the physical experience of industrial labor differs little whether under capitalism or communism, because the same
grid stretched over not only space but time, the process of production,
and, consequently, lives.[88] Time was gridded into schedules (set and
calibrated by the railroad); materials were graphed into production
quotas; bodies were regimented into units. As such, it is possible to
leave Karaganda and retire to another war, another place: Butte, Montana, in 1917. Miners dug in thousands of miles of underground tunnels to produce copper for the American war effort. Foremen for the
Anaconda Mining Company continually raised production quotas to

meet the demand, and miners were stretched to the last breath of their reserve. The farther they burrowed below ground, the higher the temperatures rose; at two thousand feet down, the temperature reached 117 degrees.[89] Dust from the drills swirled in the dank air together with the odors of man and beast, blasting powder, rotting food, and spit-drenched tobacco. Above ground, sulfurous fumes billowed up, floating over exposed heaps of roasting ore. Residents walked about town with damp rags tied over their mouths and lanterns at midday. One of the copper kings, William A. Clark, claimed the fumes were vital to health as a disinfectant for disease. The airborne arsenic, he asserted, gave Butte women their beautiful, pale complexions.[90] It was a scene Dante would have recognized even before the night of June 8, when a flume of fire roared through a mine shaft and caused the death of 168 men in the worst hard-rock mining disaster in U.S. history.

After the explosion, the Metal Mine Workers' Union called for additional safety measures. When the company refused the union's demands, fifteen thousand workers shut down the mines, and for the second time in a few years martial law was installed in Butte. For the next year and a half, troops from the National Guard ruled Butte from the thick-walled respectability of the county courthouse. In the meantime, the state legislature passed the Montana Sedition Act banning "disloyal" speeches and literature, legalizing deportation, and outlawing the Wobblies. Pinkerton detectives snuck about the city, trying to infiltrate and uncover seditious organizations. The Wobblies still went to the picket lines, however, with other unions, and in April 1920, troops opened fire on picketers in front of the Neversweat mine, killing two and injuring thirteen others. After that incident, the governor canceled the National Guard and called in U.S. Army regulars, who monitored the city while work resumed in the mines.

Yet to imply that Butte was an armed camp during the years of the city's biggest boom would be an oversimplification. Most miners did not need guns and soldiers to compel them to work. They went willingly; their paychecks and the need to cover bills and gambling debts kept them underground. And after the war, when the demand for copper fell off, miners lived in perpetual fear of being shut out of the mines. Besides, it was underground, in the zone of free-labor relations, not above ground in the midst of violent corporation-versus-labor confrontation, where more miners perished by far. Locals in

Butte today calculate death based on the work week. They say one miner died for every week of the hundred years the mines functioned. The official estimate of death by accident falls short of local lore, at two thousand; however, no one knows how many miners died of lung diseases and "natural" causes that shrunk life expectancy and left the city full of widows.

The similarities between Kazakhstan and Montana center on the transformation of two rapidly industrializing, growing, voraciously hungry countries from small-scale, local economies to economies of national and imperial magnitude powered by cheap fossil fuels. By enticing and coercing, by offering opportunities laced with threats, by dividing time, space, and materials into discrete units, Soviet functionaries and American capitalists found it possible to line up bodies to build and extract, and to build the machines that would build more machines and make it easier and faster to extract more. The machines, and the people that followed them, demanded more coal, steel, ore, oil, and gas, and ever more lives. None of these resources were renewable, except for the people. Between 1880 and 1900, 700,000 workers died on the job in the United States.[91] Between 1934 and 1940, 239,000 forced laborers died in Soviet labor camps.[92] These fatalities did not slow industrial expansion, because immigrants, legal and illegal, have always flooded U.S. borders, and in the Soviet Union more "enemies of the people" could always be uncovered, and babies could be endlessly generated. (In 1935, at the height of the industrialization drive, the Soviet government outlawed abortion and made mothers of ten or more children "heroes.") As it happened, for decades, the same teeming Central European countryside supplied both fledgling superpowers with an incessant source of able bodies. But the story does not end there. As industrial space gridded the landscape, populations of migrants and prisoners were segmented as well, by class and ethnicity.

Now, tourists speeding along Interstate 90 in Montana can stop in Butte for a few minutes and stroll out to a platform extending over the Berkeley Pit, once the "richest hill on Earth," now a cavity a mile wide and a mile deep, filled with toxins left over from a century of mining. On the platform, it doesn't take long to listen to the recorded message that describes the history of the pit and the wealth that was dug from the buff-colored cliffs, and when the message dies out, tourists can hear the eerie whizzing signals that warn off birds from landing in the pit, which is acidic enough to liquefy steel. While tourists stare into the country's largest Superfund cleanup site, what they no longer see are the neighborhoods that used to ramble over the hill that is now negative space.

Although nearly half of the city has been voided, residents of Butte still recite a mental geography established during the mining days. On the east side, they say, the Irish lived up the hill in Dublin Gulch, above the Finns in Finntown, which gave the Irish gangs the advantage in bombarding the Finnish gangs during their regular brawls. Italians and Slavs lived in Meaderville, now an imaginary space over the pit, and on the precipice of the pit, in the Cabbage Patch, lived Mexicans, Indians, and African Americans, who had houses so transitory that today only empty gridded lots have endured. On the west side of town stand the Victorian mansions of the copper kings. The mansions have castlelike turrets from which one can survey the miners' homes huddled next to the mines' black headframes.

In Karaganda, as in Butte, residents were sorted by class, ethnicity, and race. By 1941, forty-one thousand prisoners worked in KarLag, and thousands of deportees arrived every month, swelling the city's population. Soldiers patrolled the streets, while prisoners marched from walled barrack zones to fenced-off labor sites. The fenced zones were important because the NKVD needed to segregate a complex hierarchy of prisoners incarcerated along a sliding scale of unfreedom—political prisoners, German POWs, Soviet citizens of German and Polish descent interned for the war, and regular prisoners convicted on criminal charges.[93] Soviet-German Labor Army conscripts lived in one zone. German POWs lived in another, next to but separate from Japanese POWs. As the war continued, more and more suspect ethnic groups streamed into the region under guard: Ukrainians, Poles, Kalmyks, Bashkirs, Chechens.[94] Each group was assigned a village or zone and told they could not venture from their homes. The zone system meant that most people generally remained where they were deposited, which strengthened ethnic ties and minority allegiances—ironically, the very traits for which these people were deported. But even when given a choice, the free populations of Russians and Kazakhs sought to live segregated from each other. At most factories, Russians and Kazakhs lived in separate dorms, but in one factory, Russian and Kazakh workers had to share a bunkhouse, and the workers constructed a wall down the middle to divide the space.[95]

What does the NKVD's enforced, zoned, and policed segregation of prisoners and exiles have to do with immigrant ethnic groups in Butte who chose to live in separate neighborhoods? It makes sense that immigrants would seek a cushion of common language and culture to soften the blow of migration and assimilation. What is strange, however, is that in 1905 a Pole from Silesia, in the south in the Habsburg empire, had little in common with a Pole from Mazuria, who was a citizen of tsarist Russia. These two Poles arrived from different political states; they practiced different customs and spoke different dialects of Polish, if not mutually incomprehensible languages. What compelled Mazurians and Silesians, who would have little in common in the old world, to join into one Polish community in the new world?

The forces that hammered Poles and other immigrant groups into discrete ethnic enclaves belonged to the industrial age. Between 1880 and 1920 in the United States, the way people worked and produced goods altered significantly, which in turn influenced how people lived and where. Corporate bureaucracies organized production from the top down. As production decisions moved up a lengthening hierarchy, skilled laborers were replaced by foremen supervising unskilled workers. Relations between foremen and workers slid into mutual aggression as the foremen were pressed to continually increase production, and in so doing threatened workers with dismissal and pay cuts.[96] Workers responded by organizing in unions. In order to fight the unions, firms altered their hiring practices, tending to employ immigrant laborers, who, because of their primitive knowledge of English, were less likely to unionize. On the shop floor, immigrant workers were grouped together by language to allow work to progress more smoothly, and gradually the workplace became segregated. At the same time, native-born workers began to resent the strikebreaking, wage-lowering immigrants and excluded them from their social and residential circles outside the workplace. Immigrants were relegated to the lowest tier of labor and were promoted far more slowly than native-born workers. This and the experience of being labeled "foreign," "alien," and "inferior" brought members of ethnic groups together in a defensive posture. Immigrant neighborhoods, then, with their ethnic churches, schools, and fraternal orders, embodied a circle-the-wagon mentality. Each group tried to carve out its own space within hazy and porous borders defined as "nationality," which gangs of young men patrolled to inhibit others from crossing the invisible lines of race and class.[97]

In other words, the ethnic segmentation of Butte and Karaganda had less to do with race than with discipline. As hierarchies and values were used to segregate and standardize stages of production along an assembly line, they also worked to normalize and segregate workers inside and outside the factory. The gridded spaces that first arranged on a huge scale the settling of Central Asia and the Great Plains made a lasting stamp on the nature of the lives that took up residence on the plains and steppe, because at some point the abstract survey lines turned into boundaries. Boundaries fix labels in space, defining who is inside and who is outside. But boundaries can be porous, and so gradually boundary lines in Montana and Kazakhstan transformed into walls, laws, and social custom, which worked to define who was alien and who was native, who was a prisoner and who a guard, who lived in the migrant camp and who on the affluent east side. Perhaps for this reason, the same grid stretches across the American West and Soviet Central Asia—not only because of topography and efficiency but because the edifice of modernist dichotomies constructed urban spaces that employed the grid as the most effective means to control space by blocking it off into discrete and ever-divisible units. Each unit could be marked for exclusion or reward; each could be arranged in a hierarchy, supervised and observed in a constant division between the normal and the abnormal.

Despite the fact that both the United States and Soviet Union were founded on revolution and grew through rapid urbanization, leaders in both countries distrusted the revolutionary and spontaneous quality of urban space and worked to destroy it. With straight lines and the force of the grid, Soviet and American leaders planned new "garden cities" cut through with wide, rebellion-proof avenues that negated the unpredictability and anarchy of nineteenth-century cities.[98] As a result, both expanding American corporate power and expanding

Soviet party-state power etched an antirevolutionary conservatism onto twentieth-century urbanscapes. Perhaps for this reason, Karaganda and Billings do not radiate the energy of New York or Moscow but instead a feeling of listless suspension, of containers waiting to be filled, of the utopia of what Foucault calls the "perfectly governed city." It is this utopian wish for gridded order and discipline that links the railroad city of Billings with the prison city of Karaganda.

Even after World War II ended, Maria Weimar continued to work as before in Mine Number 89 as a Labor Army conscript. Some things changed: the bread ration was raised from 800 grams to a kilogram— "No one will starve on a kilogram of bread a day," she says—and the mine administrators organized a club for cultural enlightenment, where the conscripts gathered in the evenings to play music and dance. And then, one morning in 1947, Maria rose as usual, stepped outside, heading for the cafeteria, and noticed that the fence that had held her in for so long was laying on its side:[99]

> We walked out of the barracks, saw the fence, and we were frightened. "Oh, the fence fell down," I said. No one told us anything. We didn't move. We were afraid to go out. How could we go out? The head of the column walked up. He was a good man, and he said, "You are free, ladies. You are free to go wherever you want." We said to each other, "We've gotten used to it here. Where would we go?"[100]

A few decades before the barbed wire fence fell in Karaganda, another mine shutdown occurred in Butte and another farm was foreclosed near Billings; the rusted economic links in the chain of production were falling away. One less farmer was tied to the bank mortgage; another group of miners was released from the boiling recesses of the mines. Without their fence, Maria and her fellow prisoners wondered what they would do, for without it, they no longer had home, jobs, or sustenance, however meager. After World War I, unemployed miners in Butte twisted their blackened faces with similar fears. When the mine company seized up and refused to exploit them any further, miners took to the streets in protest to defend their dangerous jobs, low-paying salaries, and right to breathe poisonous air. Perhaps we do not have to look far to explore the nature of our prisons, if we allow the term some metaphorical license. What we rarely question is the fatal attraction to our chains, to the consumptive urges that drive us deeper into labor and then remorse for what our labor has destroyed. We have been conscripted to build our own fences, and we like them, or at least get used to them, so that, like Maria, a sigh of regret wheezes from the icy fog when they fall away.

7 Returning Home to Rustalgia

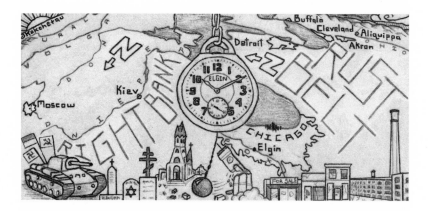

In the fall of 1997, I landed in northern Kazakhstan, hot on the trail (for a historian) of villagers who had been deported there from Ukraine in 1936.[1] At the time, Kazakhstan was in the midst of an economic crisis, and when the train pulled into Kokchetau at 3 a.m., the line of hard-bitten cab drivers hoping for a fare looked menacing. I chose one young man, trusting the manicured look of his fur hat. On the drive to the hotel, he told me he was an Olympian, a long-distance runner. He had competed all over the world, but now with no money in independent Kazakhstan to support athletes, he said remorsefully, he was driving a cab. At Kokchetau's best hotel, the receptionist sat under a circle of light in an otherwise dark lobby. She wore her winter coat and sleepily handed over a key. The room, like the rest of the city, was unheated, as cold as a tomb and shaped like one. On the cracked bathroom mirror, prostitutes had scrawled messages in lipstick that read disturbingly like suicide notes. Leaving the overhead light on for warmth, I lay in bed, sleepless, cold, and miserable, watching a fly that circled the bulb project its elongated shadow round and round on the walls. As the giant fly looped around, my homesickness sank deeper. What am I doing here? Why do I seek out places where melancholy emanates from the very walls?

Ostensibly I was writing a "biography" of Right Bank Ukraine, and since an important part of its population had been exiled to Kazakhstan, I went there too. Thinking about it now, I realize that in my Kazakh hotel room I was not so far from home as it seemed. Places are closely calibrated with a person's identity. While writing about Ukraine and Kazakhstan, I slowly edged out on a precipice of autobiography. As I did so, I approached, obliquely and unbeknownst to me, my childhood in the Midwestern rust belt.

What makes a place biographical? Conceiving the story of Right Bank Ukraine as biography wasn't an instinctive move. The place had no discreet identity, no charted boundaries or a proper spot on the map. It was just a territory, variously named by locals, and loosely defined by the reach of a certain sandy soil that yielded little in the way of cash crops. The region is located on the northern forest belt of what today is central Ukraine, on a flat plane between the former Russian, Polish, and Lithuanian empires, deep in what was once the tsarist Pale of Settlement. The population had long lived among shifting powers, and by the time the biography begins, in the mid-1920s, locals had endured six years of world war, civil war, and the Polish-Soviet war. The people who lived in the region spoke hybrid forms of Polish, Ukrainian, German, Yiddish, Hebrew, Belorussian, and Russian. They prayed in Catholic, Russian Orthodox, Ukrainian Uniate, and Lutheran churches and Hasidic and Orthodox synagogues. Just as many joined eclectic sectarian religious communities, which met in homes or the forest and drew on the surrounding religious traditions for inspiration.

Most of the rural people in this story were illiterate, yet trilingual. They lived in hard-to-reach villages, some inaccessible for months of the year, made poorer and even more remote by the ravages of war and the new Soviet-Polish border planted in 1921 a short distance away. State power was distant; ghosts and apparitions of the Virgin Mary visited more frequently than Soviet officials.[2] But in three decades, from 1925 to 1955, the poor communities of this isolated backwater were swept away and replaced with outsiders who were thought to belong because they were categorized as "Ukrainian." A few decades later, the explosion at the Chernobyl nuclear power plant made much of the territory unlivable for the next couple of centuries. In short, this ancient site of human habitation, which archaeologists in Ukraine argue was the "cradle of Slavic civilization," was fully annihilated in the space of a few generations.[3] If, like a life, a place can have a beginning and a definite end, I can think of few places where the endpoint, so critical for biographers, is more definite.

The funereal quality of the landscape inspired the idea of biography. The palpable insinuation of decay caught me by surprise when I first arrived in Right Bank Ukraine. There I visited villages of mostly elderly residents. Some were living in homes of people who had been expelled before, during, or just after World War II. They pulled out old chests to show me possessions left behind, stored carefully for fifty years in case the departing family returned. Inevitably someone would take me, unbidden, to see burial mounds, where "our Jews" were killed. I stumped across weedy Polish cemeteries, stepping lightly over cracked headstones, and stood at the thresholds of caved-in Lutheran churches. These sites sounded out loss in a cacophony that echoed across the terrain like an obituary. The fact that I made these travels in the mid-1990s—when the economy of Ukraine was in an extended nosedive; when the young and educated were seeking to leave Ukraine, for Russia, America, Israel, Europe, anywhere else; when the intercity buses no longer ran and the city of Zhitomir, where I lived, reduced heat and electricity to a few hours a day, and then at times to nothing—all suggested failure, endings, closings, death.

Local literary traditions also pointed to the application of biography to territory. In the 1930s, for example, Soviet officials carried out inspections of the region and filed "biographies" (*kharaktaristika*) usually describing a backward hinterland that bedeviled the revolution.[4] These officials, too, saw death in the end of the old regime, but they projected the birth of a new revolutionary society. Soviet power, they wrote, would bring sweeping changes, turning darkness to light, redemption, and rebirth.[5] A second category of local biographers included memoirists who had lived in Right Bank Ukraine. After they left during the interwar period, Polish landowners, German farmers,

Right Bank Ukrainian villagers. Photo by author.

and Jewish *shtetl*-dwellers remembered their lost homelands in a soft light shaded by a patina of memory.[6] Influenced by nineteenth-century romantic, nationalist literature, they endowed the land and the people who sprang from it with particular features. These autobiographies read as eulogies for homes to which the authors could never return, communities that would never be reconstituted. To have left "no place" was to have lost that ability to recall oneself and the complexities of one's identity for others. The leaving facilitated simplified, standard-ized national identities—Polish, Ukrainian, Jewish, or German—but left a painful vacuum. The act of writing a memoir was a way for au-thors to recalibrate shattered identities, to reestablish themselves on a cultural map.

Influenced by the texts I was reading, I followed this tradition of geographical biography. If I could write about a place that stood still while borders, armies, and political ideologies shifted over it, then I could tell the story of the people whom Marshall Berman described as "in the way" of progress, defined in this case by increasingly homogenized concepts of national territory.[7] For the history of the people who lived between states and national identities had yet to be written. Their stories had been eclipsed by competing national histories, Ukrainian, Jewish, Polish, and German, that narrated Right Bank Ukraine's imagined communities. These were national entities imagined mostly by the historians and Soviet officials who created them.[8] Recording a place with no definite borders, home to people with uncertain identities, served as a way to conceive of history outside of the nation-state and detached from national histories. These two forces contributed powerfully to the mournful silence extending over "no place" at the end of the century.

Yet biography as a genre has its problems. The ephemeral, psychological, anecdotal, and individual qualities of biographical writing have led historians to look at it askance. Biography is too personal, too much about the musty crannies of self-identity and self-representation to tell us about the larger world. As a genre it can lead the scholar, who is supposed to be detached, to overidentify with the subject. This lack of detachment, of course, contributes to the genre's popularity among nonacademic readers, who like to take in the exploits of great personalities as models for their own lives. The scholarly bias against biography overlooks the fact that nearly all good history writing relies on the experience of the historian, the historian's biography, to grasp and represent the past.[9] From selecting subjects, to researching and then writing about them, historians draw on their own realm of emotions and experiences. As historians write, they often dwell in a back room of conjecture, imagination, and assumption, none of which are allowed in the front-room presentation of history as scholarship. That is perhaps why we seek to know the biographies of important historians like Natalie Zemon Davis, Mikhail Bakhtin, or E. P. Thompson, because they shed light on the histories they wrote (as well as on the ones they didn't write). In other words, both biographers and historians are attached to their subjects in complicated ways. Often in histories it is clear the historian has chosen a subject or group of subjects and is betting on them, backing them to win, if not in the past, then at least in memory. Biography, I suspect, is all the more dubious for historians because it exposes the shading of history into autobiography.

Having just argued that biography and history rely on autobiography, what does the subject of my book *A Biography of No Place*, a poor, remote, agricultural, multiethnic borderland in east-central Europe have to do with me? When I was writing the history, I would have said the place held only an intellectual interest. In the narrative, I employed the first-person voice occasionally, as a heuristic device to explore history's constructed nature. But I was careful to leave my own biography and any personal identification with my subjects out of the story. Like many fellow historians I was suspicious of that sort of self-exposure as cheap and tabloid. And, on the face of it, central Ukraine had very little to do with my biography. To the best of my knowledge, I have no Slavic, Jewish, or German roots. I was born into the professional middle-class in the industrial heartland of the United States at a time when it was the world's most prosperous and powerful country. I could hardly have been born farther from rural, famished, collectivized, heavily politicized, bombed and terrorized Right Bank Ukraine, a place that stands in my mind as the epicenter of twentieth-century misery.

Then again, as I think about it, I was born in one era, of historic prosperity, and came of age in another, of decline and disintegration. In 1965 my parents settled their growing family in Elgin, Illinois. My father, a young high school teacher, had grown up on a farm nearby, and for him Elgin was the big city, the place to buy one's Sunday best. At the time, Elgin appeared prosperous, with a dozen factories, a large state asylum for the mentally insane, and a bustling commercial district that attracted shoppers from the surrounding farm communities. The major employer in town was the Elgin Watch Company, which in the 1920s made more watches than any other factory in the world.[10] The watch factory had located in Elgin in the mid-nineteenth century, breaking away from established watch manufacturers in New England, because land and labor were cheaper in the rural Midwest. The company's directors, however, declined to live in Elgin and established their headquarters in Chicago, thirty-five miles away. Low wages, critical to the industries that followed the watch factory, were crucial too for the watch company's dominance over competitors. When male

Elgin, Illinois, skyline, New Years' 1957, *Elgin Courier-News*. Courtesy of the Elgin Historical Society.

workers went on strike at the turn of the century to fight shrinking wages, the company fired them and hired scabs. Half of the factory's workers were already women, even less generously compensated than male workers and known not to cause trouble. For the following century the company suffered no more strikes, and Elgin leaders enticed other manufacturers to town with tax breaks, land grants, and arguments that Elgin was "a poor field for the agitator."[11]

The pattern of a chastened work force and low wages persisted. By 1960 unemployment was low, 2.6 percent, but additional statistics show the nature of labor and wages. Forty percent of married women worked, and 30 percent of people remained on the job past the age of sixty-five.[12] Elgin was, along with other communities in the industrial Midwest, the first third world for the American watch industry, but not the last.[13] The overseas flight of manufacturing tolled its hour early for watch manufacturers. In 1957 the Elgin Watch Company paid its last dividend. In 1958 it recorded a loss of over two million dollars. In 1963 it relocated a branch to an open-shop town in Blaney, South

Demolition of
clock tower,
Elgin Watch
Company
factory, 1966.
Courtesy
of the Elgin
Historical
Society.

Carolina, a town so desperate for jobs it renamed itself Elgin.[14] In 1965
the company filed a loss of an astonishing 6.8 million dollars. That year
the factory was shuttered, as watch production migrated overseas following the ongoing search for cheap and pliable labor that drew many
industries abroad in the second half of the twentieth century. During
the winter of 1965, the clock on the watchtower froze in an ice storm,
and that summer the watch factory bolted its doors for the last time. In
1966 a wrecking crew, working from back to front, razed the massive
plant, a solid, crenellated building that looked as if it had been built to
stand for generations. Corporate raiders bought the company from the
family owners, gutted it, and sold it again. As the company left town,
the new owners pillaged the workers' pension fund.

For a hundred years, the watch factory had been the city's economic
pillar, employing the largest number of workers, as well as guiding the

city's hand, enforcing low wages and labor discipline through control of city hall, backed up by the National Guard, quartered in an armory strategically located across from the factory. The company had also organized sporting, musical, and cultural activities and founded the Elgin Watchmaker's College. Now, with wages and pensions from the watch factory lost, the clubs and the college disbanded, and the local economy faltered. Between 1957 and 1962, commercial vacancies in Elgin increased by 40 percent. Businesses that had supplied the watch factory went under. Elgin wasn't alone. In the following two decades, the industrial Midwest bore the brunt of job losses from deindustrialization, a process that sped up each successive year.[15]

Other problems compounded the economic troubles. The Fox River, which an early Elgin mayor had touted as "a natural sewer created by Almighty God," stank by the 1960s, indeed, to the high heavens.[16] Tired of watching expired ducks float downriver bottom up, in 1968 a local eco-terrorist took action. By day a mild-mannered science teacher, James Phillips secretly turned into "the Fox" by night. He took to plugging drainpipes that dumped steaming industrial waste into the river. He capped smokestacks belching smog, left skunks on the doorsteps of corporate executives, and once sloshed fifty pounds of effluence onto the floor of the reception room of a polluting company.[17] While the police cursed the elusive saboteur, David Dominick, commissioner of the federal Water Quality Administration, praised him in 1970 in a speech before the American Society of Civil Engineers. "The Fox," he said, "by his deeds, challenges us all with the question: Do we, as individuals in a technological society, have the will to control and prevent the degradation of our environment?"[18] The Fox's actions were soon followed by an emerging Greenpeace movement, which, with other increasingly vocal environmental activists, worked to pass legislation that put federal limits on the business-friendly environmental free-for-all Elgin's city elites had long guaranteed local industries.[19]

Then there was the immigrant problem. Elgin had a proud German and Scandinavian immigrant history. But in the 1950s and 1960s, immigrants arrived in larger numbers from new locations: African Americans from the South, Latinos from Puerto Rico, Cuba, and Mexico, and later Laotian and Cambodian refugees from the Vietnam War. Undocumented Mexican immigrants, especially, were drawn to Elgin because it had an existing Mexican community, nonunionized industry, and a location just beyond the reach of the understaffed Immigration and Naturalization Services offices in Chicago. Local real estate agents and property owners contained the newcomers to substandard, high-rent housing down by the salvage yard and rail tracks. In the 1970s, however, another category of migrants, less easily contained, arrived from the immediate vicinity. The State of Illinois released long-term patients in the Elgin Mental Health Center to the care of new drug therapies. Those who had lost their ties to families elsewhere stayed in Elgin, where they became fitting mascots for the city itself—marooned, discarded, unwanted, waiting on park benches until it was time to return to the transient hotel in the evening.

Meanwhile, on higher ground, the Chicago suburbs spread in the direction of Elgin, surrounding the city with developments built for and dedicated to the white middle class. Some neighborhood families left "for the schools" in the new developments, but most of the arriving suburban residents came from other places. They locked their car doors when passing through Elgin and shopped at new malls stamped out across freshly graded farmland. Store by store, Elgin's downtown went bankrupt. By the 1980s only a handful of businesses remained. I remember a musty, basement joke shop, "Quik Shoe Repair," and a trophy engraver. The rest of the stores stood empty or fell before the frantic bulldozing commanded by city fathers, who paved over a wide swath of the downtown core in a desperate attempt to make over the graceful, nineteenth-century riverside town into a twentieth-century big-box mall surrounded by an asphalt moat.

It is easy to recognize from this description the Midwestern rust belt, not to be mistaken for belly-up Appalachian mining towns, blighted inner cities, or failing Western railroad and farm towns. For a wealthy country blessed with wealth and political stability, the United States has a surprising number of places that possess a half-abandoned quality, communities that have been bulldozed, shattered, and scarred with bullet holes, yet have suffered no war.

You know these places when you see them, driving by at the posted speed limit. There is the row of cramped houses in the hollow, built none too well from the start, listing and peeling with age and hard times. Even the finer houses on the ridge are caught in spirals of decay and ever more elaborate security installations. There are the teenagers slouching on a chain-link fence, taunting a dog too lazy to snarl. In the collapsed commercial district, I recognize the particular thickset dust on the windows, the "for lease" sign water-stained and yellowed. Broken-bricked lots surround the former shops. Something used to stand there. I ask what, but no one can remember. Fresher are the "for rent" signs on the bankrupt strip mall on the outskirts. The malls now have churches, which compete with tiny storefront chapels that moved out the traditional stone houses of prayer. The scent in the air is neutral, no smell of coal, tar, or sulfur, and there are hardly any sounds of grinding engines, humming machines, or piercing whistles. These are the muted smells and sounds of amputated careers and arrested bank accounts. Looking at the chain of churches and shops displacing one another in quick succession, feeling something between depression and despair, I think about E. P. Thompson's question—who will rescue these places from the enormous condescension of posterity?

Elgin's skyline was determined mostly by light manufacturing, which had nothing on the gray-snow, working-class turmoil of the steel town where my mother grew up. She left Aliquippa, Pennsylvania, as soon as she could and never really looked back. My parents also left Detroit in the mid-1960s. They brought with them heavy oak furniture they picked up cheap in the yard sales of the wealthy fleeing their Victorian townhouses. In time, my grandmother joined us from Aliquippa, where she was the last remnant of what had been a large, extended family. The displaced furniture and inhabitants, refugees from a spreading disaster, were crammed into my parents' 1920s Craftsman bungalow, a house too small for the burden. By the time I was conceived, the American manufacturing empire was well on its way to mortification.

In 1965, the year the watch factory closed and time stopped in Elgin, it started for me. I came of age thinking that liquidation sales were normal, so too public demolitions, and living with neighbors who on summer nights turned their houses inside out, watching TVs propped on the windowsill from couches parked on lawns. My father patched together a new car from spare parts from the three defunct VWs that lined the driveway. The usual American formulas that related race and class to deviance and crime made no sense in this overturned setting. When police came to the high school to make arrests for the murder of a neighborhood youth, they handcuffed John and Vincent, two white boys from families whose parents hadn't made good in the hollowed-out economy. The people I was told to be wary of were the former wards of the asylum. They too were white. Meanwhile, I gave my first kiss to chocolate-brown Charlie Murray and the second to Luis Perez, born in Puerto Rico. We would sneak past Luis's mother in the airless sunroom where she nodded uncomprehendingly to young Mormon missionaries sweating in ties. A devout Catholic, she invited the Mormons in each afternoon to practice English. On Friday nights when his mother had a date over, my friend Louie Hernandez would come up from his crated-together house down on Ann Street. In 1920 the Palm Sunday Tornado had run the length of Ann Street. When Louie lived there in the 1970s, the street still had that headline look of the day after the storm. Louie's mother spoke little English and read it, I think, not at all, but it was Louie who taught me to read English poetry.

My palms sweat as I write this. Historians expose *other* people's biographies, not their own. In their quest to explore the human condition, historians can hide behind their subjects, using them as a scrim on which to project their own sentiments and feelings. Let me put that another way: in my quest to explore the human condition, I have hidden behind my subjects, using them as a scrim on which to project my own sentiments and feelings. The third person voice is a very comfortable one in which to reside. Permanently. The intimacy of the first person takes down borders between the author and subject, borders that are considered by many to be healthy in a profession that is situated between the social sciences and humanities.[20]

I do not mean to equate the economic devastation of my hometown with the near total decimation of the communities of Right Bank Ukraine. These experiences are of two vastly different orders. There was no famine, genocide, or war, nothing even close, in my American rust-belt childhood—only lives that didn't pan out, and a sense that we were sitting sidetracked, waiting for something to happen. From Elgin, however, I came to understand how closely one's biography is linked to one's place. I recognized, in documents from Right Bank Ukraine, familiar voices worrying about what to do with this failing backwater, about people who are said not to be educated enough or smart enough to fix their own problems. I was familiar with the suspicion and dismissive attitude toward a place where people speak in different languages and nonstandard dialects, where the confusion of ethnicity and language is taken for inferiority, where difference is seen as disorderly and threatening. I was well aware of the suggestion that one's particular geography can spell personal failure, that an able and ambitious person should go somewhere else (as indeed I felt I had to, and did).[21] Living in Ukraine in the 1990s, when everything American was taken to be better, I fell into the role of the condescending and superior outsider in the so-called backwater. Within those ignominious feelings, I recognized the impulse to bulldoze and start over, to push on toward a brighter, cleaned-up destiny, to abandon some places and people as losers of an unannounced contest. Places like Elgin at the end of the twentieth century repeat across the industrialized world, in towns and cities stranded in postindustrial malaise. It makes the globe uncomfortably small and my travels disquietingly predictable.

Nor am I alone in my travels. I join a host of people who are fascinated with deindustrialized territories.[22] The rust belt has become an icon of American culture, used in all kinds of ways, from poetry to comedy, advertising to tourism. For tourists and adventurers the usually unnoticed rust belt comes into focus as a frontier, a place of adventure to test one's courage. In Detroit, tourists can pay forty-five dollars for a three-hour tour of collapsing buildings (cheaper than a three-hour tour of the Chernobyl Zone, but a comparable tourist experience). More daring, urban spelunkers break into crumbling buildings without a guide and blog about their adventures.[23] Consumers also travel to modernist wastelands in their imaginations. Writers and filmmakers set their dramas in deindustrialized locales, while artists publish photo books of famously emptied failure-scapes.[24] Art books, films, and fiction serve up dozens of square miles of abandoned city blocks—factories, parks, office buildings, hospitals, asylums, houses, and schools—a whole, lost Atlantis, emptied of its residents.

When artists place inhabitants in the frame, it is often to make some other point. Canadian novelist Douglas Coupland, for example, coined the term "Detroitus" to elaborate on a contemporary North American condition of feeling satiated and adrift in a new service economy oriented around, not production, but consumption. "Detroitus is the fear of Michigan. It is the queasy realization that it's probably much too late to fix whatever little bit of the economy is left after having shipped most of it away to China. Detroitus is also the fear of roughly 10 million primates needing 2,500 calories a day sitting on top of a cold rock in the middle of the North American continent, with nothing to do all day except go online and shop from jail. Detroitus is an existential fear, as it forces one to ponder the meaning of being alive at all."[25]

Coupland renders Detroit residents faceless and voiceless, invisible behind bars as prisoners and bar codes as consumers. Coupland's Detroit is meant to be caricature, but it shows up a notable feature of the fetish of modernist wastelands, which critics call "ruin porn" or "rust belt nostalgia."[26] In these portrayals, artists depict territories emptied of heroic, muscled, white, male inhabitants and taken over by dark, disfigured mutants or criminals.

Another kind of rust belt nostalgia is the embrace of deindustrialized zones as targets for redevelopment. A 2009 Levi's ad about Braddock, Pennsylvania, features three people of the two thousand who remain in one of Andrew Carnegie's first mill towns. The ad describes the rust belt as the "new frontier" of economic opportunity. The voice-over proposes that maybe Braddock got "broke on purpose so we can have work to do."[27] Meant to sound patriotic and hopeful, the ad writers instead infamously point to the money to be made in turning communities into wastelands by showing the two faces of entropy: those who profit from destruction through corporate raiding, foreclosures, and legal fees, and in the cleanup and gentrification that ensues; and those who pay the cost of continual abandonment with their livelihoods, investments, health, and futures.[28]

Capital on the move works as an ordering mechanism, sorting out in a base way who makes it and who doesn't. The winners, those who can liquidate and profit from the cycle, move on to new, cleaner places with bigger and better housing and more opportunities and services, while those whose labor and savings pay for the emptied storefronts, lost capital, brownfields, and green rivers remain in what Loïc Wacquant calls "advanced marginality." These are communities severed from the labor market, in environments of decay, dysfunction, and danger with few remaining institutions and services, little policing or commerce, and scant opportunities.[29] The image of rusting machinery, empty houses, and toxic belts surrounded by cyclone fencing appears to make visual sense of the abandonment; worthless is as worthless does. The iconic rust belt news photo of an unemployed man of color lifelessly staring at the curb bolsters the notion that individual merit determines success. That photo is meant to be assuring: work hard and you can avoid this fate. But it is yet another erasure, a pacifying illusion, and, therefore, often repeated, despite the fact that it is a false-hood.

The rust belt, in short, serves as a metaphor to express anxieties about the economy, society, race, and the nature of human life. Detroit and places like it are visible voyeuristically as porn, aesthetically as beauty, and economically as opportunity, but the violence that created these places usually goes unacknowledged. Only rarely, when writers of the rust belt speak for themselves, does a picture emerge of the de-structive force that passed through cities like Akron, Youngstown, and Buffalo. In fact, poets of the rust belt sound out like weary survivors of a slow-motion war. They describe the pains from "the phantom limb long after the amputation; the vertiginous sensation of watching someone (or something) die," "not loss like a massive destruction, but a loss like something insidious, deep, pervasive."[30]

If an enemy nation or rogue terrorists had dropped a bomb in downtown Detroit and pounded dozens of square miles of city into rubble, every schoolchild in the nation would be able to recite the facts of the event.[31] Americans would have started foundations to help the families of the victims. There would be monuments listing the names of those who suffered and sacrificed, and the Americans who amass to see the 9/11 Monument in New York would add to their pilgrimage (now blessed, sacred) Detroit. But no one set off a bomb or crashed a plane in Detroit. The low-decibel, slowly accruing violence that de-stroyed Detroit advanced instead in ways difficult to visualize and en-capsulate, which makes it nearly impossible to locate distinct perpe-trators and victims, or to recognize the destruction at all.[32]

In Cleveland, where the oily, chemical-laced Cuyahoga River caught fire repeatedly over years of furious industrial production, activists now commemorate that legacy by drinking Burning River Pale Ale while listening to the Burning River Ramblers play at the annual Burning River Festival. They sell beer and music to raise money to continue cleaning up the river, and, in the celebration of catastrophe, they show a bit of the survivor's grim pride. Cleveland residents em-brace the burning river as their bequest after the steel and chemical industries picked up and went elsewhere. The survivors stayed and domesticated industry's poisonous legacy, which, along with the mem-ory of the burning river, left behind mercury, petroleum hydrocar-bons, cancer clusters, inflated rates of infant mortality, and swollen thyroids.[33] In Cleveland, identity, history, biography, bodies, and place come together in a loving reference to a river that should never have caught fire, but did.

Communities are attached to capitalist cycles like the wings of a child's pinwheel, spinning dizzily in whatever light breeze overtakes them. The cycle keeps places in a persistent heaving of growth and decline, which gives the appearance that "all that is solid melts in the air," when, as Marx grasped, nothing was solid to begin with. The industrial culture of adequate jobs and housing forged by regular factory work appears to be permanent only as long as it lingers, and the duration of the lingering is growing ever shorter.[34]

The instinct to gloss over the sites of destruction plays out in infrastructure, laws, and culture; in limited-access freeways that steer cleanly around deindustrialized zones; in voting and tax districts redrawn to minimize the voice of and services provided to those left in such zones; in finding beauty in decay but danger in the people who inhabit it. Because capitalism is a cyclone pushing across the globe, the number of chroniclers of modernist wastelands will continue to grow.[35] Some will watch fascinated from the outside, producing more ruins porn. Others will speak in mournful tones of what is lost, what I call rustalgia. As opposed to ruins porn, rustalgia can help show how sketchy is the longstanding faith in the necessity of perpetual economic growth.

Unfortunately, however, the impulse to gaze at places of advanced marginality, and then bypass them, is seductive. In the competition between ruins porn and rustalgia, I fear porn sells better. The fascination with ruins porn shows that the more society works to avoid voyeurism, the more we are drawn to look, even if the watching is blinded and blinkered. That, at least, has been my personal trajectory. Every American-born generation of my mother's family uprooted and migrated from one place in decline to another that looked better, until that place also fell on hard times. I too skipped out of the path of entropy. But people suffer when they lose their place.[36] Knowing the costs of her family's persistent displacement, my mother frequently told us as children, "Never leave your family." As I said, I left the first chance I had, but having said that, I can't seem to leave Elgin behind. Not really.

It took me a long time to realize that the simmering, latent violence I witnessed as a child in the rust belt rematerialized in a desire to understand it. As an adult I went to places where the forces of destruction were so outsized they were impossible to miss—Ukraine, Kazakhstan, gulag territories, and nuclear wastelands. It finally dawned on me one day that I had spent my career as a historian chronicling environmental, demographic, and economic dystopias. Does that mean I had only ostensibly been writing about Soviet, and later American history, while really constructing an allegory of my own past? I don't think so. At least I hope not. Rather, because places are so closely connected to biography and identity, I believe I was able to see stories that had not yet taken shape for other historians because of the sensitivities I acquired in my past. My biography serves as a kind of archive of emotions, insecurities, sympathies, and antipathies, which I draw on as I seek out subjects and write about them. From my childhood in Elgin, I have been drawn to emptied buildings and abandoned streets, to wandering through forlorn sites, picking up discarded objects to figure out what they revealed about the people who parted with them. It is these people, the last to turn out the lights, who have most interested me, perhaps because they help tell a part of my own story, but also because I've felt their stories have been overlooked, left invisible, despite their importance. Place is inevitably at the center of these biographies because it, alone, remains to tell the tale.

ACKNOWLEDGMENTS

This book has been a couple of decades in the making. I have relied on strangers and friends to help me along the way. Most immediately, I would like to thank my colleagues at the University of Maryland, Baltimore County, for reading and listening, among them Marjoleine Kars and Susan McDonough as my first readers, plus Rebecca Boehling and Beverly Bickel of the Dresher Center for research leave, James Grubb, Constantine Vaporis, and members of the History Department writers' circle: Amy Froide, Christy Chapin, Dan Ritschel, Andrew Nolan, Meredith Oyen, and Michelle Scott. For support in research and writing, my thanks to John Jeffries, Phil Rous, and Scott Caspar. In the United States, Russia, and Ukraine I am very grateful to Julia Khmelevskaia, Igor Narskii, Nadezhda Kutepova, Natalia Manzurova, Natalia Mironova, Trisha Pritikin, Natasha Narikova, Tom Bailie, Efim Melamed, and Galina Kibitkina. Michael David-Fox and Sergei Zhuravlev provided valuable contacts. Richard White, Glennys Young, Lynne Viola, Jon Wiener, Marilyn Ivy, Glennys Young, Robert Self, Lewis Siegelbaum, Charles King, Ali Igmen, Warren Cohen, Choi Chatterjee, Steven Harris, Asif Saddiqi, Anna Veronika Wendland, Linda Nash, Steven Seegal, and Tom Okie provided intellectual backup for this work. I am extremely grateful for many inspired conversations with Maggie Paxson. At the workshop for the Program in History and Anthropology at the University of Michigan I would like to thank Paul Johnson, Christian de Pee, and Brian Porter, and at Carnegie Mellon University my thanks to Wendy Goldman, Caroline Jean Acker, Joel Tarr, and John Soluri. I am also grateful to David Moon, Catherine Evtukhov of the Leverhume Foundation Environmental History Workshop, Donna Goldstein and Magda Stawkowski of the Anthropology Department at the University of Colorado, and Anna Tsing, Donna Haraway, and Heather Swanson at the University of California Santa Cruz for opportunities to try out my ideas.

For editorial help I am indebted to Tim Mennel, Joel Score, and Nora Devlin at the University of Chicago Press. I am grateful too to Abigail Bratcher, Joe Parsons, Bill Rosenberg, Gary Oliveira, and my anonymous readers. My inspiring students Alexander Dorfman and Celso Baldivieso sent me sources and websites.

My sisters Liz Marston and Julie Hofmeister helped me put this book together. My son, Sasha Bamford-Brown, came up with the subtitle. Friends and family supported my travels, especially Marjoleine Kars, Dave Bamford, Sally Brown, William Brown, Aaron Brown, Kama Garrison, Lisa Hardmeyer, Leslie Rugaber, Hussien El-Ali, Prentis Hale, Tracy Edmunds, Sally Hunsberger, Mike Faye, Wendy Jacobson, and Leila Corchoran. Abby Brown wants to be in this book. Here she is. I bet so too does Kate Hofmeister.

NOTES

CHAPTER 1

1. Eric Sheppard, "The Spaces and Times of Globalization: Place, Scale, Networks, and Positionality," *Economic Geography* 78, no. 3 (2002): 307-30; Karen Halttunen, "Groundwork: American Studies in Place—Presidential Address to the American Studies Association, November 4, 2005," *American Quarterly* 58, no. 1 (2006): 1-15; Charles W. J. Withers, "Place and the 'Spatial Turn' in Geography and in History." *Journal of the History of Ideas* 70, no. 4 (2009): 637-58; Joseph E. Taylor, "Boundary Terminology," *Environmental History* 13, no. 3 (2008): 454-81; Doreen B. Massey, *Space, Place and Gender* (Hoboken, NJ: Wiley, 2013); Mark Bassin, Christopher David Ely, and Melissa Kirschke Stockdale, eds., *Space, Place, and Power in Modern Russia: Essays in the New Spatial History* (DeKalb: Northern Illinois University Press, 2010), 1, 11.

2. Francis X. Blouin and William G. Rosenberg, *Processing the Past: Contesting Authority in History and the Archives* (New York: Oxford University Press, 2011); Shannon McSheffrey, "Detective Fiction in the Archives: Court Records and the Uses of Law in Late Medieval England," *History Workshop Journal*, no. 65 (2008), 65-78.

3. Ann Laura Stoler, *Along the Archival Grain: Epistemic Anxieties and Colonial Common Sense* (Princeton, NJ: Princeton University Press, 2009). For more literature examining the archive critically, see, among others, Antoinette Burton, *Archive Stories: Facts, Fictions, and the Writing of History,* (Durham, NC: Duke University Press, 2005); Carolyn Steedman, *Dust: The Archive and Cultural History* (New Brunswick, NJ: Rutgers University Press, 2002); Harriet Bradley, "The Seductions of the Archive: Voices Lost and Found," *History of the Human Sciences* 12, no. 2 (May 1999): 107-22; Michael Lynch, "Archives in Formation: Privileged Spaces, Popular Archives and Paper Trails," *History of the Human Sciences* 12, no. 2 (1999): 65-87; Ann Laura Stoler, *Carnal Knowledge and Imperial Power: Race and the Intimate in Colonial Rule* (Berkeley: University of California Press, 2002), 162-204; and Jo Tollebeek, "'Turn'd to Dust and Tears': Revisiting the Archive," *History and Theory* 43, no. 2 (2004): 237-48.

4. I especially wrote "Gridded Lives" for Americans who study Soviet history because I suspected that lurking in the subtext of histories of the Soviet Union was a

gold standard of good governance, a mythical image of U.S. history, against which Soviet history failed. For a study that makes explicit the Soviet and American use of the family and childhood to promote ideology, see Margaret Peacock, *Innocent Weapons: The Soviet and American Politics of Childhood in the Cold War* (Chapel Hill: University of North Carolina Press, 2014).

5. As quoted in Withers, "Place and the 'Spatial Turn,'" 642.

6. Peter I died a few years before Tatishchev published his work promulgating the new boundary. Mark Bassin, "Russian between Europe and Asia: The Ideological Construction of Geographical Space," *Slavic Review* 50, no. 1 (Spring 1991): 1–17; Alastair Bonnett, *The Idea of the West: Culture, Politics, and History* (Houndmills, Basingstoke: Palgrave Macmillan, 2004), 45.

7. In 1721, after the victory over Sweden, Peter I had the designation of Moscovy changed from a tsardom (*tsarstvie*) to an empire (*imperiia*). Bassin, "Russia between Europe and Asia," 4.

8. Maria Shahgedanova, *The Physical Geography of Northern Eurasia* (Oxford: Oxford University Press, 2003), 608. The two continents are now, however, determined to be on the same Eurasian tectonic plate.

9. Christian S. G. Katti and Bruno Latour, "Mediating Political 'Things,' and the Forked Tongue of Modern Culture: A Conversation with Bruno Latour," *Art Journal* 65, no. 1 (April 2006): 94–115.

10. Philip J. Ethington, "Placing the Past: 'Groundwork' for a Spatial Theory of History," *Rethinking History* 11, no. 4 (December 2007): 466.

11. The word "past" grew out of the concept of passing something in space, and only in 1500 appeared, according to the *Oxford English Dictionary* to refer to the passage of time. Ibid., 478.

12. Withers, "Place and the 'Spatial Turn.'" "By "place," I do not mean a bounded site of authenticity and identity, but rather, as Doreen Massey defines it, something that is crossed by global currents, is anti-essentialist, has no definite boundaries, and is dynamic. Massey, *Space, Place, and Gender*, 5, 9, 121.

13. See, for example, William Cronon, *Changes in the Land: Indians, Colonists, and the Ecology of New England* (New York: Hill and Wang, 2011); Richard White, *"It's Your Misfortune and None of My Own": A New History of the American West* (Norman: University of Oklahoma Press, 1993); Juliana Barr, *Peace Came in the Form of a Woman: Indians and Spaniards in the Texas Borderlands* (Chapel Hill: University of North Carolina Press, 2007); Elizabeth A Fenn, *Encounters at the Heart of the World: A History of the Mandan People* (New York: Hill and Wang, 2014).

14. Almaty was the capital at the time. In 1997 the former city of Akmola, renamed Astana, became the capital of Kazakhstan.

15. Edward S. Casey, *The Fate of Place: A Philosophical History* (Berkeley: University of California Press, 1997).

16. Donna Haraway, "Situated Knowledges: The Science Question in Feminism and the Privilege of Partial Perspective," *Feminist Studies* 14, no. 3 (October 1988): 575–99. See also Christopher Sellers, "Thoreau's Body: Towards an Embodied Environmental History," *Environmental History* 4, no. 4 (October 1999): 486–514.

17. Torin Monahan and Jill A. Fisher, "Benefits of 'Observer Effects': Lessons from the Field," *Qualitative Research* 10, no. 3 (June 2010): 358.

18. For a wonderful history that does reflect on the process of doing history, see Ronald Fraser's social history of the servants of his parents' mansion edited against his description of psychoanalysis. Fraser, *In Search of a Past: The Rearing of an English Gentleman, 1933–1945* (New York: Atheneum, 1984).

19. William Cronon, "AHA Presidential Address: 'Storytelling,'" *American Historical Review* 118, no. 1 (February 2013): 1–20.

20. For more on the essence of storytelling in order to live, see Rebecca Solnit, *The Faraway Nearby* (New York: Viking, 2013), 3. For the connections between space and social relations, see Massey, *Space, Place, and Gender*, 2–9.

21. Esther Peeren and Maria del Pilar Blanco, eds., *Popular Ghosts: The Haunted Spaces of Everyday Culture* (London: Bloomsbury Academic, 2010).

22. Herbert Henke, "Der dornige Weg zum Wissen: Autobiographische Skizzen," *Feniks,* no. 11 (September 1995), 2–76.

23. On the impulse to dissemble about one's past and the pressures in Stalinist society to reshape and cultivate one's self-image, see Sheila Fitzpatrick, *Tear off the Masks! Identity and Imposture in Twentieth-Century Russia* (Princeton, NJ: Princeton University Press, 2005); Jochen Hellbeck, *Revolution on My Mind: Writing a Diary under Stalin* (Cambridge, MA: Harvard University Press, 2006).

24. Henri Lefebvre, Edward Soja, and David Harvey, especially, assert that people's lives occur multidimensionally, spatially as well as temporarily. Taylor, "Boundary Terminology," 455.

25. Patricia Yaeger, "Ghosts and Shattered Bodies," *South Central Review* 22, no. 1 (Spring 2005): 102.

26. There is a growing literature in slavery studies about "claims making" among enslaved people. See Alejandro de la Fuente, "Slave Law and Claims-Making in Cuba: The Tannenbaum Debate Revisited," *Law and History Review* 22/2 (Summer 2004): 339–69; Rebecca J. Scott and Jean M. Hébrard, *Freedom Papers: An Atlantic Odyssey in the Age of Emancipation* (Cambridge, MA: Harvard University Press, 2012).

27. On unreliable narrators, see Kate Brown, "Downwinders," *Aeon* (December 3, 2012), http://www.aeonmagazine.com/world-views/kate-brown-nuclear -downwinders/ (accessed December 4, 2012). On the importance of words left unsaid, see Patricia Yaeger, *Dirt and Desire: Reconstructing Southern Women's Writing, 1930–1990* (Chicago: University of Chicago Press, 2000), 9–17.

28. Michel Foucault, *Madness and Civilization: a History of Insanity in the Age of Reason* (New York: New American Library, 1967).

CHAPTER 2

1. A version of this chapter was published as "The Eclipse of History: Japanese America and a Treasure Chest of Forgetting," *Public Culture* 9 (Fall 1996).

2. Recent histories of this event and postwar reparations include Kimi Cunning-

ham Grant, *Silver Like Dust: One Family's Story of America's Japanese Internment* (New York: Pegasus Books, 2012); Brian Masaru Hayashi, *Democratizing the Enemy: The Japanese American Internment* (Princeton, NJ: Princeton University Press, 2010); Bill T. Manbo and Eric L. Muller, *Colors of Confinement: Rare Kodachrome Photographs of Japanese American Incarceration in World War II* (Chapel Hill: University of North Carolina Press, 2012); David A Neiwert, *Strawberry Days: How Internment Destroyed a Japanese American Community* (New York: Palgrave Macmillan, 2005); Yoon Pak, *Wherever I Go, I Will Always Be a Loyal American: Seattle's Japanese American School-children during World War II* (Hoboken, NJ: Taylor and Francis, 2013); Greg Robinson, *By Order of the President: FDR and the Internment of Japanese Americans* (Cambridge, MA: Harvard University Press, 2001); Lawson Fusao Inada, ed., *Only What We Could Carry: The Japanese American Internment Experience* (Berkeley, CA: Heyday Books, 2000); Eric K. Yamamoto, *Race, Rights, and Reparation: Law and the Japanese American Internment* (New York: Wolters Kluwer Law & Business, 2013); and Alice Yang Murray, *Historical Memories of the Japanese American Internment and the Struggle for Redress* (Stanford, CA: Stanford University Press, 2008).

3. Aleksandr Ėtkind attributes to Hannah Arendt and Vassilii Grossman the notion that history that has been repressed or forgotten will return in unexpected ways, like a nightmare. Ėtkind, *Warped Mourning: Stories of the Undead in the Land of the Unburied* (Stanford, CA: Stanford University Press, 2013), 30–34.

4. Louis Fiset, *Camp Harmony: Seattle's Japanese Americans and the Puyallup Assembly Center* (Urbana: University of Illinois Press, 2009), 12.

5. Saidiya Hartman, *Lose Your Mother: A Journey along the Atlantic Slave Route* (New York: Farrar, Straus and Giroux, 2008), 115.

6. The U.S. Congressional Committee on Alien Nationality and Sabotage on February 13, 1942, recommended "the immediate evacuation of all persons of Japanese lineage and all others, aliens and citizens alike, whose presence shall be deemed dangerous or inimical to the safety of the defense of the United States from all strategic areas." A letter writer to a Seattle paper put it more simply: "footloose Japs could do plenty of damage." Fiset, *Camp Harmony*, 38–39.

7. The term *evacuation* is commonly used for the temporary relocation of residents endangered by hurricanes, floods, and the like; its use in the case of the Japanese American internment suggests that government officials expected the fury of an anti-Japanese backlash on the West Coast to be as uncontrollable and unpredictable as a natural disaster. Evacuation can also mean a withdrawal of troops from a fortified zone or of civilians from an inhabited area; a more general definition of *evacuate* is "to purge" or "to empty out." The purging or isolation of persons of suspected nationalities from the general population during World War II was not limited to the United States. The Canadian government interned Chinese nationals. Germans in British India were imprisoned. And the Soviet government carried out an extensive policy of "cleansing" its border regions of potentially traitorous nationalities, including Germans, Poles, Tatars, Ingushi, Chechens, and Karelians. The Nazi government is, of course, infamous for taking the most extreme and fi-

nite measures to remove "diseased" nationalities, Jews and Gypsies, from the body politic.

8. See Susan Buck-Morss, *Dialectics of Seeing: Walter Benjamin and the Arcades Project* (Cambridge, MA: MIT Press, 1989), 38.

9. Monica Itoi Sone, *Nisei Daughter* (Seattle: University of Washington Press, 1979).

10. Mary Young, "Setting Sun: Popular Culture Images of the Japanese and Japanese Americans and Public Policy," *Explorations in Ethnic Studies* 16, no. 1 (January 1993): 51–62. Other songs of the time picked up on this theme: "A Jap Is a Sap," "The Japs Haven't Got a Chinaman's Chance," "Mow the Japs Down," "Oh, You Little Son of an Oriental."

11. Jeanne Wakatsuki Houston and James D. Houston, *Farewell to Manzanar: A True Story of Japanese American Experience during and after the World War II Internment* (Boston: Houghton Mifflin, 1973).

12. In the two days following Pearl Harbor, FBI agents and police in Seattle arrested 116 Japanese nationals. The arrests included community association and business leaders, teachers, martial arts instructors, farmers, and fishermen with knowledge of coastal waters. Fiset, *Camp Harmony*, 26–28; quote on 55.

13. See Sone, *Nisei Daughter*; Wakatsuki Houston, *Farewell to Manzanar*.

14. Henry Lefebvre, *Everyday Life in the Modern World*, trans. Sacha Rabinovitch (New Brunswick, NJ: Transaction Books, 1990), 22.

15. Fiset, *Camp Harmony*, 26.

16. Wakatsuki, *Farewell to Manzanar*, 94.

17. Ibid., 117.

18. Roland Barthes, *Mythologies* (New York: Hill and Wang, 1994), 152.

19. Elizabeth Becker, "Private Idaho," *New Republic*, May 4, 1992.

20. See Hales, *Levittown: Documents of an Ideal American Suburb*, http://tigger.uic.edu/~pbhales/Levittown.html (accessed January 15, 2014).

21. Orin Starn argues that American ethnographers working in the internment camps helped create the representation of the camps as quasi-utopian centers of social adjustment, where Japanese Americans were forging new communities based on the principles of democratic self-rule and hard work, a process that was to be the prelude to their full inclusion in the American national community. Anthropological literature and photographs released by the War Relocation Authority depict internees at work happily making furniture, going to school, housecleaning, growing cabbages—all as productive members of society. Barbed-wire fences, guard towers, and the desert location were removed from the frame of reference. Starn, "Engineering Internment: Anthropologists and the War Relocation Authority," *American Ethnologist* 13, no. 4 (November 1986): 700–720.

22. On the transformation of immigrants into "aliens," see Mae M. Ngai, *Impossible Subjects: Illegal Aliens and the Making of Modern America* (Princeton, NJ: Princeton University Press, 2004). Quote from Wakatsuki Houston and Houston, *Farewell to Manzanar*, 94.

23. "Minutes of Meeting of Community Council and Block Commissioners with Mr. S. T. Kimball", January 4, 1945. Panama Hotel basement.

24. Greg Robinson, *A Tragedy of Democracy: Japanese Confinement in North America* (New York: Columbia University Press, 2009), 275–80.

25. "War Relocation Authority Minidoka Project Report," February 28, 1945, Panama Hotel basement.

26. Robinson argues that Myer had opposed the internments from the start as unjustified and racially motivated. Robinson, *Tragedy of Democracy*, 279.

27. Barthes, *Mythologies*, 143.

28. "War Relocation Authority Minidoka Project Report."

29. Fiset, *Camp Harmony*, 12.

30. Janis L. Edwards, "Ethnic Contradiction and Reconciliation in Japanese American Internment Memorials," in G. Mitchell Reyes, ed., *Public Memory, Race, and Ethnicity* (Newcastle upon Tyne: Cambridge Scholars, 2010), 79.

31. Fiset, *Camp Harmony*, 58.

32. Jamie Ford, *Hotel on the Corner of Bitter and Sweet: A Novel* (New York: Ballantine, 2009).

33. Gail Dubrow with Donna Graves, *Sento at Sixth and Main: Preserving Landmarks of Japanese American Heritage* (Seattle: Seattle Arts Commission, 2002); Phuong Le, "Japanse Past Displayed in the International District Hotel," *Seattle Post-intelligencer*, July 23, 1999; Paula Block, "Tea and Treasures: A Hotel Gets Hip, From the Basement Up," *Seattle Times*, November 3, 2002.

34. "Historic Panama Hotel Bed and Breakfast," http://www.panamahotel.net /bathhouse%20tours.htm.

35. Ngai, *Impossible Subjects*, 227.

36. "Misteaching History on Racial Segregation: Ignoring Purposeful Discriminatory Government Policies of the Past Contributes to the Ongoing Achievement Gap," *Economic Policy Institute*, http://www.epi.org/publication/misteaching -history-racial-segregation-ignoring/ (accessed January 14, 2014).

37. Douglas S. Massey, "Residential Segregation and Neighborhood Conditions in U.S. Metropolitan Areas," in *America Becoming: Racial Trends and Their Consequences*, ed. Neil Smelser, William Julius Wilson, and Faith Mitchell (Washington, DC: National Academy Press, 2001). For instance, the more segregated communities of black Americans are, the higher their rates of lung cancer. The reverse is true for white Americans. Awori J. Hayanga, Steve B. Zeliadt, and Leah M. Backhus, "Residential Segregation and Lung Cancer Mortality in the United States," *JAMA Surgery* 148, no. 1 (January 2013): 37–42.

38. John W Dower, *War without Mercy: Race and Power in the Pacific War* (New York: Pantheon, 1986).

39. Edwards, "Ethnic Contradiction," 75.

40. Robinson, *Tragedy of Democracy*.

41. Former internees had higher rates of suicide, suffered chronic health problems, and lived shorter lives. Forty percent of Nisei men died before the age of

sixty. G. Jensen, "The Experience of Injustice: Health and Consequences of the Japanese American Internment" (PhD diss. Ann Arbor, 1997), as cited in Edwards, "Ethnic Contradiction," 201.

CHAPTER 3

1. A version of this chapter was published as "Chernobyl: History in the Dead Zone," *Chronicle of Higher Education*, September 23, 2005, B6–B9.

2. *Kiddofspeed*, http://www.kiddofspeed.com/chapter1.html.

3. Mary Mycio broke the story of the hoax, using me, an assistant professor taken in by the website, as the lead character of the story. Mycio, "Account of Chernobyl Trip Takes Web Surfers for a Ride," *Los Angeles Times*, July 6, 2004, http://articles.latimes.com/2004/jul/06/world/fg-chernobyl6.

4. Mycio later published the book *Wormwood Forest: A Natural History of Chernobyl* (Washington, DC: Joseph Henry Press, 2005).

5. Aleksandr Esaulov, *Chernobyl': Letopis' mertvogo goroda* (Moscow: Evropa, 2006), 65–83.

6. Natalia Manzurova and Cathie Sullivan, *Hard Duty: A Woman's Experience at Chernobyl* (Tesuque, NM: Sullivan and Manzurova, 2006), 35.

7. Ihor F. Kostin, *Chernobyl: Confessions of a Reporter* (New York: Umbrage, 2007).

8. *Kiddofspeed*, http://www.kiddofspeed.com/chapter5.html (accessed January 10, 2014).

9. Thom Davies, "A Visual Geography of Chernobyl: Double Exposure," *International Labor and Working-Class History*, no. 84 (Fall 2013), 116–39.

10. Eduard Vlasov, "The World According to Bakhtin: On the Description of Space and Spatial Forms in Mikhail Bakhtin's Works," *Canadian Slavonic Papers/Revue Canadienne Des Slavistes* 37, nos. 1/2 (March 1995): 50.

11. James Lawson, "Chronotope, Story, and Historical Geography: Mikhail Bakhtin and the Space-Time of Narratives," *Antipode* 43, no. 2 (March 2011): 386.

12. Katerina Clark and Michael Holquist, *Mikhail Bakhtin* (Cambridge, MA: Harvard University Press, 1984), 22, 46–48.

13. Hana Owen, "Bakhtinian Thought and the Defence of Narrative: Overcoming Universalism and Relativism," *Cosmos and History: The Journal of Natural and Social Philosophy* 7, no. 2 (July 2011): 143.

14. Clark and Holquist, *Mikhail Bakhtin*, 142–43.

15. Sarah Cameron, "The Hungry Steppe: Soviet Kazakhstan and the Kazakh Famine, 1921–1934" (PhD diss., Yale University, 2010).

16. Mycio, "Account of Chernobyl Trip."

17. Historians and scholars for many decades have experimented with first-person narrative voices, most often in memoir form For some wonderful explorations of history and narrator, see Saidiya Hartman, *Lose Your Mother: A Journey along the Atlantic Slave Route* (New York: Farrar, Straus and Giroux, 2008); Richard White, *Remembering Ahanagran: Storytelling in a Family's Past* (New York: Hill and

Wang, 1998); Alice Yaeger Kaplan, *French Lessons: A Memoir* (Chicago: University of Chicago Press, 1993); Ronald Fraser, *In Search of a Past: The Rearing of an English Gentleman, 1933–1945* (New York: Atheneum, 1984).

18. Philip J. Ethington, "Placing the Past: 'Groundwork' for a Spatial Theory of History," *Rethinking History* 11, no. 4 (December 2007): 471.

19. For a telling account of the devastation by a vice-mayor of Pripyat, see Esaulov, *Chernobyl'*.

20. Alfred John DiMaio, *Soviet Urban Housing: Problems and Policies* (New York: Praeger 1974), 60; Alexei Osipovich Kudriavtsev, *Ratsional'noe ispol'zovanie territorii pri planirovke i zastroike gorodov SSSR* (Moscow, 1971), 3.

21. Evgenii Ternei, "Zhivaia legenda mertvogo goroda," *Zerkalo nedeli*, April 29–May 5, 1995, http://www.zerkalo-nedeli.com.

22. For a study using letters and diaries of the last Soviet generation that finds affirmation of Soviet values and way of life, see Alexei Yurchak, *Everything Was Forever, Until It Was No More: The Last Soviet Generation* (Princeton, NJ: Princeton University Press, 2006). For an examination of the improvement in the Soviet economy, see G. I. Khanin. "The 1950s: The Triumph of the Soviet Economy." *EuropeAsia Studies* 55, no. 8 (December 2003): 1199.

23. Esaulov, *Chernobyl'*, 65–83.

24. Kostin, *Chernobyl*, 23, 70, 74, 76.

25. "Dopovida zapiska UKDB," March 12, 1981, and N. K. Vakulenko, "O nedostatochnoi nadezhnosti kontrol'noizmeritel'nykh proborov," October 16, 1981, in *Secrets of the Chernobyl Disaster* (Minneapolis, MN: East View Publications, 2003). On the efforts of a local reporter to tell the same story, see Ternei, "Zhivaia legenda mertvogo goroda."

26. Susan Buck-Morss, *The Dialectics of Seeing: Walter Benjamin and the Arcades Project* (Cambridge, MA: MIT Press, 1989), 95.

27. On the need to be more self-conscious about how documents have come to be selected and archived, see Francis X. Blouin and William G. Rosenberg, *Processing the Past: Contesting Authority in History and the Archives* (New York: Oxford University Press, 2011), 65–66, 73.

CHAPTER 4

1. Kathleen Day, "Sting Reveals Security Gap at Nuclear Agency," *Washington Post*, July 12, 2007, A1.

2. Author interview with Anna Miliutina, June 21, 2010, Kyshtym. After a major accident in 1957, plant managers gradually introduced a safety regime of sanitation and monitoring. "Stenogrammy na vtoroi Ozerskoi gorodskoi partkonferentsii, 30 Nov. 1957, Ob'edinennyi Gosudarstvennyi Arkhiv Cheliabinskoi Oblasti, Cheliabinsk, Russia (OGAChO) 2469/1/117, 205, 238.

3. Valentina Pesternikova, Nadezhda Okladnikova, Margarita Sumina, and Victor Doshchenko, "Occupational Diseases from Radiation Exposure at the First Nuclear Plant in the USSR," *Science of the Total Environment* 142 (1994): 9–17; Angelina

Gus'kova, *Atomnaia otrasl' strany: Glazami vracha* (Moscow: Real'noe vremia, 2004), 82.

4. See Kate Brown, *Plutopia: Nuclear Families, Atomic Cities, and the Great Soviet and American Plutonium Disasters* (New York: Oxford University Press, 2013), 187–96. On the dangers of this exposure, see G. Thompson, "Unmasking the Truth: The Science and Policy of Low-Dose Ionizing Radiation," *Bulletin of the Atomic Scientists* 68, no. 3 (May 2012): 44–50. On the revised totals of waste in the Techa River, see M. O. Degteva et al., "Reevaluation of Waterborne Releases of Radioactive Materials from the Mayak Production Association into the Techa River in 1949–1951," *Health Physics* 102, no. 1 (January 2012): 25–38.

5. V. N. Novoselov and V. S. Tolstikov, *Atomnyi sled na Urale* (Cheliabinsk: Rifei, 1997), 171.

6. Elaine Scarry, *The Body in Pain: The Making and Unmaking of the World* (New York: Oxford University Press, 1987), 1–7.

7. On the constructed quality of considering some workers "nuclear" and others nonnuclear, see Gabrielle Hecht, *Being Nuclear: Africans and the Global Uranium Trade* (Cambridge, MA: MIT Press, 2012).

8. Mira Kossenko, a former radiobiologist at the Maiak plant, noted that dose measurements taken over the years by Soviet monitors on the Techa River were deemed so unreliable by Japanese researchers that they refused to use the data. Author interview with Kossenko, May 13, 2012, Redwood City, CA.

9. S. A. Roach and S. M. Rappaport, "But They Are Not Thresholds: A Critical Analysis of the Documentation of Threshold Limit Values," *American Journal of Industrial Medicine* 17 (1998): 727–53; Gregg Mitman, Michele Murphy, and Christopher Sellers, "Introduction, A Cloud Over History," in *Landscapes of Exposure: Knowledge and Illness in Modern Environments*, ed. Mitman, Murphy, and Sellers (Chicago: University of Chicago Press, 2004),13.

10. Karen Dorn Steele, "U.S., Soviet Downwinders Share Legacy of Cold War," *Spokesman Review*, July 13, 1992, A4.

11. For a filmmaker's view of the archives, see the documentary film *Chelyabinsk: The Most Contaminated Spot on the Planet*, directed by Slawomir Grünberg (Chip Taylor Production, 1995).

12. For a promotional brochure advertising the data, see Ministry of Health of Russia, *Muslyumovo: Results of 50 Years of Observation* (Chelyabinsk, 2001). For a discussion of the debates on and dismissive attitudes toward Soviet science about radiation health, see Donna Goldstein and Magdalena E. Stawkowski, "James V. Neel and Yuri E. Dubova: Cold War Debates and the Genetic Effects of Low-Dose Radiation," *Journal of the History of Biology*, online edition (July 2014).

13. From 2000 to 2004, the Department of Energy did fund some studies that looked into the linkage between ionizing radiation, multiple sclerosis, and Parkinson's. In areas such as Spokane County, downwind from Hanford, researchers found a significant elevation in the frequency of multiple sclerosis. Walter B. Eidbo and Merle P. Prater, "Linkage—Multiple Sclerosis and Ionizing Radiation," paper presented at Conference of Radiation Control Program Directors Radon Meeting

(2004). See also the work of Swedish researchers looking at diagnostic and occupational exposure to hospital X-rays. Olav Axelson, Anne-Marie Landtblom, and Ulf Flodin, "Multiple Sclerosis and Ionizing Radiation," *Scandinavian Journal of Work and Environmental Health* 19, no. 6 (1993): 399–404. DOE presently has a low-dose medical research program in conjunction with NASA. Most of this research is related to genetics (http://lowdose.energy.gov/about_projects_doe_nasa.aspx). In 2007 the DOE funded studies of low-dose exposure to radiation and made progress in determining "dose-dependent changes in gene and protein expression, which differ from those at high dose exposures." Just as scientists were finally making progress in distinguishing specific bodily changes from low-dose exposures, funding for this research was steadily reduced between 2011 and 2013. The research was deemed "completed," yet the department has issued no final reports. Quote from Rod Adams, "Why Was DOE's Low Dose Radiation Research Program Defunded in 2011," *Atomic Insights*, November 26, 2013, atomicinsights.com. For a review of this literature and a plea for more research, see C. K. Hill, "The Low-Dose Phenomenon: How Bystander Effects, Genomic Instability, and Adaptive Responses Could Transform Cancer-Risk Models," *Bulletin of the Atomic Scientists* 68, no. 3 (May 2012): 51–58.

14. *Atomnaia otrasl' strany*, 111. In 2014 Alexander Akleev, director of the Experimental Research Station (ONIS) that deals with patients from Techa River, informed activists that the institute no longer performs analyses for diagnoses of chronic radiation syndrome. Conversation with Nadezhda Kutepova, April 5, 2014, Washington, DC.

15. Despite the fact that the Biological Effects of Ionizing Radiation (BEIR) VII Committee of the National Academy of Sciences' Board on Radiation Effects Research concluded in 2005 that "there is no threshold of exposure below which low levels of ionizing radiation can be demonstrated to be harmless," and that in addition to cancer "other degenerative health effects have been demonstrated" from low-dose exposure, these insights have not been incorporated into regulation or lawsuits.

16. H. M. Parker to S. T. Cantril, "Action Taken on Report on Visit to Site W, April 9April 13, 1945 by G. Failla," July 10, 1945, HW71973, DOE Public Reading Room (PRR), Richland, WA; Parker, Control of Ground Contamination, August 19, 1954, HW 32808, PRR.

17. Scott Kirsch writes how in 1962 the dissenting AEC scientist Harold Knapp caused problems within the commission by proposing to run tests on children and milk cows downwind of the Nevada test site. Other researchers were monitoring the environment around the test site, but Knapp was asking to do something different. He proposed to collate data on exposed people with their places of exposure. This proposition caused a ripple of protest within the agency, and Knapp was denied access to the monitoring results of the Nevada tests. Kirsch, "Harold Knapp and the Geography of Normal Controversy: Radioiodine in the Historical Environment," in Mitman, Murphy, and Sellers, *Landscapes of Exposure*, 167–81.

18. Gus'kova, *Atomnaia otrasl' strany*, 87; Novoselov and Tolstikov, *Atomnyi sled*, 247.

19. V. N. Novoselov and V. S. Tolstikov, *Taina "Sorokovki"* (Ekaterinburg: Ural'skii rabochii, 1995), 247–48.

20. V. Larin, *Kombinat "Maiak": Problema na veka* (Moscow: KMK Scientific Press, 2001), 202–3.

21. Gregg Mitman, "In Search of Health: Landscape and Disease in American Environmental History," *Environmental History* 10, no. 2 (April 2005): 184–210.

22. Siddhartha Mukherjee, *The Emperor of All Maladies: A Biography of Cancer* (New York: Scribner, 2010).

23. Linda Nash, "Finishing Nature: Harmonizing Bodies and Environments in Late-Nineteenth-Century California," *Environmental History* 8, no. 1 (January 2003): 25–52.

24. See National Archive, Atlanta (NAA), Record Group 326. The first medical studies emanating from the Manhattan Project were filed under "toxicology," and radiobiology generally was encoded "T," short for toxicology. On borrowing from industrial safety standards, see Barton C. Hacker, *The Dragon's Tail: Radiation Safety in the Manhattan Project, 1942–1946* (Berkeley: University of California Press, 1987), 51.

25. Linda Nash, "Purity and Danger: Historical Reflections on the Regulation of Environmental Pollutants," *Environmental History* 13, no. 4 (October 2008): 644; Christopher Sellers, "Discovering Environmental Cancer: Wilhelm Hueper, Post–World War II Epidemiology, and the Vanishing Clinician's Eye," *American Journal of Public Health* 87, no. 11 (1997): 1824–35.

26. For one of the earliest studies, see L. Jacobson and R. Overstreet, "Absorption and Fixation of Fission Products and Plutonium by Plants," June 1945, Bancroft Library, Special Collections, Ernest O. Lawrence Papers (EOL), Berkeley, CA, reel 43, (box 28), folder 40.

27. "Summary Medical Research Program," NAA, 326876, box 24, "Fish Program."

28. Nash, "Finishing Nature," 44. See also Christopher Sellers, "Factory as Environment: Industrial Hygiene, Professional Collaboration and the Modern Sciences of Pollution," *Environmental History Review* 18, no. 1 (April 1994): 55–83.

29. On employee fears of illness from contaminations over the decades at Hanford, see H. M. Parker, "Action Taken on Report on Visit to Site W by G. Failla," July 10, 1945, HW71973, PRR; Hofmaster to Jackson, July 24, 1951, H. M. Jackson Papers (HMJ), box 28, folder 23, University of Washington Special Collections; Stafford Warren, "Case of Leukemia in Mr. Donald H. Johnson," February 7, 1945, NAA, RG 4nn3268505, box 54, MD 700.2, "Enclosures"; K. R. Heid to W. F. Mills, July 30, 1979, and Michael Tiernan, August 10, 1979, RLHT595-0013-DEL, PRR.

30. Nash, "Purity and Danger," 653–55.

31. Guidelines for public exposures were developed in the late 1950s. See interview with Lauriston Sale Taylor by Gilbert Whittemore, August 11, 1990, Niels Bohr Library and Archive, section II, http://www.aip.org/history/ohilist/5153_2.html.

32. See Brown, *Plutopia*, 178–84.

33. Novoselov and Tolstikov, *Atomnyi sled*, 170.

34. For the exception, see "Experiments to Test the Validity of the Linear rdose/mutation Rate Relation at Low Dosage," RG 4nn326876, Box 24, "Summary Medical Research Program," NAA.

35. Christopher Sellers, "Body, Place and the State: The Makings of an 'Environmentalist' Imaginary in the Post–World War II U.S." *Radical History Review*, no. 74 (Spring 1999), 52–54.

36. Sarah S. Lochlann Jain, *Malignant: How Cancer Becomes Us* (Berkeley: University of California Press, 2013), 80. On the erasure of human subjects in randomized control trials for cancer drugs, see page 117.

37. Sanjiv Pandita, "Environment and Labour in China: Change is Led from Below," *International Labor and Working-Class History*, no. 85 (Spring 2014), 201–6.

38. David Richardson, Steve Wing, and Alice Stewart, "The Relevance of Occupational Epidemiology to Radiation Protection Standards," *New Solutions* 9, no. 2 (1999): 133–51.

39. Sander Greenland, "Underestimating Effects: Why Causation Probabilities Need to Be Replaced in Regulation, Policy, and the Law," *Bulletin of the Atomic Scientists* 68, no. 3 (2012): 76–83.

40. In the Hanford Environmental Dose Reconstruction (HEDR) case, researchers set out to reconstruct the doses people living downwind from the plant might have received over the decades. The study focused on environmental monitoring as a way to estimate dose exposure. See J. E. Till, "Environmental Dose Reconstruction," in *Proceedings of the Thirty-First Annual Meeting of the National Council on Radiation Protection and Measurements (NCRP), Washington, DC, April 12–13, 1995* (Bethesda, MD: National Council on Radiation Protection, 1997). Using HEDR's estimates and computer programs, scientists of the Hanford Thyroid Disease Study (HTDS) examined 3,440 people they were able to locate in the seven exposed counties. The study found cases of thyroid cancer and thyroid disease among the participants, but determined, based on HEDR dose estimates, that the risk was about the same regardless of radiation doses. Center for Disease Control, "Summary of the Hanford Thyroid Disease Study Final Report," June 2002.

41. "Karta ekologicheskogo sostoianiia Cheliabinskoi oblasti," (Cheliabinsk, 1994); A. E. Ivanova, V. G. Semyonova, N. S. Gavrilova, G. N. Evdokushkina, and L. A. Gavrilov, "Mortality Trends: Role of Particular Age Groups and Causes of Death in Their Shaping," *Obshchestvenno zdorov'e i profilaktika zabolevanii* 6 (2004): 3–9.

42. Most copper ore contains a small amount of copper, about 1% or less, the rest is pollution or waste. Smelters emit toxic metals such as lead, arsenic and mercury, none of which break down. They remain on location contaminating waterways, soil, house dust and gardens until cleaned up. Marianne Sullivan, *Tainted Earth: Smelters, Public Health, and the Environment* (New Brunswick, NJ: Rutgers University Press, 2013), 3, 15.

43. A new field of narrative medicine is emerging to incorporate biography and narrative in healing processes. Lorrie Klosterman,"Narrative Medicine Heals

Bodies and Souls" *Utne Reader*, September–October 2009, 3. The field of medical anthropology has been exploring the question of relations between landscapes, health, and bodies for some time. See, for example, João Guilherme Biehl, *Vita: Life in a Zone of Social Abandonment* (Berkeley: University of California Press, 2005); Barbara Rose Johnston and Holly M. Barker, *Consequential Damages of Nuclear War: The Rongelap Report* (Walnut Creek, CA: Left Coast Press, 2008); and, for a popular exploration, Kristen Iversen, *Full Body Burden: Growing Up in the Nuclear Shadow of Rocky Flats* (New York: Crown, 2012).

44. Dipesh Chakrabarty, "The Climate of History: Four Theses," *Critical Inquiry* 35 (Winter 2009).

CHAPTER 5

1. Parts of this essay were published as "For the Love of Memory: The Hasids Return to Ukraine," *CultureFront Magazine* 8, no. 1 (Spring 1999).

2. The sectarian movements, as recorded by Soviet security officials, encompassed populations of the Volynia, Podillia, and Kiev provinces. See Olena Pchilka, "Ukrain'ski narodni legendy ostann'ogo chasu," *Etnografichnyi visnyk* 1 (1925): 43, 47.

3. Gershon David Hundert, ed., *Essential Papers on Hasidism: Origins to Present* (New York: New York University Press, 1991), 4–5; Martin Buber, "My Way to Hasidism," in Hundert, *Essential Papers*, 501; and *Evreiskaia entsiklopedia* (St. Petersburg, 1913), 966. There are many theories as to why Hasidism developed specifically in Right Bank Ukraine. See Simon Dubnov, "The Beginnings: The Baal Shem Tov (Besht) and the Center in Podillia," and Benzion Dinur, "The Origins of Hasidism and its Social and Messianic Foundations," both in Hundert, *Essential Papers*, 25–57, 86–87; Murray Jay Rosman, *Founder of Hasidism: A Quest for the Historical Ba'al Shem Tov* (Berkeley: University of California Press, 1996); Yitzhak Buxbaum, *The Light and Fire of the Baal Shem Tov* (New York: Continuum, 2006); Adam Teller, "Hasidism and the Challenge of Geography: The Polish Background to the Spread of the Hasidic Movement," *AJS Review: The Journal of the Association for Jewish Studies* 30, no. 1 (2006): 1–29; and Shmuel Yosef Agnon and S Goïzman, *Rasskazy o Baal'-Shem-Tove* (Moscow: Tekst: Knizhniki, 2011).

4. Karel C. Berkhoff, *Harvest of Despair: Life and Death in Ukraine under Nazi Rule* (Cambridge, MA: Harvard University Press, 2008), 175–96; Ulrich Herbert, *Hitler's Foreign Workers: Enforced Foreign Labor in Germany under the Third Reich* (Cambridge: Cambridge University Press, 2006), 167–71, 279–82.

5. Herbert, *Hitler's Foreign Workers*, 164–65, 227–28, 244–46, 268–67.

6. Anna Knisch to Semen Knisch (no date), United States Holocaust Memorial Museum (USHMM) LM0358, reel 3, microfilm from the State Archive of the Kiev Oblast (DAKO) 4826/1/2, p. 8.

7. Historians of the medieval world, on the contrary, found Christian and Jewish cultures that exhibited a reciprocal influence and shared social polemics. See Ivan G. Marcus, *Rituals of Childhood: Jewish Acculturation in Medieval Europe* (New Haven, CT: Yale University Press, 1996); Elisheva Baumgarten, *Mothers and Chil-*

dren: Jewish Family Life in Medieval Europe (Princeton, NJ: Princeton University Press, 2004).

8. Pchilka, "Ukrainskii nardoni legendy"; David Blackbourn, *Marpingen: Apparitions of the Virgin Mary in Nineteenth-Century Germany* (New York: Knopf, 1994).

9. For contemporary examples, see Vera Shevzov, "Miracle-Working Icons, Laity, and Authority in the Russian Orthodox Church, 1861-1917," *Russian Review* 58, no. 1 (January 1999): 40, 45. For similar rationalizations in the 1950s, see Monica Black, "Miracles in the Shadow of the Economic Miracle: The 'Supernatural '50s' in West Germany,'" *Journal of Modern History* 84, no. 4 (December 2012): 833-60.

10. The idea of social issues as "pathology" and "epidemic" was often evoked in articulating the impression of social disintegration in Russia at the end of the nineteenth century. See Irina Paperno, "Constructing the Meaning of Suicide: The Russian Press in the Age of the Great Reforms," in *Imperial Russia: New Histories for the Empire*, ed. Jane Burbank and David L. Ransel (Bloomington: Indiana University Press, 1998), 305-32.

11. Ivan Alekseevich Sikorskii, "Psikhopaticheskaia epidemiia 1892 goda v Kievskoi guberni," *Sbornik nauchno-literaturnykh statei: po voprosam obshchestvennoi psikhologii, vospitaniia i nervno-psikhicheskoi gigieniy* 5 (1900): 44-114.

12. Olga Semyonova Tian-Shanskaia, *Village Life in Late Tsarist Russia*, ed. David L. Ransel (Bloomington: Indiana University Press, 1993).

13. In addition to work as a psychiatrist, Sikorskii was an early racial anthropologist committed to preserving the Aryan qualities of the descendents of Rus' from degenerate neighbors, including Jews, Poles, and the "German element," in the Ukrainian borderlands. See Faith Hillis, *Children of Rus': Right-Bank Ukraine and the Invention of a Russian Nation* (Ithaca, NY: Cornell University Press, 2013), 103.

14. Sikorskii, "Psikhopaticheskaia epidemiia, 59-64.

15. Nykanor Dmytruk, "Z novogo pobutu," *Ethnografichnyi visnyk* 2 (1926), 31-37. For discussion of this event, see Kate Brown, *A Biography of No Place: From Ethnic Borderland to Soviet Heartland* (Cambridge, MA: Harvard University Press, 2004), 69.

16. Haraway calls this "mobile positioning." Haraway, "Situated Knowledges," 583.

17. Gilbert Meilaender, "Dependent Rational Animals: Why Human Beings Need the Virtues and The MacIntyre Reader," *First Things*, October 1999, http://www.firstthings.com/article/2007/01/dependent-rational-animals-why-human-beings-need-the-virtues-and-the-macintyre-reader-35.

CHAPTER 6

1. This article was originally published in *American Historical Review* 106, no. 1 (February 2001): 17-48. KarLag stands for Karagandinskaia lager, the Karaganda Labor Camp.

2. Iurii Aleksandrovich Poliakov and V. B. Zhiromskaia, eds., *Vsesoiuznaia perepis'*

naseleniia 1937 goda—obshchie itogi: Sbornik dokumentov (Moscow: ROSSPĖN, 2007), 180.

3. The same commentators who frequently remark on the repetition and monotony of Soviet urban spaces and who attribute these qualities to socialist authoritarian state control and uninspired top-down planning overlook, or momentarily forget, the monotony and repetition of the American subdivision located in thriving centers of capitalism.

4. The grid, however, on high, flat ground is not inevitable. Old Central Asian cities along the silk route, such as Tashkent, Samarkand, and Kashgar, center on the mosque and market, from which streets wind around without any specific pattern. In the American Southwest, Mesa Verde is an intricate labyrinth built into the cliffs of a mesa, and Pueblo Bonito circles around like a contemporary soccer stadium.

5. Italo Calvino, *Invisible Cities*, trans. William Weaver (New York: Harcourt Brace Jovanovich,1978), 11. Henri Lefebvre argues that the passage from one mode of production to another must entail the production of a new space. He calls for a study of history that looks at "interconnections, distortions, displacements, mutual interactions and their links with the spatial practice of the particular society or mode of production." Lefebvre, *The Production of Space*, trans. Donald Nicholson-Smith (Oxford: Blackwell, 1994), 42–46. As well, Marshall Berman notes the necessity for revolutions to produce new spatial patterns. See Berman's discussion of Chernyshevsky's Crystal Palace, in *All That Is Solid Melts into Air: The Experience of Modernity* (New York: Simon and Schuster, 1982), 241–44.

6. The title and jurisdictions of Soviet federal and republic security branches changed frequently. In 1934 the Unified State Political Administration (OGPU) was subsumed into the National Commissariat of Internal Affairs (NKVD), which was responsible for the gulag network and special settlements. In 1946 the bureau in charge of state security was renamed the NKVD-MVD, the Ministry of Internal Affairs. To reduce confusion, in this article I will refer to the Soviet security organs generally as the NKVD.

7. Soviet security forces maintained broad and variegated categories of incarceration, arrest, and exile. Those arrested were assigned to prisons or labor camps. Those deported were restricted to living within a limited area, called a "special settlement" or "labor settlement." For literature on the Soviet penal system, see Edwin Bacon, *The Gulag at War: Stalin's Forced Labour System in the Light of the Archives* (New York: New York University Press, 1994); Viktor P. Danilov and S. A. Krusil'nikov, eds., *Spetspereselentsy v Zapadnoi Sibiri, 1933–1938* (Novosibirsk: ĖKOR, 1994); Galina Mikhailovna Ivanova, *Gulag v sisteme totalitarnogo gosudarstva* (Moscow: Moskovskiĭ obshchestvennyĭ nauchnyĭ fond, 1997); Michael Jakobson, *The Origins of the GULAG: The Soviet Prison-Camp System, 1917–1934* (Lexington, KY, 1993); Lynne Viola, *The Unknown Gulag: The Lost World of Stalin's Special Settlements* (Oxford: Oxford University Press, 2007); Steven Anthony Barnes, *Death and Redemption: The Gulag and the Shaping of Soviet Society* (Princeton, NJ: Princeton Uni-

versity Press, 2011); Wilson T. Bell, "Was the Gulag an Archipelago? De-Convoyed Prisoners and Porous Borders in the Camps of Western Siberia," *Russian Review* 72, no. 1 (January 2013): 116–41. For statistics, see J. Otto Pohl, *The Stalinist Penal System: A Statistical History of Soviet Repression and Terror, 1930–1953* (Jefferson, NC: McFarland, 1997); and V. H. Zemskov, "Spetsposelentsi," *Sotsiologicheskie issledovaniia* 11 (1990): 3–17.

8. Deborah Cohen and Maura O'Connor, *Comparison and History: Europe in Cross-National Perspective* (New York: Routledge, 2004).

9. For an interesting review of the comparison of Nazi Germany and Stalinist Soviet Union as similar "totalitarian" states, see Ian Kershaw and Moshe Lewin, eds., *Stalinism and Nazism: Dictatorships in Comparison* (Cambridge: Cambridge University Press, 1997). For a discussion on the changing concept of totalitarian states, see Abbott Gleason, *Totalitarianism: The Inner History of the Cold War* (New York: Oxford University Press, 1995). For recent scholarship fashioning German and Russian histories as "entangled," see Michael David-Fox and Alexander M. Martin, *Fascination and Enmity: Russia and Germany as Entangled Histories, 1914–1945* (Pittsburgh, PA: University of Pittsburgh Press, 2012); Omer Bartov and Eric D. Weitz, *Shatterzone of Empires: Coexistence and Violence in the German, Habsburg, Russian, and Ottoman Borderlands* (Bloomington: Indiana University Press, 2013).

10. In contrast, before the Cold War, in the 1930s and during World War II, historians, political scientists, and journalists looked for and found similarities between the Soviet Union and United States. Not just left-leaning activists but right-minded businessmen and politicians saw affinities with the Soviet Union and made trips there to exchange information. For example, Rufus Woods, an influential and politically conservative Washington state newspaperman and one of the chief promoters of the Grand Coulee Dam, made several trips to the Soviet Union in the early 1930s. Though a conservative, Woods admired the Soviet industrialization drive and thought the same pattern of building big could revitalize the West. See Robert E. Ficken, *Rufus Woods, the Columbia River and the Building of Modern Washington* (Pullman: Washington State University Press, 1995). On New Dealers in the USSR, see Amity Shlaes, *The Forgotten Man: A New History of the Great Depression* (New York: Harper Perennial, 2008), 47–85. For studies comparing, favorably, the United States and the Soviet Union, see William T. R. Fox, *The Super-Powers: The United States, Britain, and the Soviet Union—Their Responsibility for Peace* (New York: Harcourt, Brace and Company, 1944); I. A. Startsev, *Amerika i Russkoe obshchestvo* (Moscow: Izd-vo Akademii nauk SSSR, 1942); Merle Elliott Tracy, *Our Country, Our People, and Theirs* (New York: Macmillan, 1938); Edmund Wilson, *Travels in Two Democracies* (New York: Harcourt, Brace and Company, 1936).

11. Jonathan A. Becker, *Soviet and Russian Press Coverage of the United States: Press, Politics, and Identity in Transition* (New York: St. Martin's Press, 1999).

12. Lefebvre, *Production of Space*, 55, 62.

13. As Iain Chambers writes, "The falling away of earlier dualities—the real and artificial, the original and false—leads to casting previous epistemological certain-

ties into an instructive confusion." Chambers, *Migrancy, Culture, Identity* (London: Routledge, 1994), 58.

14. See Michel Foucault on the art of coercive assignment, *Discipline and Punish: The Birth of the Prison*, trans. Alan Sheridan (New York: Vintage, 1995). In the Soviet Union, the enemy and citizen-traitor was most often identified as someone sympathetic to capitalism or "bourgeois-nationalist" states. Meanwhile, in the United States, from the World War I–era Palmer Raids to the House Un-American Activities Committee hearings, socialists, communists, and "fellow travelers" constituted a threatening category of disloyal citizens. See Alan M. Ball, *Russia's Last Capitalists: The Nepmen, 1921–1929* (Berkeley: University of California Press, 1987); Victor S. Navasky, *Naming Names* (New York: Hill and Wang, 2003).

15. As Foucault does in *Discipline and Punish*, 167–200.

16. As David Rollison phrases it: "The organization (and imagination) of space is deeply implicated in the maintenance of existing power structures." Rollison, "Exploding England: The Dialectics of Mobility and Settlement in Early Modern England," *Social History* 24 (January 1999): 1–16.

17. Lefebvre points out how the Spanish-American town was laid down on the basis of the grid, which reflected the political and administrative authority of the new urban power. The grid enabled the Spanish colonizers to arrange space in terms of a hierarchy and to segregate space into discrete units designated for different functions. Lefebvre, *Production of Space*, 151.

18. James C. Scott, *Seeing Like a State: How Certain Schemes to Improve the Human Condition Have Failed* (New Haven, CT: Yale University Press, 1998), 2.

19. For a study of how territory west of Chicago was charted and commodified in this way, see William Cronon, *Nature's Metropolis: Chicago and the Great West* (New York: Norton, 1991).

20. Sim van der Ryn and Peter Calthorpe, *Sustainable Communities: A New Design Synthesis for Cities, Suburbs, and Towns* (San Francisco: Sierra Club Books, 1986), 3. Scott contrasts gridded industrial cities with the *medina* of an old Middle Eastern city, where each neighborhood and quarter is unique, "the sum of millions of designs and activities," without an overall plan or map. Scott, *Seeing Like a State*, 184.

21. For a discussion of changing stories about the American West, see William Cronon, "A Place for Stories: Nature, History and Narrative," *Journal of American History* 78 (1992): 1347–76.

22. As quoted in John William Reps, *The Forgotten Frontier: Urban Planning in the American West before 1890* (Columbia: University of Missouri Press, 1981), 454.

23. Carroll Van West, *Capitalism on the Frontier: Billings and the Yellowstone Valley in the Nineteenth Century* (Lincoln: University of Nebraska Press, 1993), 120.

24. Ibid., 119.

25. Waldo Orlando Kliewer, "The Foundations of Billings, Montana" (MA thesis, University of Washington, 1938), 11, 20.

26. West, *Capitalism on the Frontier*, 124.

27. See Reps, *Forgotten Frontier*; Cronon, *Nature's Metropolis*; Richard White, *The*

Organic Machine: The Remaking of the Columbia River (New York: Hill and Wang, 1995).

28. In 1930 the Karaganda mines produced all of three thousand tons of coal, a drop from the 1913 prerevolutionary figure of seventy-two hundred tons. See O. Malybaev, *Bor'ba KPSS za sozdanie i razvitie tret'ei ugol'noi bazy SSSR* (Alma-Ata: Kazakhskoe gos. izd-vo, 1961), 64.

29. "Politburo Resolutions," Secret Sector of the All-Union Resettlement Committee of the SNK SSSR, Rossiiskii Gosudarstvennyi Arkhiv Ekonomiki [Russian State Economics Archive] (hereafter, RGAE), 1/5675/48a.

30. The administrative center of KarLag formed its own town, located outside the city of Karaganda. KarLag had divisions that stretched throughout Karaganda province. By the beginning of 1936, there were 37,958 prisoners and 806 staff persons in KarLag. S. Dil'manov and E. Kuznetsova, *Karlag* (Alma-Aty, 1997).

31. Gridded cities built during the industrial drive include Magnitogorsk, Nizhnii Tagil, Orsk, Novokuznetsk, Makeevka, Komsomol'sk, Bratsk, Magadan, and Noril'sk. For a discussion of Soviet urban planning and the creation of Magnitogorsk *ex nihilo*, see Stephen Kotkin, *Magnetic Mountain: Stalinism as a Civilization* (Berkeley: University of California Press, 1995), 72–85, 108–23. For discussions of urban architecture and history in the socialist world, see the blog http://www.secondworldurbanity.org/.

32. See Berman's discussion of the Russian revolutionary modern city, "the dream of modernization without urbanization," in *All That Is Solid*, 241–44. For an echo of this vision of deurbanized urban space enacted in Karaganda, see Sabit Mukanov, *Karaganda* (Moscow: Foreign Languages Publishing House, 1954).

33. The land was reallocated from the Letovichnii and Bliukherovskii *miasosovkhozi*, meat collective farms, which implies that it had previously been allocated to Kazakh pastoralists. See "Dokladnaia zapiska o pereselenii i khoziaistvennom ustroistva Ukrainskikh pereselentsev v Kazakhskoi ASSR," October 11, 1936, Gosudarstvennyi Arkhiv Rossiiskoi Federatsii (State Archive of the Russian Federation; hereafter, GARF), 9479/1/36, 23–26. In another document, the amount of land for the thirty-seven settlements is given at 955,740 acres. Pliner to Ezhov, Agranov, and Berman, GARF 9479/1/36, 36–39. See, as well, Pohl, *Stalinist Penal System*, 40. On the growing economic impetus behind the spread of the gulag labor camp system, see Ivanova, *Gulag v sisteme totalitarnogo gosudarstva*, 84–88.

34. For further correspondence on the subdivision, transfer, and valuation of formerly "uninhabited land" belonging to Kazakh-based livestock breeding farms, reallocated as farmland for NKVD use, see Director of the Land Fund of the Labor Colony, NKVD Shkele to GULAG NKVD Pliner, November 5, 1936, RGAE 5675/1/140, l. 12; All-Union Department of Resettlement, Berman to Miroshnikov on the incorporation of the department into the NKVD, July 4, 1936, RGAE 5675/1/165, l. 25.

35. *Billings Herald*, June 1, 1882, as quoted in West, *Capitalism on the Frontier*, 133.

36. Mukhanov, *Karaganda*.

37. As Berman writes, "This equation of money, speed, sex and power is far from exclusive to capitalism. It is equally central to the collective mystique of 20th

century socialism." In both societies, he points out, popular self-image was dedicated to whole peoples on the move. The crucial point, he notes in his discussion of Johann Wolfgang Goethe's modernist vision in *Faust*, is "to spare nothing, to overleap all boundaries, . . . all natural and human barriers fall before the rush of production and construction." Berman, *All That Is Solid*, 49, 64.

38. A crew of seven men built a public bath, a hospital, and a school in one month. A. S. Elagin, B. N. Abisheva, and K. Nurpeisov, eds., *Karaganda, Istoriia gorodov Kazakhstana* (Alma-Ata: Nauka, 1989).

39. As quoted in Reps, *Forgotten Frontier*, 693.

40. Kliewer, "Foundations of Billings, Montana," 22.

41. Kotkin, *Magnetic Mountain*, 106.

42. Richard White, *"It's Your Misfortune and None of My Own": A New History of the American West* (Norman: University of Oklahoma Press, 1993), 216.

43. See accounts of deportees to Kazakhstan in Stanisław Ciesielski and Anton Kuczynski, eds., *Polacy w Kazachstanie: Historia i wspolczesnosc* (Wrocław: Wydawnictwo Uniwersytetu Wrocławskiego, 1996); Krzysztof Samborski, "Zyczliwosci zadnoi," *Dziennik Polski*, July 6, 1995; Jerzy Sierociuk, "Archipelag Kokczetaw," *Przeglad Akademicki* 13–14 (1994). Vieda Skultans writes that people exiled to Siberia or imprisoned in labor camps emphasized the vastness and absence of human habitation as a way of representing their own lack of personal memories embedded in the landscape. Skultans, *The Testimony of Lives: Narrative and Memory in Post-Soviet Latvia* (London: Routledge, 1998), 28.

44. As Lefebvre writes, "The notion of a space which is at first empty, but is later filled by a social life and modified by it, also depends on this hypothetical initial 'purity,' identified as 'nature' and as a sort of ground zero of human reality." This kind of "empty" space, he argues, is merely another form of a representation of space. Lefebvre, *Production of Space*, 190.

45. In fact, ranchers now in the Great Plains, facing soil erosion caused by overgrazing, are reinventing grazing methods that follow the old patterns of the bison herds.

46. Mukanov, *Karaganda*; Elagin, Abisheva, and Nurpeisov, *Karaganda*; T. Y. Barag, *Karaganda* (Moscow: Gos. izd-vo Arkhitektury i gradostroitel'stva, 1950); Malybaev, *Bor'ba KPSS*.

47. Malybaev, *Bor'ba KPSS*, 15.

48. Ibid., 102.

49. For accounts of pre-Soviet and Soviet-era Kazakh history, see Martha Brill Olcott, *The Kazakhs*, 2nd ed. (Stanford, CA: Stanford University Press, 1995); Elizabeth E. Bacon, *Central Asians under Russian Rule: A Study in Culture Change*, 2nd ed. (Ithaca, NY: Cornell University Press, 1980); A. K. Akhmetov, ed., *History of Kazakhstan: Essays* (Almaty: Gylym, 1988); M. K. Kozibaev and K. S. Algazhumanov, *Totalitarnii sotsializm: Real'nost' i posledstviia* (Almaty, 1997).

50. White, *"It's Your Misfortune,"* 87.

51. Rollison argues there are two ways to transform land into property. The first is to turn people off the land. The second is to eradicate all signs of the old cul-

ture. In this way, he writes, the "massive manipulations and transformations of landscape that have resulted from the spread of capitalist values destroyed human memory." David Rollison, *The Local Origins of Modern Society: Gloucestershire 1500–1800* (London: Routledge, 1992), 73.

52. West, *Capitalism on the Frontier*, 175.

53. From *Billings Post*, April 17, 1884, as cited in Kliewer, "Foundations of Billings, Montana."

54. See Olcott, *Kazakhs*; A. K. Akshiyev, et al., eds., *Istoriia Kazakhstana* (Almaty, 1993), 310.

55. Author interview with M. K. Kozybaev, Almaty, September 1997.

56. Charles Phillips and Alan Axelrod, eds., *Encyclopedia of the American West* (New York: Macmillan, 1996), 4:1092.

57. This abbreviated account of Crow history relates only the metanarrative of Indian victimization. For a far more complex view of the Crows' adaptability and pragmatism in founding the Crow Reservation, which accelerated the tribe's transition to a modern self-consciousness, see Frederick E. Hoxie, *Parading through History: The Making of the Crow Nation in America, 1805–1935* (Cambridge: Cambridge University Press, 1995).

58. See Olcott, *Kazakhs*, chap. 8.

59. See Tsentral'nii Gosudarstvennyi Arkhiv Kinofotodokumentov Respubliki Kazakhstan (hereafter, TsGAK RK), photo numbers: 5-4377, 5-3655, 5-4380 (1930).

60. "Twenty Years of the Billings Gazette," *Billings Gazette*, 1905.

61. West, *Capitalism on the Frontier*, 145.

62. The NKVD Resettlement Bureau directed its agents in Kazakhstan to draw up new boundaries from land funds appropriated from Kazakh nomads. Report from Alma-Ata on Karaganda Oblast', RGAE 5675/1/140 (Autumn 1936), ll. 13–19. In 1931 the Resettlement Bureau of the NKVD started to deport *kulaks* (rich peasants) to Kazakhstan and later, in 1936, groups of Poles and Germans. The pioneering nature of the deportation program was similar to that of the founding of Kar-Lag. As one official wrote of the program in 1936: "Most new industrial bases are located in the Karaganda Oblast'. There the sparse population in the newly constructed regions creates a severe problem. In a series of events, resettlement has enlivened vacant regions and makes possible the development of agriculture." Just how marginal the land was is captured in the following excerpt from the report: "Almost all parcels suggested have little to no water source." From Land Fund (OMZ) to Pliner, November 2, 1936, RGAE 5675/1/40, 4. See also Director of the Land Fund of the Labor Colony, NKVD Shkele to GULAG NKVD Pliner, November 5, 1936, RGAE 5675/1/140, 12. On the 1936 deportations, see GARF 5446/18a/209 (23/I/36); on Ukrainian Republic proposals to deport, see the Central State Archives of Government Organizations of Ukraine (hereafter, TsDAHOU) 1/16/12 (February 25, 1936); TsDAHOU 1/16/12, l. 346 (November 25, 1935); on NKVD preparations in Kazakhstan, see Berman to Yagoda, April 16, 1936, GARF 9479/1/36, 7–11, and July 13, 1936, GARF 9479/1/36, 12–16.

63. The settlements were largely sited on "uninhabited steppe, in droughty, un-irrigated zones" with eight to seventeen inches of annual precipitation, which evaporated at a high rate in the intense Kazakh sun and wind. For descriptions of the topography, see Berman to Yagoda, July 13, 1936, GARF 9479/1/36, 1, 2–16, the State Archive of the Kochetau Oblast' (hereafter, GAKO), 906/1/29; and George J. Demko, *The Russian Colonization of Kazakhstan, 1896–1916* (Bloomington: Indiana University Press, 1969), 15.

64. The NKVD also sketched out new towns to accompany the communities, lay-ing out streets for new schools, hospitals, stores, and homes. Land and responsi-bilities changed hands frequently between state enterprises and bureaus, but land was always under the control of one large bureaucratic organization or another, whether a branch of internal security, regional government, or an economic bu-reau. For example, the Labor Settlement Division of the NKVD-Gulag was in charge of the distribution network, cultural and educational facilities, medical services, and agricultural-veterinarian expertise for deportees to Kazakhstan until transfer to the land bank and regional government in the late 1930s. See "Obiasnitel'naia zapiska NKVD SSSR za 1937 god," GARF 9479/1/41, 11.

65. The NKVD of Karaganda Oblast' in Kazakhstan reported that the settlers from Ukraine arrived "disoriented," with misinformation about Kazakhstan. They had been told it was to the south and had a warm climate and to sell all their warm clothes and bring salt, because there was little salt to be found there. Some families brought with them no warm clothes and up to ninety pounds of salt. See Berman to Yagoda, April 16, 1936, GARF 9479/1/36, 7–11.

66. A local official in charge of deportation reported in a secret document that 90 percent of the deportees shared the opinion of Friedrich Ralov: "I'm very happy to be resettled; it will get me better work than I have now in the collective farm." Many other resettlement officers reported a similar sentiments from other vil-lages, but they also reported tearful goodbyes and reluctant departures. State Ar-chives of the Zhitomir Oblast' (hereafter, DAZO), 42/1/372; P-87/1/3, 27–30, and P-42/1/327, 76. The assertion that deportees would be happy to be deported sounds hard to believe until one considers that the deportations occurred amid a century of voluntary migration from the overcrowded agricultural terrain of European Russia to the virgin lands of Kazakhstan. Between 1880 and 1980, over five million people migrated to Kazakhstan in search of virgin soil and opportunity. For statis-tics, see V. Moiseenko, "Migratsiia naseleniia v perepiskakh Rossii i SSSR," *Voprosy statistiki* 3 (1997): 30–36.

67. Of the 70,000 deportees, 64,319 arrived in the Karaganda Region by October 1936. See GARF 9479/1/36, 19.

68. Author interview with Maria Andzejevskaya, Tulgari, Kazakhstan, Septem-ber 29, 1997.

69. See DAZO, P-42/1/372 (1936), 29, 78, 87, 163–41, for lists of persons requesting permission to be deported from the Right Bank border zone of Ukraine to Kazakh-stan.

70. Deportees could not travel more than twenty-five kilometers beyond their assigned settlements. See "Postanovlenie SNK SSSR o trudovykh poseleniiakh OGPU v zapadnoi Sibiri i Kazakhstane," June 9, 1933, GARF 5446/57/25, ll. 21–22. Not that that law stopped deportees from leaving the special settlements. NKVD officials reported "massive flight of the deportees to various places in the USSR" and ordered that the guard be increased on the railroads and in the special settlements. Berman to Zalin, GARF, June 1937, 9479/1/38, 1–2. In the Kokchetav Province (*oblast'*) of northern Kazakhstan, 9 percent of the deportees fled in the first year. GAKO 11/1/39, 144.

71. J. C. Murphy, *The Comical History of Montana: A Serious Story for Free People* (San Diego, 1912), 40.

72. Author interview at the Karaganda German Cultural Center, Kazakhstan, October 13, 1997.

73. It may sound strange to talk of 1937, one of the chief years of the Great Terror, as a good year. However, the agricultural success in 1937 of the deportees was such that NKVD officials worried about the growth of *kulaks* in the settlements. See Pohl, *Stalinist Penal System*, 63. Meanwhile, Zemskov argues that 1937 represented "a peak of liberalization of the labor exile regime." V. H. Zemskov, "Ob uchete spetskontingenta NKVD vo vsesoiuznykh perepisei naseleniia 1937," *Sotsiologicheskie issledovaniia* 2 (1991): 75.

74. Author interview with Bernice McGee, Livingston, Montana, April 20, 1998.

75. Author interview with Maria Andzejevskaya, Tulgari, Kazakhstan, April 29, 1997. "Special settlements" of the kind in which Maria lived functioned usually at a loss to the state, which supported them in the face of continual requests for subsidies to get through the next year. Like homesteaders on the plains, special settlers in Kazakhstan were caught in a cycle. In the fall, they paid their taxes and loans back to state banks; in the spring, they needed more loans and subsidies for planting. See Danilov, *Spetspereselentsi*, 8.

76. West, *Capitalism on the Frontier*, 136.

77. Dil'manov and Kuznetsova, *Karlag*.

78. White, *"It's Your Misfortune,"* 236. See, as well, Scott on schemes for agricultural modernization that emphasized technical expertise, planning, and central control, which produced commercial and political monopolies and diminished the autonomy of the farmer. Scott, *Seeing Like a State*, 271.

79. West, *Capitalism on the Frontier*, 169.

80. Margarete Buber-Neumann, *Under Two Dictators*, trans. Edward Fitzgerald (London: V. Gollancz, 1950), 111.

81. The order read: "Among the Germans of the Volga there are thousands and hundreds of thousands diversants and spies, preparing terrorist acts and diversion." Postanovlenie SNK SSSR i TsK VKP(b), August 26, 1941, and ukaz Verkhovnogo Soveta SSSR, August 28, 1941, "O pereselenii nemtsev iz Saratovskoi, Stalingradskoi oblastei i Respubliki Nemtsev Povol'zhya," as reproduced in G. A. Karpikova, ed., *Iz istorii Nemtsev Kazakhstana, 1921–1975 gg.: Sbornik dokumentov* (Almaty: Gotika, 1997), 95. The total number of persons deported under this cate-

gory amounted to 1,093,490, of whom 393,537 were living in Kazakhstan in 1949. Zemskov, "Spetsposelentsi," 10, 12.

82. Fred C. Koch, *The Volga Germans: In Russia and the Americas, from 1763 to the Present* (University Park: Pennsylvania State University Press, 1977), 214.

83. Nels Anderson, *Men on the Move* (Chicago: University of Chicago Press, 1940), 227.

84. Ibid.

85. See Steve Hochstadt on the forces of economic propulsion and agricultural poverty that led to a growing and increasingly powerless migrant labor force, in *Mobility and Modernity: Migration in Germany, 1820-1989* (Ann Arbor: University of Michigan Press, 1999), 211–12.

86. Mikolaj Iwanow, *Pierwszy naród ukarany: Stalinizm wobec polskiej ludnosci kresowej, 1921–1938* (Warsaw: Państwowe Wydawn. Nauk, 1991); Ciesielski and Kuczynski, *Polacy w Kazachstanie*; Robert Conquest, *The Nation Killers: The Soviet Deportation of Nationalities* (London: Macmillan, 1970); Alexander Nekrich, *The Punished Peoples: The Deportation and Fate of Soviet Minorities at the End of the Second World War*, trans. George Sanders (New York: Norton, 1978); Genrich Strons'kii, *Zlet i podinnya: Pol's'kii natsional'nii raion v Ukraini y 20-30 roki* (Ternopil, 1992). On the universalization of the image of displaced persons into an ideal "type," see Liisa H. Malkki, *Purity and Exile: Violence, Memory, and National Cosmology among Hutu Refugees in Tanzania* (Chicago: University of Chicago Press, 1995), 8–14.

87. Author interview with Maria Weimar, Karaganda, October 1997.

88. As Lefebvre writes, "It is within space that time consumes or devours living beings." Lefebvre, *Production of Space*, 57.

89. On the particular "workscape" of coal mining, see Thomas G. Andrews, *Killing for Coal: America's Deadliest Labor War* (Cambridge, MA: Harvard University Press, 2010).

90. Mary Murphy, *Mining Cultures: Men, Women, and Leisure in Butte, 1914-41* (Urbana: University of Illinois Press, 1997), 4.

91. This figure derives from the four million workers in manufacturing; of these, as well, half a million annually were injured in accidents. Edward L. Ayers, ed., *American Passages: A History of the United States* (Fort Worth, TX: Harcourt College, 2000).

92. Pohl, *Stalinist Penal System*, table 25, p. 48. Not that American labor fatalities and Soviet labor camp casualties are compatible. NKVD-directed industries made up between 15 and 75 percent of total Soviet production in various industrial branches. Thousands more free Soviet workers died on the job throughout the 1930s.

93. The NKVD orders were explicit: "Labor Army conscripts do not have the right to create mixed settlements. They should be housed in special enclaves, separate from the workers." GARF 9479/1/57, 7–8.

94. By 1949 there were in Kazakhstan 820,165 deportees living in guarded "special settlements." The categories of special settlers consisted of the following state-designated ethnic-political groups: Germans, Chechens, Ingushi, Kara-

chaevs, Balkirs, Kalmyks, Russian collaborators with Germany under General Vlasov (*Vlatsovsti*), Ukrainian nationalists (*Ounovtsi*), and deportees from Georgia and Crimea. Zemskov, "Spetsposelentsi," 3-17.

95. See Terry Martin, *The Affirmative Action Empire: Nations and Nationalism in the Soviet Union, 1923-1939* (Ithaca, NY: Cornell University Press, 2001), 152.

96. Yda Schreuder, "Labor Segmentation, Ethnic Division of Labor, and Residential Segregation in American Cities in the Early Twentieth Century," *Professional Geography* 41 (1989): 131-43.

97. In both the Soviet and American cities, ethnic enclaves never reached a pure form; people moved in and out of them but often with difficulty.

98. Marshall Berman, commenting on Baudelaire's depiction of nineteenth-century Paris, writes that it is no coincidence that Baudelaire's "primal encounters" could never occur in contemporary urban spatial complexes: "For most of our century, urban spaces have been systematically designed and organized to ensure that collisions and confrontations will not take place . . . The distinctive sign of 19th century urbanism was the boulevard, a medium for bringing explosive material and human forces together; the hallmark of the 20th century urbanism has been the highway, a means of putting them asunder." Berman, *All That Is Solid*, 165.

99. Maria Weimar, as part of the "Labor Army," was freed in 1947. See Pohl, *Stalinist Penal System*, 76. However, the zones containing other categories of prisoners from KarLag marked the cityscape until 1955, when the last categories of unfree persons in Karaganda province were released. KarLag was closed in 1956, and in the countryside around Karaganda deportees termed "special settlers" were gradually granted mobility in a series of laws from 1954 to 1974. Karpikova, *Iz istorii Nemtsev Kazakhstana*; Dil'manov and Kuznetsova, *Karlag*, 12; and V. H. Zemskov, "Massovoe osvobozhdenie spetsposelentsev i ssyl'nykh, 1954-1966 gg.," *Sotsiologicheskie issledovaniia* 4 (1991): 5-25.

100. Author interview with Maria Weimar, Karaganda, audiotape, October 1997.

CHAPTER 7

1. Parts of this chapter were published as "A Place in Biography for Oneself," *American Historical Review* 114 (June 2009): 596-605.

2. On miraculous sightings and belief in unclean forces in Right Bank Ukraine in the 1920s, see Nykanor Dmytruk, "Pro chudesa na Ukraini roku 1923-go," *Ethnografichnyi visnyk* 1 (1925): 50-65; Dmytruk, "Z novogo pobutu," *Ethnografichnyi visnyk* 2 (1926): 31-37; Dmytruk, "'Chudesa' na Poltavshchyni, 1928," *Etnografichnyi visnyk* 8 (1929): 168-80; Vasyl' Kravchenko, "Osapatova dolyna," *Etnografichnyi visnyk* 2 (1926): 108-11; Olena Pchilka, "Ukrain'ski narodni legendy ostann'ogo chasu," *Etnografichnyi visnyk* 1 (1925): 43-47; Ludmila Vinogradov, "Polesskaia demonologiia" in Anna Skrypnyk, ed., *Polissia—mova, kul'tura, istoriia* (Kiev, 1996).

3. On Polesia as the cradle of Slavic civilization, see Stefaniia Gvozdevich, "Arkhaichnyi elementy u rodil'ni obriadovosty polishchukiv" in Anna Skrypnyk, ed., *Polissia—mova, kul'tura, istoriia* (Kiev: Asotsiatsiia etnolohiv, 1996), 247-51.

4. See "Kharakteristika Dzerzhinskogo natsional'nogo pol'skogo raiona BSSR," Gosudarstvennyi Arkhiv Rossiiskoi Federatsii (GARF) 3316/64/1537, (1934): 17–22. For a similar report on the political-national-geographic qualities of the Polish autonomous regions of Soviet Ukraine, see GARF 3316/64/1537, (1934): 33–42. For a report on Polish areas of Belorussia, see GARF, 3316/28/775, (1935): 27.

5. The personal *kharakteristika*, or autobiographical description, was a distinct part of Soviet political life, what Jochen Hellbeck describes as an individual's public "work toward self-perfection." The authors of the *kharakteristiki* on the national minority regions in the borderlands applied narratives and adjectives of personal socialist transformation and treachery collectively to the minority territories, as if they, "the Poles" or "the Germans," acted as one body. The fact that Soviet officials used the terminology and language of a *kharakteristika* and applied them to a territory, rather than an individual, shows how the concept of "biography" had spread by the 1930s to nationally inscribed territories. Hellbeck, *Revolution on My Mind: Writing a Diary under Stalin* (Cambridge, MA: Harvard University Press, 2006): 7. See also Sheila Fitzpatrick, *Tear off the Masks! Identity and Imposture in Twentieth-Century Russia* (Princeton, NJ: Princeton University Press, 2005); Igal Halfin, *From Darkness to Light Class, Consciousness, and Salvation in Revolutionary Russia* (Pittsburgh, 2000).

6. Zofia Kossak-Szczucka, *Pożoga: Wspomnienia z Wołynia, 1917–1919* (Kraków: Nakł. Krakowskiej Spółki Wydawniczej, 1923); Maria Dunin-Kozicka, *Burza od wschodu: Wspomnienia z Kijowszczyzny, 1918–1920* (Łódź: Wydawn. "Artus," 1990); Anna Zahorska's books *Uchodzy* (1922), *Odrutowana okolica* (Warsaw: Biblioteka Domu Polskiego, 1925), and *Trucizny* (Warsaw: Dom Książki Polskiej,1928); Kazimierz Leczycki, "Brat z tamtej strony." *Słowo*, no. 61 (Wilno, 1923); Jerzy Stempowski, *W dolinie Dniestru i inne eseje Ukraińskie: Listy o Ukrainie* (Warsaw: LNB, 1993); V. G. Bogoraz, *Evreiskoe mestechko v revoliutsii* (Moscow, 1926); L. Aizenberg, "Mestechko Kaminski i ego obivateli," *Evreiskaia letopis'* 4 (1926): 81; L. M. Aizenberg, "Chudo tsadika v kassastionnom senate," *Evreiskaia letopis'* 4 (1926); Herbert Henke, "Der dornige Weg zum Wissen: Autobiographische Skizzen," *Feniks*, no. 11 (September 1995), 2–76.

7. Marshall Berman, *All That Is Solid Melts into Air: The Experience of Modernity* (New York: Simon and Schuster, 1982).

8. On Poles of Ukraine, see W. Tągoborski, *Polacy Związku Radzieckiego: Ich pochodzenie, udział w Rewolucji Padźiernikowej i budownictwie socjalistycznym* (Moscow, 1929); Mikołaj Iwanow, *Pierwszy naród ukarany: Stalinizm wobec polskiej ludności kresowej, 1921–1938* (Warsaw: Państwowe Wydawn. Nauk, 1991); Janusz M. Kupczak, *Polacy na Ukrainie w latach 1921–1939* (Wrocław: Wydawn, Uniwersytetu Wrocławskiego, 1994); Genrikh Strons'kyi, *Zlet i podinnia: pol'skii natsional'nii raion v Ukrainy u 20–30 roki* (Ternopil', 1992); Antoni Urbanski, *Z czarnego szlaku i tamtych rubieży: Zabytki polskie przepadłe na Podolu, Wołyniu, Ukraine* (Gdansk: Graf,1991). On Germans of Ukraine, see Meir Buchsweiler, *Volksdeutsch in der Ukraine am Vorabend und Beginn des Zweitern Weltkriegs: Ein Fall Doppelter Loyalität?* (Gerlingen: Bleicher, 1984); Bogdan Chyrko, *Nemtsi v Ukraini 20–30-ti rr. XX ct* (Kiev, 1994) S. Nikel,

Die Deutschen in Wolhynien (Kharkiv, 1936); Nikolaus Arndt, *Die Deutschen in Wolhynien: Ein Kulturhistorischer Überblick* (Würzburg: Kraft, 1994); Alfred Karasek, *Die Deutschen Siedlungen in Wolhynien* (Plauen: G. Wolff, 1931); Hugo Karl Schmidt, *Die Evangelisch-Lutherische Kirche in Wolhynien* (Marburg: Elwert, 1992). For histories of Jews, see I. A. S Khonigsman, *Evrei Ukrainy: Kratkii ocherk istorii* (Kiev: Ukrainsko-finskiĭ in-t menedzhmenta i biznesa, 1992); *Istoriia Evreev na Ukraine i v Belorussii: Ėkspeditsii, pami'atniki, nakhodki: Sbornik nauchnykh trudov* (Sankt-Peterburg: Peterburgskiĭ evreĭskiĭ universitet, 1994); Mikhail Mitsel', *Evrei Ukrainy v 1943–1953 Gg.: Ocherki Dokumentirovannoĭ Istorii* (Kiev: Dukh i litera, 2004); Avrahm Yarmolinsky, *The Jews and Other Minor Nationalities under the Soviets* (New York: Vanguard Press, 1928). On the Nazi German creation of the idea of "Volksdeutsch" in Right Bank Ukraine, see Wilhelm Fielitz, *Das Stereotyp des Wolhyniendeutschen Umsiedlers: Popularisierungen zwichen Sprachinselforschung und Nationalsozialistischer Propaganda* (Marburg: Elwert, 2000). Since the publication of *A Biography of No Place*, several histories of the Polish-Ukrainian borderlands and their mixed populations have appeared. See, for example, Omer Bartov and Eric D. Weitz, *Shatterzone of Empires: Coexistence and Violence in the German, Habsburg, Russian, and Ottoman Borderlands* (Bloomington: Indiana University Press, 2013); Timothy Snyder, *Bloodlands: Europe between Hitler and Stalin* (New York: Basic Books, 2010); Daniel Adam Mendelsohn, *The Lost: A Search for Six of Six Million* (New York: HarperCollins, 2006).

9. On the life experiences that emerged in the work of Mikhail Bakhtin and Dmitri Likhachev, both gulag survivors, see Aleksander Ėtkind, *Warped Mourning: Stories of the Undead in the Land of the Unburied* (Stanford, CA: Stanford University Press, 2013), 69.

10. The factory produced an average of one million movements annually from 1920 through 1928, more than half of U.S. domestic watch production and more than twice that of the closest competitor. E. C. Alft, *Elgin: An American History, 1835–1985* (Elgin, IL: Crossroads Communications,1999), elginhistory.com (accessed November 22, 2007), chap. 7, sect. 3.

11. Ibid., chap. 5, sect. 1.

12. Ibid., chap. 10, sect. 7.

13. In Jefferson Cowie's history of RCA, he shows how the corporation first moved divisions from Camden, New Jersey, after World War II to the Midwest, which, he writes, served "much like the Mexican border decades later," as a region of low-wages for "competitive-sector, female-made" goods. Cowie, *Capital Moves: RCA's Seventy-Year Quest for Cheap Labor* (Ithaca, NY: Cornell University Press, 1999), 34.

14. Alft, *Elgin*, chap. 10, sect. 6.

15. Between 1979 and 1986, 19 percent of all manufacturing jobs in Ohio, Michigan, Indiana, Illinois, and Wisconsin disappeared. James Rhodes, "Youngstown's Ghost? Memory, Identity and Deindustrialization," *International Labor and Working-Class History*, no. 84 (Fall 2013), 56.

16. Alft, *Elgin*, chap. 7, sect. 3.

17. "The Kane County Pimpernel," *Time*, October 5, 1970. For Phillips's self-

published memoir, see Ray Fox, aka Jim Phillips, *Raising Kane: The Fox Chronicles* (Kansas, 1999).

18. As cited in Douglas Martin, "James Phillips, 70, Environmentalist Who Was Called the Fox," *New York Times*, October 22, 2001.

19. For a recent history of the early environmental movement, see Adam Rome, *The Genius of Earth Day: How a 1970 Teach-In Unexpectedly Made the First Green Generation* (New York: Hill and Wang, 2014).

20. For a wonderful series of essays on the border between author and subject, and its place in historical writing, see "Round Table: Self and Subject," *Journal of American History* 89, no. 1 (June 2002): 15–53.

21. In 1999 George McKelvey, the mayor of the infamously deindustrialized Youngstown, Ohio, commented sarcastically, "Someone in Washington obviously said 'Let's dump on Youngstown. There's nobody there smart enough to even know what we're doing.'" For quote and an analysis of the internalization of a community as a site of loss, see John Russo and Sherry Lee Linkon, "Collateral Damage: Deindustrialization and the Uses of Youngstown," in Jefferson Cowie and Joseph Heathcott, *Beyond the Ruins: The Meanings of Deindustrialization* (Ithaca, NY: ILR Press, 2003), 209.

22. As Dolores Hayden points out, "Despair about placelessness is as much a part of the American experience as pleasure in the sense of place." "The American Sense of Place and the Politics of Space," in *American Architecture: Innovation and Tradition*, ed. David G. De Long, Helen Searing, and Robert A. M. Stern (New York: Rizzoli, 1986), 184.

23. Among many, many sites, see "Dereliction Addiction," http://uexplorer .wordpress.com/; "The Bohemian Blog," http://www.thebohemianblog.com/p /urban-exploration-urbex.html

24. The list of sources on deindustrialized spaces is very long. For examples, see C. Campbell, "Residual Landscapes and the Everyday: An Interview With Edward Burtynsky," *Space and Culture* 11, no. 1 (2008): 39–50; Jennifer Baichwal, dir., *Manufactured Landscapes* (Zeitgeist Films, 2006); Dan Austin and Sean Doerr, *Lost Detroit: Stories behind the Motor City's Majestic Ruins* (Charleston, SC: History Press, 2010); Bill McGraw, "Life in the Ruins of Detroit," *History Workshop Journal* 63, no. 1 (2007): 288–302; N. Millington, "Post-Industrial Imaginaries: Nature, Representation and Ruin in Detroit, Michigan," *International Journal of Urban and Regional Research* 37, no. 1 (2013): 279–96; Andrew Moore, Philip Levine, and Akron Art Museum, *Detroit Disassembled* (Bologna: Damiani Editore; Akron, OH: Akron Art Museum, 2010). For an issue dedicated to deindustrialization around the globe, see *International Labor and Working-Class History*, no. 84 (Fall 2013).

25. Douglas Coupland, "Unclassy: The Old Class Definitions Are Becoming Obsolete," *FT Magazine*, January 10, 2014, http://www.ft.com/cms/s/2/81e53694-78c5 -11e3-a148-00144feabdc0.html#axzz2qluc1woi.

26. Tim Strangleman, "'Smokestack Nostalgia,' 'Ruin Porn' or Working-Class Obituary: The Role and Meaning of Deindustrial Representation," *International Labor and Working-Class History*, no. 84 (Fall 2013), 23–38.

27. Sue Halpern, "Mayor of Rust, John Fetterman," *New York Times Magazine*, February 11, 2011; Sean Posey, "The Battle for Braddock, January 24, 2013, rustwire.com.

28. For an especially vivid depiction of the two sides of entropy, see Paige Williams, "Drop Dead, Detroit!" *New Yorker*, January 27, 2014, 32–39. For a Marxist analysis of this process based on the lost value in immobile property transferred to new sites, see Don Mitchell, "Working-Class Geographies: Capital, Space, and Place," in *New Working-Class Studies*, ed. John Russo and Sherry Lee Linkon (Ithaca, NY: Cornell University Press, 2005), 78–97.

29. Thomas J. Sugrue, *The Origins of the Urban Crisis: Race and Inequality in Postwar Detroit* (Princeton, NJ: Princeton University Press, 1996); William J. Wilson, *When Work Disappears: The World of the New Urban Poor* (New York: Knopf, 1996); Loïc J. D. Wacquant, *Urban Outcasts: A Comparative Sociology of Advanced Marginality* (Cambridge, MA: Polity, 2008).

30. Jason Segedy, "Looking Ahead after Growing Up with Decline," November 6, 2013, rustwire.com. My thanks to Steve Seegal for alerting me to this site.

31. In 1989 Detroit had 5,215 abandoned buildings. McGraw, "Life in the Ruins," 294.

32. For a definition of "slow violence," see Rob Nixon, *Slow Violence and the Environmentalism of the Poor* (Cambridge, MA: Harvard University Press, 2011), 2–3.

33. "Clyde, Ohio, Child-Cancer Cluster Confounds Parents, Medical Investigators," *Plain* Dealer/Cleveland.com, http://www.cleveland.com/nation/index.ssf/2010/12/clyde_ohio_child-cancer_cluste.html (accessed January 29, 2014); "America's Infant Mortality Crisis," http://www.aljazeera.com/programmes/fault lines/2013/09/20139248355279581.html (accessed January 29, 2014).

34. On the impermanence of the period of high wages and industrial growth in the midcentury United States, see Cowie and Heathcott, *Beyond the Ruins*, 14.

35. See, for example, an oral history project centered on Sparrow's Point, Maryland, a community created around the Sparrows Point Steel Mill in Baltimore. "Sparrows Point," http://millstories.umbc.edu/sparrows-point/.

36. Helen M. Cox and Colin A. Holmes, "Loss, Healing, and the Power of Place," *Human Studies* 23, no. 1 (January 2000): 70.

BIBLIOGRAPHY

Agnon, Shmuel Yosef, and S. Goĭzman. *Rasskazy o Baal'-Shem-Tove*. Moscow: Tekst: Knizhniki, 2011.

Aizenberg, L. "Chudo tsadika v kassastionnom senate," *Evreiskaia letopis'* 4 (1926)
———. "Mestechko Kaminski i ego obivateli." *Evreiskaia letopis'* 4 (1926).

Alft, E. C. *Elgin: An American History, 1835–1985*. 1984; Elgin, IL: Crossroads Communications, 1999.

Anderson, Nels. *Men on the Move*. University of Chicago Sociological Series. Chicago, IL: University of Chicago Press, 1940.

Andrews, Thomas G. *Killing for Coal: America's Deadliest Labor War*. Cambridge, MA: Harvard University Press, 2010.

Arndt, Nikolaus. *Die Deutschen in Wolhynien: Ein Kulturhistorischer Überblick*. Würzburg: Kraft, 1994.

Austin, Dan, and Sean Doerr. *Lost Detroit: Stories behind the Motor City's Majestic Ruins*. Charleston, SC: History Press, 2010.

Ayers, Edward L., ed. *American Passages: A History of the United States*. Fort Worth, TX: Harcourt College, 2000.

Bacon, Edwin. *The Gulag at War: Stalin's Forced Labour System in the Light of the Archives*. New York: New York University Press, 1994.

Bacon, Elizabeth E. *Central Asians under Russian Rule: A Study in Culture Change*. 2nd ed. Ithaca, NY: Cornell University Press, 1980.

Baichwal, Jennifer, director. *Manufactured Landscapes*. Distributed by Zeitgeist Films, 2006.

Ball, Alan M. *Russia's Last Capitalists: The Nepmen, 1921–1929*. Berkeley: University of California Press, 1987.

Barag, T. Y. *Karaganda*. Moscow: Gos. izd-vo Arkhitektury i gradostroitel'stva, 1950.

Barnes, Steven Anthony. *Death and Redemption: The Gulag and the Shaping of Soviet Society*. Princeton, NJ: Princeton University Press, 2011.

Barr, Juliana. *Peace Came in the Form of a Woman: Indians and Spaniards in the Texas Borderlands*. Chapel Hill: University of North Carolina Press, 2007.

Barthes, Roland. *Mythologies*. New York: Hill and Wang, 1994.

Bartov, Omer, and Eric D Weitz. *Shatterzone of Empires: Coexistence and Violence in the German, Habsburg, Russian, and Ottoman Borderlands*. Bloomington: Indiana University Press, 2013.

Bassin, Mark. "Russia between Europe and Asia: The Ideological Construction of Geographical Space." *Slavic Review* 50, no. 1 (Spring 1991): 1–17.

Bassin, Mark, Christopher David Ely, and Melissa Kirschke Stockdale. *Space, Place, and Power in Modern Russia : Essays in the New Spatial History*. DeKalb: Northern Illinois University Press, 2010.

Baumgarten, Elisheva. *Mothers and Children: Jewish Family Life in Medieval Europe*. Princeton, NJ: Princeton University Press, 2004.

Becker, Elizabeth. "Private Idaho." *New Republic*. May 4, 1992.

Becker, Jonathan A. *Soviet and Russian Press Coverage of the United States: Press, Politics, and Identity in Transition*. New York: St. Martin's Press, 1999.

Bell, Wilson T. "Was the Gulag an Archipelago? De-Convoyed Prisoners and Porous Borders in the Camps of Western Siberia." *Russian Review* 72, no. 1 (January 2013): 116–41.

Berkhoff, Karel C. *Harvest of Despair: Life and Death in Ukraine under Nazi Rule*. Cambridge, MA: Harvard University Press, 2008.

Berman, Marshall. *All That Is Solid Melts into Air: The Experience of Modernity*. New York: Simon and Schuster, 1982.

Biehl, João Guilherme. *Vita: Life in a Zone of Social Abandonment*. Berkeley: University of California Press, 2005.

Black, Monica. "Miracles in the Shadow of the Economic Miracle: The 'Supernatural '50s' in West Germany.'" *Journal of Modern History* 84, no. 4 (December 2012): 833–60.

Blackbourn, David. *Marpingen: Apparitions of the Virgin Mary in Nineteenth-Century Germany*. New York: Knopf, 1994.

Blouin, Francis X., and William G. Rosenberg. *Processing the Past: Contesting Authority in History and the Archives*. New York: Oxford University Press, 2011.

Bogoraz, V. G. *Evreiskoe mestechko v revoliutsii*. Moscow, 1926.

Bonnett, Alastair. *The Idea of the West: Culture, Politics, and History*. Houndmills, Basingstoke: Palgrave Macmillan, 2004.

Bradley, Harriet. "The Seductions of the Archive: Voices Lost and Found." *History of the Human Sciences* 12, no. 2 (May 1999): 107–22.

Brown, Kate. *A Biography of No Place: From Ethnic Borderland to Soviet Heartland*. Cambridge, MA: Harvard University Press, 2004.

———. *Plutopia: Nuclear Families, Atomic Cities, and the Great Soviet and American Plutonium Disasters*. New York: Oxford University Press, 2013.

Buber-Neumann, Margarete. *Under Two Dictators*. Trans. Edward Fitzgerald. London: V. Gollancz, 1949.

Buchsweiler, Meir. *Volksdeutsche in der Ukraine am Vorabend und Beginn des Zweiten Weltkriegs: Ein Fall Doppelter Loyalität?* Gerlingen: Bleicher, 1984.

Buck-Morss, Susan. *The Dialectics of Seeing: Walter Benjamin and the Arcades Project*. Cambridge, MA: MIT Press, 1989.

Burton, Antoinette M. *Archive Stories: Facts, Fictions, and the Writing of History*. Durham, NC: Duke University Press, 2005.

Buxbaum, Yitzhak. *The Light and Fire of the Baal Shem Tov*. New York: Continuum, 2006.

Calvino, Italo. *Invisible Cities*. Trans. William Weaver. New York: Harcourt Brace Jovanovich, 1978.

Cameron, Sarah. "The Hungry Steppe: Soviet Kazakhstan and the Kazakh Famine, 1921–1934." PhD diss., Yale University, 2010.

Campbell, C. "Residual Landscapes and the Everyday: An Interview With Edward Burtynsky." *Space and Culture* 11, no. 1 (2008): 39–50.

Casey, Edward S. *The Fate of Place: A Philosophical History*. Berkeley: University of California Press, 1997.

Chambers, Iain. *Migrancy, Culture, Identity*. London: Routledge, 1994.

Ciesielski, Stanisław, and Anton Kuczynski, eds. *Polacy w Kazachstanie 1940–1946: Historia i wspolczesnosc*. Wrocław: Wydawnictwo Uniwersytetu Wrocławskiego, 1996.

Clark, Katerina, and Michael Holquist. *Mikhail Bakhtin*. Cambridge, MA: Harvard University Press, 1984.

Cohen, Deborah, and Maura O'Connor. *Comparison and History: Europe in Cross-National Perspective*. New York: Routledge, 2004.

Conquest, Robert. *The Nation Killers: The Soviet Deportation of Nationalities*. London: Macmillan, 1970.

Cowie, Jefferson. *Capital Moves: RCA's Seventy-Year Quest for Cheap Labor*. Ithaca, NY: Cornell University Press, 1999.

Cowie, Jefferson, and Joseph Heathcott. *Beyond the Ruins: The Meanings of Deindustrialization*. Ithaca, NY: ILR Press, 2003.

Cox, Helen M., and Colin A. Holmes. "Loss, Healing, and the Power of Place." *Human Studies* 23, no. 1 (January 2000): 63–78.

Cronon, William. "AHA Presidential Address: 'Storytelling.'" *American Historical Review* 118, no. 1 (February 2013): 1–20.

———. *Changes in the Land: Indians, Colonists, and the Ecology of New England*. New York: Hill and Wang, 2011.

———. *Nature's Metropolis: Chicago and the Great West*. 1st ed. New York: W. W. Norton, 1991.

———. "A Place for Stories: Nature, History and Narrative," *Journal of American History* 78 (1992): 1347–76.

Danilov, Viktor Petrovich, and S. A. Krasil'nikov, eds. *Spetspereselentsy v zapadnoǐ Sibiri, 1933–1938*. Novosibirsk: ÈKOR, 1994.

David-Fox, Michael, and Alexander M. Martin. *Fascination and Enmity: Russia and Germany as Entangled Histories, 1914–1945*. Pittsburgh, PA: University of Pittsburgh Press, 2012.

Davies, Thom. "A Visual Geography of Chernobyl: Double Exposure." *International Labor and Working-Class History*, no. 84 (Fall 2013), 116-39.

Day, Kathleen. "Sting Reveals Security Gap at Nuclear Agency." *Washington Post*, July 12, 2007, A1.

Degteva, M. O., N. B. Shagina, M. I. Vorobiova, L. R. Anspaugh, and B. A. Napier. "Reevaluation of Waterborne Releases of Radioactive Materials from the Mayak Production Association into the Techa River in 1949-1951." *Health Physics* 102, no. 1 (January 2012): 25-38.

De Long, David Gilson, Helen Searing, and Robert A. M. Stern, eds. *American Architecture: Innovation and Tradition*. New York: Rizzoli, 1986.

Demko, George J. *The Russian Colonization of Kazakhstan, 1896-1916*. Bloomington: Indiana University Press, 1969.

DiMaio, Alfred John. *Soviet Urban Housing: Problems and Policies*. New York: Praeger, 1974.

Dmytruk, Nykanor. "Pro chudesa na Ukraini roku 1923-go." *Ethnografichnyi visnyk* 1 (1925): 50-65.

———. "Z novogo pobutu." *Ethnografichnyi visnyk* 2 (1926): 31-37.

———. "'Chudesa' na Poltavshchyni, 1928." *Etnografichnyi visnyk* 8 (1929): 168-80.

Dower, John W. *War without Mercy: Race and Power in the Pacific War*. New York: Pantheon, 1986.

Dunin-Kozicka, Maria. *Burza od wschodu: Wspomnienia z Kijowszczyzny, 1918-1920*. Łódź: Wydawn. "Artus," 1990.

Elagin, A. S., B. N. Abisheva, and K. Nurpeisov, eds. *Karaganda: Istoriia gorodov Kazakhstana*. Alma-Ata: Nauka, 1989.

Esaulov, Aleksandr. *Chernobyl': Letopis' mertvogo goroda*. Moscow: Evropa, 2006.

Ethington, Philip J. "Placing the Past: 'Groundwork' for a Spatial Theory of History." *Rethinking History* 11, no. 4 (December 2007): 465-93.

Ėtkind, Aleksandr. *Warped Mourning: Stories of the Undead in the Land of the Unburied*. Stanford, CA: Stanford University Press, 2013.

Fenn, Elizabeth A. *Encounters at the Heart of the World: A History of the Mandan People*. New York: Hill and Wang, 2014.

Ficken, Robert E. *Rufus Woods, the Columbia River and the Building of Modern Washington*. Pullman: Washington State University Press, 1995.

Fielitz, Wilhelm. *Das Stereotyp Des Wolhyniendeutschen Umsiedlers: Popularisierungen Zwischen Sprachinselforschung und Nationalsozialistischer Propaganda*. Marburg: Elwert, 2000.

Fiset, Louis. *Camp Harmony: Seattle's Japanese Americans and the Puyallup Assembly Center*. Urbana: University of Illinois Press, 2009.

Fitzpatrick, Sheila. *Tear Off the Masks! Identity and Imposture in Twentieth-Century Russia*. Princeton, NJ: Princeton University Press, 2005.

Ford, Jamie. *Hotel on the Corner of Bitter and Sweet: A Novel*. New York: Ballantine, 2009.

Foucault, Michel. *Discipline and Punish: The Birth of the Prison*. Trans. Alan Sheridan. New York: Vintage, 1995.

———. *Madness and Civilization; a History of Insanity in the Age of Reason*. New York: New American Library, 1967.

Fox, William T. R. *The Super-Powers: The United States, Britain, and the Soviet Union—Their Responsibility for Peace*. New York: Harcourt, Brace and Company, 1944.

Fraser, Ronald. *In Search of a Past : The Rearing of an English Gentleman, 1933-1945*. New York: Atheneum, 1984.

Gleason, Abbott. *Totalitarianism: The Inner History of the Cold War*. New York: Oxford University Press, 1995.

Goldstein, Donna, and Magdalena E. Stawkowski. "James V. Neel and Yuri E. Dubova: Cold War Debates and the Genetic Effects of Low-Dose Radiation." *Journal of the History of Biology*, online edition (July 2014).

Grant, Kimi Cunningham. *Silver Like Dust: One Family's Story of America's Japanese Internment*. New York: Pegasus Books, 2012.

Grünberg, Slawomir, director. *Chelyabinsk: The Most Contaminated Spot on the Planet*. Chip Taylor Production, 1995.

Gus'kova, A. K. *Atomnaia otrasl' strany: Glazami vracha*. Moscow: Real'noe vremia, 2004.

Hacker, Barton C. *The Dragon's Tail: Radiation Safety in the Manhattan Project, 1942-1946*. Berkeley: University of California Press, 1987.

Hales, Peter Bacon. *Levittown: Documents of an Ideal American Suburb*. http://tigger.uic.edu/~pbhales/Levittown.html (accessed January 15, 2014).

Halpern, Sue. "Mayor of Rust, John Fetterman." *New York Times Magazine*, February 11, 2011.

Halttunen, Karen. "Groundwork: American Studies in Place—Presidential Address to the American Studies Association, November 4, 2005." *American Quarterly* 58, no. 1 (2006): 1-15.

Haraway, Donna. "Situated Knowledges: The Science Question in Feminism and the Privilege of Partial Perspective." *Feminist Studies* 14, no. 3 (October 1988): 575-99.

Hartman, Saidiya. *Lose Your Mother: A Journey along the Atlantic Slave Route*. New York: Farrar, Straus and Giroux, 2008.

Hayanga, Awori J., Steve B. Zeliadt, and Leah M. Backhus. "Residential Segregation and Lung Cancer Mortality in the United States." *JAMA Surgery* 148, no. 1 (January 2013): 37-42.

Hayashi, Brian Masaru. *Democratizing the Enemy: The Japanese American Internment*. Princeton, NJ: Princeton University Press, 2010.

Hecht, Gabrielle. *Being Nuclear: Africans and the Global Uranium Trade*. Cambridge, MA: MIT Press, 2012.

Hellbeck, Jochen. *Revolution on My Mind: Writing a Diary under Stalin*. Cambridge, MA: Harvard University Press, 2006.

Henke, Herbert. "Der dornige Weg zum Wissen: autobiographische Skizzen." *Feniks*, no. 11 (September 1995), 2-76.

Herbert, Ulrich. *Hitler's Foreign Workers: Enforced Foreign Labor in Germany under the Third Reich.* Cambridge: Cambridge University Press, 2006.

Hill, C. K. "The Low-Dose Phenomenon: How Bystander Effects, Genomic Instability, and Adaptive Responses Could Transform Cancer-Risk Models." *Bulletin of the Atomic Scientists* 68, no. 3 (May 2012): 51–58.

Hillis, Faith. *Children of Rus': Right-Bank Ukraine and the Invention of a Russian Nation.* Ithaca, NY: Cornell University Press, 2013.

Hochstadt, Steve. *Mobility and Modernity: Migration in Germany, 1820–1989.* Ann Arbor: University of Michigan Press, 1999.

Hoxie, Frederick E. *Parading through History: The Making of the Crow Nation in America, 1805–1935.* Cambridge: Cambridge University Press, 1995.

Hundert, Gershon David, ed. *Essential Papers on Hasidism: Origins to Present.* New York: New York University Press, 1991.

Inada, Lawson Fusao, ed. *Only What We Could Carry: The Japanese American Internment Experience.* Berkeley, CA: Heyday Books, 2000.

Ivanova, A. E., V. G. Semyonova, N. S. Gavrilova, G. N. Evdokushkina, L. A. Gavrilov, "Mortality Trends: Role of Particular Age Groups and Causes of Death in Their Shaping,"." *Obshchestvenno zdorov'e i profilaktika zabolevanii* 6 (2004): 3–9.

Ivanova, Galina Mikhailovna. *Gulag v sisteme totalitarnogo gosudarstva.* Moscow: Moskovskiĭ obshchestvennyĭ nauchnyĭ fond, 1997.

Iversen, Kristen. *Full Body Burden: Growing Up in the Nuclear Shadow of Rocky Flats.* New York: Crown, 2012.

Iwanow, Mikolaj. *Pierwszy naród ukarany: Stalinizm wobec polskiej ludnosci kresowej, 1921–1938.* Warsaw: Państwowe Wydawn. Nauk, 1991.

Jain, Sarah S. Lochlann. *Malignant: How Cancer Becomes Us.* Berkeley: University of California Press, 2013.

Johnston, Barbara Rose, and Holly M. Barker. *Consequential Damages of Nuclear War: The Rongelap Report.* Walnut Creek, CA: Left Coast Press, 2008.

Kaplan, Alice Yaeger. *French Lessons: A Memoir.* Chicago: University of Chicago Press, 1993.

Karasek, Alfred. *Die Deutschen Siedlungen in Wolhynien.* Plauen: G. Wolff, 1931.

Karpikova, G. A., ed. *Iz istorii Nemtsev Kazakhstana, 1921–1975 gg.: Sbornik dokumentov.* Almaty: Gotika, 1997.

Katti, Christian S. G., and Bruno Latour. "Mediating Political 'Things,' and the Forked Tongue of Modern Culture: A Conversation with Bruno Latour." *Art Journal* 65, no. 1 (April 2006): 94–115.

Kershaw, Ian, and Moshe Lewin, eds. *Stalinism and Nazism: Dictatorships in Comparison.* Cambridge: Cambridge University Press, 1997.

Khanin, G. I. "The 1950s: The Triumph of the Soviet Economy." *Europe-Asia Studies* 55, no. 8 (December 2003): 1187–1212.

Khonigsman, I. A. S. *Evrei Ukrainy: Kratkiĭ ocherk istorii.* Kiev: Ukrainsko-finskiĭ in-t menedzhmenta i biznesa, 1992.

Klosterman, Lorrie. "Narrative Medicine Heals Bodies and Souls." *Utne Reader,* September–October 2009.

Koch, Fred C. *The Volga Germans: In Russia and the Americas, from 1763 to the Present*. University Park: Pennsylvania State University Press, 1977.

Kossak-Szczucka, Zofia. *Pożoga; Wspomnienia z Wołynia, 1917–1919*. Kraków: Nakł. Krakowskiej Spółki Wydawniczej, 1923.

Kostin, Ihor F. *Chernobyl: Confessions of a Reporter*. New York: Umbrage, 2007.

Kotkin, Stephen. *Magnetic Mountain: Stalinism as a Civilization*. Berkeley: University of California Press, 1995.

Kravchenko, Vasyl'. "Osapatova dolyna." *Etnografichnyi visnyk* 2 (1926): 108–11.

Kudriavtsev, Alekseĭ Osipovich. *Ratsional'noe ispol'zovanie territoriĭ pri planirovke i zastroĭke gorodov SSSR*. Moscow, 1971.

Kupczak, Janusz M. *Polacy na Ukrainie w latach 1921–1939*. Wrocław: Wydawn, Uniwersytetu Wrocławskiego, 1994.

Larin, V. *Kombinat "Maiak": Problema na veka*. Moscow: KMK Scientific Press, 2001.

Lawson, James. "Chronotope, Story, and Historical Geography: Mikhail Bakhtin and the Space-Time of Narratives." *Antipode* 43, no. 2 (March 2011): 384–412.

Leczycki, Kazimierz. "Brat z tamtej strony." *Słowo*, no. 61. Wilno, 1923.

Lefebvre, Henri. *Everyday Life in the Modern World*. Trans. Sacha Rabinovitch. New Brunswick, NJ: Transaction Books, 1990.

———. *The Production of Space*. Trans. Donald Nicholson- Smith. Oxford: Blackwell, 1994.

Lynch, Michael. "Archives in Formation: Privileged Spaces, Popular Archives and Paper Trails." *History of the Human Sciences* 12, no. 2 (1999): 65–87.

Malkki, Liisa H. *Purity and Exile: Violence, Memory, and National Cosmology among Hutu Refugees in Tanzania*. Chicago: University of Chicago Press, 1995.

Malybaev, O. *Bor'ba KPSS za sozdanieĭ razvitie tret'eĭ ugol'noĭ bazy SSSR*. Alma-Ata: Kazakhskoe gos. izd-vo, 1961.

Manbo, Bill T., and Eric L. Muller. *Colors of Confinement: Rare Kodachrome Photographs of Japanese American Incarceration in World War II*. Chapel Hill: University of North Carolina Press, 2012.

Manzurova, Natalia, and Cathie Sullivan. *Hard Duty: A Woman's Experience at Chernobyl*. Tesuque, NM: Sullivan and Manzurova, 2006.

Marcus, Ivan G. *Rituals of Childhood: Jewish Acculturation in Medieval Europe*. New Haven, CT: Yale University Press, 1996.

Martin, Terry. *The Affirmative Action Empire: Nations and Nationalism in the Soviet Union, 1923–1939*. Ithaca, NY: Cornell University Press, 2001.

Massey, Doreen B. *Space, Place, and Gender*. Hoboken, NJ: Wiley, 2013.

McGraw, Bill. "Life in the Ruins of Detroit." *History Workshop Journal* 63, no. 1 (2007): 288–302.

McSheffrey, Shannon. "Detective Fiction in the Archives: Court Records and the Uses of Law in Late Medieval England." *History Workshop Journal*, no. 65 (2008), 65–78.

Mendelsohn, Daniel Adam. *The Lost: A Search for Six of Six Million*. New York: HarperCollins, 2006.

Millington, N. "Post-Industrial Imaginaries: Nature, Representation and Ruin in Detroit, Michigan." *International Journal of Urban and Regional Research* 37, no. 1 (2013): 279–96.

"Misteaching History on Racial Segregation: Ignoring Purposeful Discriminatory Government Policies of the Past Contributes to the Ongoing Achievement Gap." *Economic Policy Institute*. http://www.epi.org/publication/misteaching -history-racial-segregation-ignoring/ (accessed January 14, 2014).

Mitman, Gregg. "In Search of Health: Landscape and Disease in American Environmental History." *Environmental History* 10, no. 2 (April 2005): 184–210.

Mitman, Greg, Michelle Murphy, and Christopher Sellers, eds. *Landscapes of Exposure: Knowledge and Illness in Modern Environments*. Chicago: University of Chicago Press, 2004.

Mitsel', Mikhail. *Evrei Ukrainy v 1943–1953 gg.: Ocherki dokumentirovannoĭ istorii.* Kiev: Dukh i litera, 2004.

Moiseenko, V. "Migratsiia naseleniia v perepiskakh Rossii i SSSR." *Voprosy statistiki* 3 (1997): 30–36.

Monahan, Torin, and Jill A. Fisher. "Benefits of 'Observer Effects': Lessons from the Field." *Qualitative Research* 10, no. 3 (June 2010): 357–76.

Moore, Andrew, Philip Levine, and Akron Art Museum. *Detroit Disassembled*. Bologna: Damiani Editore; Akron, OH: Akron Art Museum, 2010.

Mukherjee, Siddhartha. *The Emperor of All Maladies: A Biography of Cancer*. New York: Scribner, 2010.

Mukanov, Sabit. *Karaganda*. Moscow: Foreign Languages Publishing House, 1954.

Murphy, J. C. *The Comical History of Montana: A Serious Story for Free People*. San Diego, 1912.

Murphy, Mary. *Mining Cultures: Men, Women, and Leisure in Butte, 1914–41*. Urbana: University of Illinois Press, 1997.

Murray, Alice Yang. *Historical Memories of the Japanese American Internment and the Struggle for Redress*. Stanford, CA: Stanford University Press, 2008.

Mycio, Mary. "Account of Chernobyl Trip Takes Web Surfers for a Ride." *Los Angeles Times*, July 6, 2004. http://articles.latimes.com/2004/jul/06/world/fg -chernobyl6 (accessed July 6, 2004).

———. *Wormwood Forest: A Natural History of Chernobyl*. Washington, DC: Joseph Henry Press, 2005.

Nash, Linda. "Finishing Nature: Harmonizing Bodies and Environments in Late-Nineteenth-Century California." *Environmental History* 8, no. 1 (January 2003): 25–52.

———. "Purity and Danger: Historical Reflections on the Regulation of Environmental Pollutants." *Environmental History* 13, no. 4 (October 2008): 651–58.

Navasky, Victor S. *Naming Names*. New York: Hill and Wang, 2003.

Neiwert, David A. *Strawberry Days: How Internment Destroyed a Japanese American Community*. New York: Palgrave Macmillan, 2005.

Nekrich, A. M. *The Punished Peoples: The Deportation and Fate of Soviet Minorities at the End of the Second World War.* Trans. George Sanders. New York: Norton, 1978.

Ngai, Mae M. *Impossible Subjects: Illegal Aliens and the Making of Modern America.* Princeton, NJ: Princeton University Press, 2004.

Nixon, Rob. *Slow Violence and the Environmentalism of the Poor.* Cambridge, MA: Harvard University Press, 2011.

Novoselov, V. N. and V. S. Tolstikov. *Atomnyi sled na Urale.* Chliabinsk: Rifei, 1997.

———. *Taĭna "Sorokovki."* Ekaterinburg: Ural'skiĭ rabochiĭ, 1995.

Olcott, Martha Brill. *The Kazakhs.* 2nd ed. Stanford, CA: Hoover Institution Press, Stanford University Press, 1995.

Owen, Hana. "Bakhtinian Thought and the Defence of Narrative: Overcoming Universalism and Relativism." *Cosmos and History: The Journal of Natural and Social Philosophy* 7, no. 2 (July 2011): 136–56.

Pak, Yoon. *Wherever I Go, I Will Always Be a Loyal American: Seattle's Japanese American Schoolchildren during World War II.* Hoboken, NJ: Taylor and Francis, 2013.

Pchilka, Olena. "Ukrain'ski narodni legendy ostann'ogo chasu." *Etnografichnyi visnyk* 1 (1925): 43–47.

Peacock, Margaret. *Innocent Weapons: The Soviet and American Politics of Childhood in the Cold War.* Chapel Hill: University of North Carolina Press, 2015.

Peeren, Esther, and Maria del Pilar Blanco, eds. *Popular Ghosts: The Haunted Spaces of Everyday Culture.* London: Bloomsbury Academic, 2010.

Pesternikova, Valentina, Nadezhda Okladnikova, Margarita Sumina, and Victor Doshchenko. "Occupational Diseases from Radiation Exposure at the First Nuclear Plant in the USSR." *Science of the Total Environment* 142 (1994): 9–17.

Phillips, Charles, and Alan Axelrod, eds. *Encyclopedia of the American West.* 4 vols. New York : Macmillan, 1996.

Pohl, J. Otto. *The Stalinist Penal System: A Statistical History of Soviet Repression and Terror, 1930–1953.* Jefferson, NC: McFarland, 1997.

Poliakov, Iuriĭ Aleksandrovich, and V. B. Zhiromskaia, eds. *Vsesoiuznaia perepis' naseleniia 1937 goda—obshchie itogi: Sbornik dokumentov.* Moscow: ROSSPĖN, 2007.

Reps, John William. *The Forgotten Frontier: Urban Planning in the American West before 1890.* Columbia: University of Missouri Press, 1981.

Reyes, G. Mitchell, ed. *Public Memory, Race, and Ethnicity.* Newcastle upon Tyne: Cambridge Scholars, 2010.

Rhodes, James. "Youngstown's Ghost? Memory, Identity and Deindustrialization." *International Labor and Working-Class History*, no. 84 (Fall 2013), 56.

Robinson, Greg. *By Order of the President: FDR and the Internment of Japanese Americans.* Cambridge, MA: Harvard University Press, 2001.

———. *A Tragedy of Democracy: Japanese Confinement in North America.* New York: Columbia University Press, 2009.

Rollison, David. "Exploding England: The Dialectics of Mobility and Settlement in Early Modern England." *Social History* 24, no. 1 (January 1999): 1–16.

———. *The Local Origins of Modern Society: Gloucestershire 1500–1800*. London: Routledge, 1992.

Rosman, Murray Jay. *Founder of Hasidism: A Quest for the Historical Ba'al Shem Tov*. Berkeley, CA: University of California Press, 1996.

Roach, S. A., and S. M. Rappaport. "But They Are Not Thresholds: A Critical Analysis of the Documentation of Threshold Limit Values." *American Journal of Industrial Medicine* 17 (1998): 727–53.

Scarry, Elaine. *The Body in Pain: The Making and Unmaking of the World*. New York: Oxford University Press, 1987.

Schmidt, Hugo Karl. *Die Evangelisch-Lutherische Kirche in Wolhynien*. Marburg: Elwert, 1992.

Schreuder, Yda. "Labor Segmentation, Ethnic Division of Labor, and Residential Segregation in American Cities in the Early Twentieth Century." *Professional Geography* 41 (1989): 131–43.

Scott, James C. *Seeing Like a State: How Certain Schemes to Improve the Human Condition Have Failed*. New Haven, CT: Yale University Press, 1998.

Scott, Rebecca J., and Jean M. Hébrard. *Freedom Papers an Atlantic Odyssey in the Age of Emancipation*. Cambridge, MA: Harvard University Press, 2012.

Secrets of the Chernobyl Disaster. Minneapolis, MN: East View Publications, 2003.

Sellers, Christopher. "Body, Place and the State: The Makings of an 'Environmentalist' Imaginary in the Post–World War II U.S." *Radical History Review*, no. 74 (Spring 1999), 31–64.

———. "Discovering Environmental Cancer: Wilhelm Hueper, Post–World War II Epidemiology, and the Vanishing Clinician's Eye." *American Journal of Public Health* 87, no. 11 (1997): 1824–35.

———. "Factory as Environment: Industrial Hygiene, Professional Collaboration and the Modern Sciences of Pollution." *Environmental History Review* 18, no. 1 (April 1994): 55–83.

———. "Thoreau's Body: Towards an Embodied Environmental History." *Environmental History* 4, no. 4 (October 1999): 486–514.

Sheppard, E. "The Spaces and Times of Globalization: Place, Scale, Networks, and Positionality*." *Economic Geography* 78, no. 3 (2002): 307–30.

Shevzov, Vera. "Miracle-Working Icons, Laity, and Authority in the Russian Orthodox Church, 1861–1917." *Russian Review* 58, no. 1 (January 1999): 26–48.

Shales, Amity. *The Forgotten Man: A New History of the Great Depression*. New York: Harper Perennial, 2008.

Sikorskii, Ivan Alekseevich. "Psikhopaticheskaia epidemiia 1892 goda v Kievskoi Guberni." *Sbornik nauchno-literaturnykh statei: Po voprosam obshchestvennoi psikhologii, vospitaniia i nervno-psikhicheskoi gigieniy* 5 (1900): 44–114.

Skultans, Vieda. *The Testimony of Lives: Narrative and Memory in Post-Soviet Latvia*. London: Routledge, 1998.

Snyder, Timothy. *Bloodlands: Europe between Hitler and Stalin*. New York: Basic Books, 2010.

Solnit, Rebecca. *The Faraway Nearby*. New York: Viking 2013.

Sone, Monica Itoi. *Nisei Daughter*. Seattle: University of Washington Press, 1979.

Starn, Orin. "Engineering Internment: Anthropologists and the War Relocation Authority." *American Ethnologist* 13, no. 4 (November 1986): 700–720.

Startsev, I. A. *Amerika i Russkoe obshchestvo*. Moskva: Izd-vo Akademii nauk SSSR, 1942.

Steedman, Carolyn. *Dust: The Archive and Cultural History*. New Brunswick, NJ: Rutgers University Press, 2002.

Steele, Karen Dorn. "U.S., Soviet Downwinders Share Legacy of Cold War." *Spokesman Review*, July 13, 1992, A4.

Stempowski, Jerzy. *W dolinie Dniestru i inne eseje Ukraińskie: Listy o Ukrainie*. Warsaw: LNB, 1993.

Stoler, Ann Laura. *Along the Archival Grain: Epistemic Anxieties and Colonial Common Sense*. Princeton, NJ: Princeton University Press, 2009.

———. *Carnal Knowledge and Imperial Power: Race and the Intimate in Colonial Rule*. Berkeley: University of California Press, 2002.

Strangleman, Tim. "'Smokestack Nostalgia,' 'Ruin Porn' or Working-Class Obituary: The Role and Meaning of Deindustrial Representation." *International Labor and Working-Class History* 84, no. 1 (Fall 2013): 23–37.

Sugrue, Thomas J. *The Origins of the Urban Crisis: Race and Inequality in Postwar Detroit*. Princeton, NJ: Princeton University Press, 1996.

Taylor, Joseph E. "Boundary Terminology." *Environmental History* 13, no. 3 (2008): 454–81.

Teller, Adam. "Hasidism and the Challenge of Geography: The Polish Background to the Spread of the Hasidic Movement." *AJS Review: The Journal of the Association for Jewish Studies* 30, no. 1 (2006): 1–29.

Ternei, Evgenii. "Zhivaia legenda mertvogo goroda." *Zerkalo nedeli*, April 29–May 5, 1995.

Thompson, G. "Unmasking the Truth: The Science and Policy of Low-Dose Ionizing Radiation." *Bulletin of the Atomic Scientists* 68, no. 3 (May 2012): 44–50.

Tian-Shanskaia, Olga Semyonova. *Village Life in Late Tsarist Russia*. Edited by David L. Ransel. Bloomington: Indiana University Press, 1993.

Till, J. E. "Environmental Dose Reconstruction." In *Proceedings of the Thirty-First Annual Meeting of the National Council on Radiation Protection and Measurements (NCRP), Washington, DC, April 12–13, 1995*. Bethesda, MD: National Council on Radiation Protection, 1997.

Tollebeek, Jo. "'Turn'd to Dust and Tears': Revisiting the Archive." *History and Theory* 43, no. 2 (2004): 237–48.

Tracy, Merle Elliott. *Our Country, Our People, and Theirs*. New York: Macmillan, 1938.

Van der Ryn, Sim, and Peter Calthorpe. *Sustainable Communities: A New Design Synthesis for Cities, Suburbs, and Towns*. San Francisco: Sierra Club Books, 1986.

Viola, Lynne. *The Unknown Gulag: The Lost World of Stalin's Special Settlements*. Oxford: Oxford University Press, 2007.

Vlasov, Eduard. "The World According to Bakhtin: On the Description of Space and Spatial Forms in Mikhail Bakhtin's Works." *Canadian Slavonic Papers/Revue Canadienne Des Slavistes* 37, nos. 1/2 (March 1995): 37–58.

Wacquant, Loïc J. D. *Urban Outcasts: A Comparative Sociology of Advanced Marginality.* Cambridge, MA: Polity, 2008.

Wakatsuki Houston, Jeanne, and James D. Houston. *Farewell to Manzanar: A True Story of Japanese American Experience during and after the World War II Internment.* Boston: Houghton Mifflin, 1973.

West, Carroll Van. *Capitalism on the Frontier: Billings and the Yellowstone Valley in the Nineteenth Century.* Lincoln: University of Nebraska Press, 1993.

White, Richard. *"It's Your Misfortune and None of My Own": A New History of the American West.* Norman: University of Oklahoma Press, 1993.

———. *The Organic Machine: The Remaking of the Columbia River* New York: Hill and Wang, 1995.

———. *Remembering Ahanagran: Storytelling in a Family's Past.* New York: Hill and Wang, 1998.

Williams, Paige. "Drop Dead, Detroit!" *New Yorker*, January 27, 2014.

Wilson, Edmund. *Travels in Two Democracies.* New York: Harcourt, Brace and Company, 1936.

Wilson, William J. *When Work Disappears: The World of the New Urban Poor.* New York: Knopf, 1996.

Withers, Charles W. J. "Place and the 'Spatial Turn' in Geography and in History." *Journal of the History of Ideas* 70, no. 4 (2009): 637–58.

Yaeger, Patricia. *Dirt and Desire: Reconstructing Southern Women's Writing, 1930–1990.* University of Chicago Press, 2000.

———. "Ghosts and Shattered Bodies." *South Central Review* 22, no. 1 (Spring 2005): 87–108.

Yamamoto, Eric K. *Race, Rights, and Reparation: Law and the Japanese American Internment.* New York: Wolters Kluwer Law & Business, 2013.

Yarmolinsky, Avrahm. *The Jews and Other Minor Nationalities under the Soviets.* New York: Vanguard Press, 1928.

Young, Mary. "Setting Sun: Popular Culture Images of the Japanese and Japanese Americans and Public Policy." *Explorations in Ethnic Studies* 16, no. 1 (January 1993): 51–62.

Yurchak, Alexei. *Everything Was Forever, Until It Was No More: The Last Soviet Generation.* Princeton, NJ: Princeton University Press, 2006.

Zahorska, Anna. *Uchodzy.* 1922.

———. *Odrutowana okolica.* Warsaw: Biblioteka Domu Polskiego, 1925.

———. *Trucizny.* Warsaw: Dom Książki Polskiej, 1928.

Zemskov, V. H. "Massovoe osvobozhdenie spetsposelentsev i ssyl'nykh, 1954–1966 gg." *Sotsiologicheskie issledovaniia* 4 (1991): 5–25.

———. "Ob uchete spetskontingenta NKVD vo vsesoiuznykh perepisei naseleniia 1937." *Sotsiologicheskie issledovaniia* 2 (1991): 75.

———. "Spetsposelentsi." *Sotsiologicheskie issledovaniia* 11 (1990): 3–17.

INDEX